Anonymous

The Border Counties Business Directory

Comprising Roxburghshire, Selkirkshire, Peeblesshire and Berwickshire

Anonymous

The Border Counties Business Directory
Comprising Roxburghshire, Selkirkshire, Peeblesshire and Berwickshire

ISBN/EAN: 9783337340384

Printed in Europe, USA, Canada, Australia, Japan

Cover: Foto ©Suzi / pixelio.de

More available books at **www.hansebooks.com**

THIRD EDITION.

THE BORDER COUNTIES

COMPRISING

ROXBURGHSHIRE, SELKIRKSHIRE, PEEBLESSHIRE, BERWICKSHIRE, & HADDINGTONSHIRE.

BUSINESS DIRECTORY.

Price---Two Shillings and Sixpence.

PUBLISHER—
CHARLES LAMBURN,
22 MONTGOMERY STREET, EAST,
GLASGOW.

ROXBURGHSHIRE.

THIS County, which lies on the south-eastern border of Scotland, is bounded by Northumberland on the east, Dumfriesshire on the south-west, by the county of Selkirk on the west, by Berwickshire on the north, and by Northumberland and part of Cumberland on the south. The area of the shire contains 670 square miles, or 428,494 acres. The county is divided by its waters into several districts, of which the chief and largest is Teviotdale, which forms the south-west corner of the county, comprehends the alpine territory, which is drained by the Liddle and its tributaries, and contains 120 square miles. The third division lies between the Gala and Leader streams, measuring 26 square miles; and the fourth, which is situated north of the Tweed, is included in "the Merse," and comprehends 27 square miles. In size, Roxburgh is the fourteenth, and in population the seventeenth of the counties of Scotland.

The southern parts of Roxburghshire are very mountainous. The following are the principal mountains and eminences, with their respective altitudes above the level of the sea—Cheviot, 2,682 feet; Auchopecairn, 2,382; Chill Hill, Millenwood Fells, and Windhead Fells, each 2,000; Tudhope Fell, 1,730; Carter Fell, 1,602; Meggs Hill, 1,480; Ruberslaw, 1,392: Eildon Hills, 1,330; Dunnian, 1,021; Minto Hills, 858; and Minto Craigs, 649.

The manufactures of Roxburghshire is that of articles manufactured from wool, the seats of which are at Hawick, Jedburgh, and Kelso, where flannels, blankets, tartans, woollen cloth, lambs'-wool yarn, and hosiery are extensively manufactured. The salmon fisheries of the Tweed are of consequence, and yield handsome rents to the proprietors.

The principal railway line in connection with this county is the North British, with its several branches.

The County of Roxburgh comprises thirty entire parishes, and five parts of parishes; it contains only one royal burgh—Jedburgh. The present member for the county is the Earl of Dalkeith. The lord-lieutenant is Lord Reay. Population in 1891 was 53,741.

ANCRUM is a small village in the united parishes of Ancrum and Longnewton, 11 miles W. from Kelso, 11 E. from Hawick, and 4 N. from Jedburgh, situated on the right bank of the Water of Ale. The parish extends 6 miles in length, and has an acreage of 10,295.

Business Directory.

Blacksmiths.
Maben, William, Ancrum
Turnbull, Mark, Old Belses

Boot and Shoe Makers.
Bell, John & Co , Ancrum
Ormiston, John, Ancrum

Butchers.
Veitch, James, Ancrum
Wight, Andrew, Ancrum

Drapers and Clothiers.
Kennedy, James, Ancrum
Turnbull, Richard, Ancrum

Farmers—see end of Directory.

Grocers and General Merchants.
Bell, John, Ancrum
Black, Jane, Ancrum
Hogg, George (& baker), Ancrum
Temple, George, Ancrum

Hotels and Inns.
Commercial Inn (Stabling) James Galloway, Ancrum
Cross Keys (Stabling),—John Buchanan, Ancrum

Joiners and Cartwrights.
Scott, Thomas, Ancrum
White, John, Longnewton

Market Gardeners.
Bell, John, Ancrum
Hume, Miss, Ancrum
Ormiston (and florist), Ancrum

Millers.
Drummond, A. & A., Longnewton
Jeffrey, James, Belses
Scott, John, Nether Ancrum

Traction Engine Proprietors.
Henderson & Watson, (and contractors), Ancrum

BEDRULE—SEE JEDBURGH.
BOWDEN—SEE LILLIESLEAF.
CAVERS—SEE DENHOLM.
CRAILING—SEE JEDBURGH.
DARNICK—SEE MELROSE.

DENHOLM.

With the Parish of CAVERS.

DENHOLM is a small village in the parish of CAVERS, 5 miles from Jedburgh, and the same distance from Hawick, situated on the banks of the river Teviot. The parish has an acreage of 18,254.

Business Directory.

Blacksmiths.

Laing, Joseph, Denholm
Robson, John, Denholm

Boot and Shoe Makers.

Hume, Robert, Denholm
Park, Thomas, Denholm

Butchers.

Beattie, Thomas, Denholm
Johnstone, William, Denholm

Drapers.

Beattie, George, Denholm
Turnbull, Robt. (tailor), Denholm
Turnbull, Robert S., Denholm

Farmers—see end of Directory.

Grocers and General Merchants.

Little, Miss, Denholm
Mack, Mrs., Denholm
Scott, Jas. (and saddler), Denholm

Hotels and Inns.

Cross Keys Inn—Andw. Anderson, Denholm
Fox and Hounds - Wm. Sanderson, Denholm
Temperance—Jn. Robson, Denholm

Joiners and Wrights.

Furness, Alex. R., Denholm
Little, Adam (builder), Denholm
Miller, John, Post Office, Denholm
Scott, Elliot, Denholm

Miscellaneous.

Baker—Wm. Carruthers, Denholm
Horse Dealer—W. Clark, Denholm
Surgeon—J. D. Brown, Denholm
Wood Merchant—Geo. Cairns, Denholm

ECKFORD—SEE KELSO.

EDNAM—SEE KELSO.

GATTONSIDE—SEE MELROSE.

HAWICK,

Including HOBKIRK, KIRKTOWN, MINTO, ROBERTON, TEVIOT HEAD, and WILTON.

HAWICK is a thriving manufacturing town, a parliamentary burgh, and capital of its parish, 50 miles S. by E. from Edinburgh, 20 S.W. from Kelso, 11 S. from Selkirk, and 45 N. from Carlisle, situated on the high road between the last-named city and Edinburgh, on the Waverley branch line of the North British Railway, for which there is a station. The village of WILTON, on the north bank of the Teviot, is now included in the burgh boundaries, the river being spanned by two stone bridges. The public buildings are the Town Hall, Temperance Hall, Cottage Hospital, and the Exchange. The Town Hall and Municipal Buildings includes Free Library, Reading Room, and a Science and Art Institute and Museum. The market is held on Thursday, and there are auction sales of stock every alternate Monday and Saturday, and special sales during the summer. The fairs are held on the 17th of May, the 21st of September, and the 8th of November. A tryst is likewise held in October, at which horses and cattle are exposed for sale; and there is a wool fair held on the first Thursday after St. Boswell's fair in July. Population, 19,204.

HAWICK parish comprises an area of 6,112 acres.

HOBKIRK, or HOPEKIRK, is a mountainous parish, 7 miles from Hawick, 11 miles long and about one and a half in breadth; it adjoins the parishes of Cavers, Bedrule, Southdean, Castleton and Kirktown. Acreage 16,193.

KIRKTOWN is a parish 3 miles from Hawick, bounded by Lilliesleaf, Ancrum, Bedrule, Cavers, Wilton, and the County of Selkirk. Acreage, 5,602.

ROBERTON is a parish 5 miles from Hawick. Acreage, 29,419.

WILTON is a parish adjoining Hawick. Acreage, 8,760.

Business Directory.

Ærated Water Manufacturers.

Craig, John (and chemist and druggist), 17 High st
Dalgleish, M., 14 Kirk wynd
Maben, Thomas, 52 High st
Pirrie, Alexander, 52 High st

Antique Dealer.

Thomson, A., Exchange arcade

Architects and Surveyors.

Alison, James P., 21 Bridge st
Inglis, John, Bridge st
Manuel, John, Municipal buildings

Auctioneers and Valuators.

Atkinson, R. F., O'Connell st
Milligan, Charles, Tannage Close, 63 High st
Oliver, A, & Son, Trinity st

Baby Linen and Ladies' Underclothing Establishments

Armstrong, Miss, 11 Oliver place
Easton, Miss M., 2 High st
Jardine, Miss, Drumlanrig square
Millar, Mrs., 1 Wilton place
Miller, M., 12 Wilton place

Bakers.

Anderson, Thomas, 12 Bridge st
Bell, John Scott, 1 Sandbed
Bell, Thomas, Union st
Brydon, Thomas, 16 High st
Murray, James, 23 High st
Scott, George, 10 High st
Scott, James, 25 Howgate
Scott, Thomas, 55 High st
Walker, John, 1 Wellington st
Wright, G., 2 Allars crescent
Young, John, 12 Sandbed
Young, R. & Sons, 75 High st

Banks.

British Linen Co. Bank, High st—Gilbert Davidson, agent
Commercial Bank, Litd., Tower Knowe
Hawick Heritable Investment Bank Ltd., 35 High st
Hawick Security Savings Bank, 35 High st
National Bank of Scotland, Litd., High st—Robert Purdom, agent
Royal Bank of Scotland, High st

Blacksmiths.

Allan, Thomas, Murray place
Bowie, Thomas, Havelock st
Clark, Peter, 1 Orrock pl
Craik, Alex. & Chisholm, Baker st
Kedie, James, 18 Drumlanrig sq
Kerr, John, 55 High st
Ovens, J., Old Gas Works
Scott, Gideon, 62 High st
Tait, Wm., Commercial rd
Telfer, William, Crown Close High st
Williamson, James, 21 High st

Booksellers and Stationers.

Davidson, A. W., 41 High st
Goodfellow J. C., 63 High st
Grieve, George C. (and printer), 6 Tower Knowe
Henderson, A. (& printer), 8a Bridge st
Henderson, W. (and printer), 35 High st
Kennedy, W. & J., 2 Sandbed
Watt, Allan, (& printer), Station Buildings

Boot and Shoemakers.

Ballantyne, George, 14 Howgate
Blackie, John, 56 High st
Bell, Richard, 7 Kirkstyle
Burnet, R. & W., 5 Howgate
Elliot, Robert, 2 O'Connell st
Graham, Michael, Silver st
Gray, John, 20 High st
Jackson, Simon, 9 Howgate
Johnston, John, 6 O'Connell st
Kyle, Adam, 1 Gladstone st
Macnee, Robert, 1 Oliver place
Nicol, Mrs., 11 High st
Rae, John, 21 High st

Rutherford, And., 2 Gladstone st
Scott, C. & Son, 6 Sandbed
Shiel, J. & Son, 3 Buccleugh st
Stothart, James, 29 High st
Tyler. H. P., 1 Oliver place
White, George, 21 Howgate

Builders and Contractors.

Anderson, Hugh, 37 High st
Bell, & Turnbull, Commercial road
Eckford, John, 1 Wilton hill
Marshall, John, & Sons, Lothian st
Oliver, & Pennicuik, Croft road
Scott, Adam, 18 Bourtree place

Butchers.

Bell Brothers, 77 High st
Burns, Robert, 28 High st
Burns, Thomas, 1 Melgund place
Clarke, Andrew, 6 Loan
Clark, John, Dovemount place
Hutton, W., 8 Howgate
Inglis, Mrs., 10 O'Connell st
Kay, A. & Sons, 3 High st
Kenroway, T., Howgate
Millar, John, 6 Cross wynd
Reid, John, 4 High st
Scott, R., 55 High st
Spreng, H., 13 Howgate
Stoddart, Wm., 9a Bridge st
Tait, Robert, 11 Wellington st
Telfer, James, Backdamgate

Cabinetmakers and Upholsterers

Hobkirk, W. & T. (and joiners), 3 Allars crescent
Hunter, J. & Son, 2 Princes st
Inglis, A. & Son (& joiners), Bridge street
Milligan, Charles (cabinetmaker and undertaker), Tannage close, 63 High st
Russel, Philp, 8 Oliver place
Scott, W. & Sons, 4 Buccleuch st
Scott & Wight, 58 High st
Temple, Robert, Bourtree place

Coach Proprietors and Posting Establishments.

Anderson, Wm., Imperial Hotel Stables
Brown, James, 13 Kirk wynd
Fleming, George, Croft road
Graham, John, Drumlanrig square
Kennedy, William, Crown Hotel, High st, and Tower Hotel, Tower Knowe
Proudfoot, J., Tenterfield, Ladylaw
Short, John, Bourtree place
Whillens, Thomas, Slitrig crescent —see advt
Wright, J. & R., 52 High st

Chemists and Druggists

Blaine, T. J. S., 5 High st
Craig, John (& Ærated Water Manufacturer), 17 High st
Kennedy, David, 37 High st
Maben, Thomas, 5 Oliver place
Ross, W. R., 48 High st
Turnbull, W. S, 2 Dovemount place

China and Glass Merchants.

Anderson, G. S., Teviot rd
Currie, A., 19 Howgate
Currie, Miss, 1 Princes st
Guthrie, I. & M., 53 High st
Scott, Francis. 26 High st
Scott, J., 13 Wellington st
Shaw, Mrs., 68 High st
Wilson, Wm. (and rag), 5 Teviot rd

Coal Merchants.

Blaikie, Geo. & Co., 63 High st
Cairns, James, 33 Lothian st
Hart, Adam, Leckieshedge, Wilton
Lothian Coal Co., Railway Station
Miller, Robert, 7 Albion place
Robson, Andrew, Bourtree hill
Rutherford, Thomas, (and hay and straw merchant), 1 Wellogate pl and Railway Station
Smith, David, 21 Havelock st
Turnbull, John, 74 High st
Waldie, R. & Co., 1 Laing terrace

Confectioners.

Hutchison, Wm., 66 High st
Kyle, R , 4 Buccleuch st
Nisbet, Wm., 6 O'Connell st
Purvis & Gowans, 1High st
Shiel, Miss, 3 Buccleuch st
Shiel, Miss, 2 Princes st
Temple, John, 63 High st
Welsh, Robert, 12 Oliver pl

Contractors.

Bowie, Gilbert, Bourtree place
Hart, Adam, Lockieshedge Wilton
M'Donald, D. & Son, 1 Laing ter

Corn and Seed Merchants.

Drummond, A., Sandbed
Grieve Walter, 4 Dovecote st
Haldane, James, 4 Howgate
Scott, Wm., (and hay and straw merchant), 6 Oliver pl—see ad
Turnbull, T. & W., Hawick mill

Cutlers.

Clark, Peter, Orrock place
Mackenzie, F., 15 Howgate
Milligan, Robert, Tannage lane

Cycle and Bicycle Makers and Agents.

Gaylor, D., 59 High st
Millligan, Robert, Tannage lane
Scott John, (Bicycle maker and Cycle Agent), 52 High st

Drapers, Dressmakers, and Milliners.

Aitken, James, 15 High st
Alexander, G. & Co., 11 High st
Burnet, J. & A., 39 High st
Colosseum Co., 14 High st
Davidson, J., 4 Wellington st
Gentles & Co., 44 High st
Irving, Frank, 2 Howgate
Jardine, Miss, 10 Drumlanrig sq
Lockie & Co, 37 Drumlanrig sq
Miller, Robert, 49 High st
Park, D. S., 19 High st
Paterson, Mrs 7 Tower knowe
Renwick, Andrew, 3 Oliver place
Wright, Joseph, 7 Bourtree place

Dressmakers—see also Drapers.

Bragg, Miss, 1 Drumlanrig sq
Drysdale, Miss, (scientific dressmaking taught), 25 Beaconsfield terrace
Forbes, Miss, 60 Sandbed

Drysalters.

Kennedy, D., 37 High st
Simpson, R., Walters wynd

Dyers.

Rule & Leyden, Teviot road
Turnbull, John & Sons, Slitrig cres

Egg Merchant.

Rodger, J. B. (agent for T. Howden, Leith,) 19 Howgate

Engineers.

Davidson, Wm., Commercial rd
Melrose, Jas. & Sons, Slitrig cres

Farmers—see end of Directory.

Fishmongers, Game and Poultry Dealers.

Armstrong, George, 17 Howgate
Davidson Brothers, 70 High st
Dougall, T., 11 Howgate
Hall, George & Son, 40 High st
Riddle, John, 1 Drumlanrig sq
Simpson, A., 7 Kirk wynd
Simpson, J. & Son, 62 High st

Fruiterers and Greengrocers.

Cumming, John, Bridge st
Dewar, Mrs, 1 Melgund place
Hewitson, Miss, 13 Wilton place
Irving, R., 5a Bridge st
Ormiston, Mrs., Station buildings
Purvis & Gowans, 1 High st
Turnbull, A., 16 Bridge st
Tait, William, 72 High st
Virtue, R. M., 46 High st

Furniture Dealers, &c. (Secondhand.)

Laidlaw, Mrs., Dickson st
Thomson, A., Exchange arcade

Grocers and General Merchants.
(Marked 'e' are Spirit Dealers.

e Aitken, Mrs., 13 Wilton path
e Anderson, John (licensed), 8 Dickson st
Anderson, Walter, 11 Lothian st
Baptie, M. 5 Union st
Blake, A. H. & Co., 4 Oliver place
Borthwick, James, 70 High st
e Brodie, Mrs., 6 Albion place
Brydon, J. & Sons, 8 High st
Burnet, W., 2 Kirk wynd
Co-operative Store Co., 69 High st

Darling, G. & J., Bourtree place
Doig, C., 20 Kirk wynd
Eckford, Andrew, 21 High st
e Elliot, Jas. O., 2 Buccleuch st
Elliot, W. & F., 18 Bourtree place
e Forsyth, W. W., 4 Howgate
Gray, James, 1 Drumlanrig place
e Halliday, David, 1 Union st
e Henderson, J. A., 5 Loan
e Henderson, John, 3 Drumlanrig sq
e Hogg, James, 9 High st
e Hume, Walter, 16 Howgate
Hunter, Thomas, 9 Dickson st
e Jardine, John, 7 O'Connell st
Jardine, T., Wilton hill
Jeffrey, John, 3 Howgate
Kirkpatrick, W., 4 Heron hill ter
e Lambert, J. & Son, 8 Sandbed
Lipton, Thomas L., 45 High st
London, &c., Tea Co., 18 High st
Marchbank, J., 29 Drumlanrig sq
Nelson, Thomas, 4 Wellington st
Nichol, George, 9 Wilton place
e Oliver, Thomas, 1 Buccleuch st
e Peden, William, 73 High st
Richardson, Thomas, 5 Alice bank
e Robertson, John, 10 Wilton place
Robson, James, 1 Havelock st
e Scott, Alexander, 2 Dickson st
Scott, Mrs., 9 Havelock st
Scott, Walter, 12 Howgate
Shiel, David, 14 Park st
Shipley, R., 1 Wellogate place
e Tait, E., 3 Wilton path
e Turnbull, James, 51 High st
e Turnbull, J. & Son, Tower Knowe
Wilson, Mungo, 5 Silver st

Hairdressers.

Bonsor, T. W., 16 Bridge st
Fairgrieve, W., Princes st
Flockhart, T., 9 Cross wynd
Law, John, 25 Howgate
Mackenzie, Francis, 15 Howgate
Martin, P., 2 Round close
Moellendorff, F. C., 42 High st
Park, William, 62 High st
Walker, Mrs., 6 O'Connell st
Waugh, George, Oliver place

Hatters Hosiers and Glovers.

Hume, John, 8 Oliver place
Shiel, Thomas, 25 High st
-Weir, William, James, 57 High st

Hay and Straw Merchant.

Scott, William, (& Corn Merchant), Oliver, pl—see advt

Hosiery Manufacturers.

Dicksons & Laings, Wilton mills
Drummond, James, 7 Kirkstyle
Elliot, Wm., & Sons, Slitrig cres
Henderson, J. & Co., Victoria rd
Hogg George & Sons, Mill bank
Hunter, & Young, Commercial rd
Innes, A. P. & Co., Victoria rd
Kersel, R. & Co., Gladstone st
Laing, John & Sons, Slitrig Crescent
Lockie, Wm. & Co., Drumlanrig sq
Lyle, & Scott, Lothian st
Pringle, R. & Son, Walters wynd
Renwick, James & Co., Commercial road
Reyburn, Bros., Duke st
Scott, Peter & Co., Bucclengh st
Trotter, Wm., 16 Howgate
Turner, Rutherford & Co. Mansfield
Wilson, W. & Sons., Allers cres

Hotels—Family and Commercial.

Those marked 'e' are Temperance Hotels.

Bridge Hotel — Angus M'Intosh, Sandbed
Buccleuch Hotel — William Reid, Trinity st
e Caver's Hotel,—Bridge st
Central Hotel—1 Bridge st
Crown Hotel, 22 High st, & Tower Hotel, Tower Knowe—William Kennedy, proprietor—see advt
Half-Moon Hotel, — Daniel Wight, proprietor, 64 High st
Imperial Hotel—Philip M'Govern, Oliver place
e Murray's Hotel, 15 High st
Station Hotel—James Wilson, proprietor, Dovemount place
Victoria Hotel—John M'Dougal, 52 High st
e Washington Hotel—Bridge st
Waverley Hotel—Robert Elliot, 78 High st
e Wight's Hotel—29 High st

Ironmongers and Hardwaremen.
Armstrong, John, 5 Tower knowe
Deans, David D., 5 Oliver place
Kerr, John, 1 Murray place
Paisley, Walter, 43 High st
Paterson. John, 60 High st
Rae, Walter, 11 Dickson st
Russell, Robert, Bourtree place

Joiners.
Beattie, John, Bourtree place
Brunton, John, 11 Round Close
Graham, John, 20 Drumlanrig sq
Grieve, Robert, 16 Havelock st
Inglis, James, 7 Kirkstyle
Riddle, Wm., Commercial road
Scott, Walter & Son, Orrock place
Scott, Wm. & Son, Mansfield rd
Smith & Scott, 4a Oliver place

Ladies and Children's Outfitter.
Brown, Mrs D., 10 Bridge st

Lathsplitters.
M'Mahon, P., 45 High st
Scott, P., 4a Oliver crescent

Laundries.
Anderson's, Trinity st
Harris, Mrs, 4 Mill Path

Machine Makers.
Meller, Moses & Sons, Ltd. (hosiery), Commercial rd
Singer Manufacturing Co., (sewing) 7 Bridge st

Medical Practitioners.
Bannerman, Goo. G., 27 Bridge st
Barrie, W. T., 18 N. Bridge st
Brydon, James, 4 Sandbed
Hamilton, J. R., 17 Bridge st
Lorraine, Herbt. J. B., 28 Bridge st
M'Leod, D. J. A., 14 Buccleuch st
Peterkin, George, 17 Bridge st

Millers.
Steam Flour Mills, Havelock st
Turnbull, T. & W., Hawick mill

Milliner—see also Drapers, &c.
Davidson, Miss, 48 High st

Mill Furnishers.
Kyle, William, Commercial road
Scott, George, Bourtree place
Tait, William, Commercial road

Music Teachers.
Blackwood, Thos., (violinist and teacher of music), 11 Bourtree place
Grant, Adam, (and music seller), 10 Bridge st
Reid, Miss, Craig Ian, Eskdaill terrace

Newspaper Publishers and Printers.
Hawick Advertiser—W. Morrison, & Co. Ltd., 4 Bridge st
Hawick Express — A. H. Craw, High st
Hawick News—Vair & M'Nairn, 24 High st

Nurserymen Seedsmen & Florists.
Forbes, John, Buccleuch Nurseries
Frazer, Wm., Wilton Lodge
Hall T. C. & Sons, Glenburnie
Lamb, W., 54 High st
Scott, James, 50 High st
Turnbull, William, Bramblehall
Wood, Geo., Summerfield Nurseries

Painters and Decorators.
Haig, James, Oliver place
Jardine, Alexander, 41 High st
Laidlaw, T. H., 13 High st
May, George, 13 Howgate
Nichol, John D., 7 Wellington st
Scott, Francis, 27 High st

Photographers.
Bell, Richard, Exchange Arcade
Dalgleish & Wilkinson, 59 High st
Evans, Thomas, 47 High st
Murray, J. E. D., 6 Bridge st
Robinson, George, A., 25 Bridge st

Picture Frame Makers.
Inglis, Alexander, 10 High st
Kyle, Andrew, Bourtree place
Smith, Peter, 47 High st

Plasterers.
Davidson Wm., & Sons, 4

Croft road
Huggan, James, 2 Langlands bank

Plumbers, Gasfitters, and Tinsmiths.

Armstrong, John, Sandbed
Bell, James, 21 High st
Grieve, Walter & Co., (and Slaters) 16 Buccleuch st
Kerr, Andrew, Drumlanrig sq
Kerr, George, 1 Murray pl
Miller, J. & Son, (and Slaters), 1 O'Connell, st—see adv
Murray, John & Son, (and Slaters), 19 Bridge st
Paisley, Walter, 43 High st
Rae, & Murdoch, 26 Drumlanrig st
Rae, Walter, 13 Dickson st
Russell, Robt., Bourtree place
Smith, John, 12 Cross wynd

Posting Establishments—see Coach Proprietors.

Poulterers and Game Dealers—see Fishmongers.

Printers—see also Booksellers and Newspapers Publishers

Deans, R. & Co., 10 High st
Henderson, A., 8a Bridge st
Henderson, W., 35 High st
Watson, James, 72 High st

Reed and Heddle Makers.

Baron & Hogarth, Commercial rd
Nelson & Son, 12 Teviot Crescent

Restaurants.

Bruce, John 12 Baker st (Break fasts, Teas, Dinners, &c., at exceedingly moderate charges)
Davidson, N. M., 1 Bourtree place

Saddlers and Harness Makers.

Davies, George, 6 High st
Hills, Wm., 3 Oliver place
Law, A., 11 Bourtree place
Stothart, Joseph, 8 Bridge st

Saw Mill Proprietor.

Smith, David, Commercial rd

Schools—Boarding and Day.

Brand, James, Bride st
Brodie, R., Wilton Lodge
Reid, Miss (assisted by certified English and German Governesses Art Master of S. Kensington. Private day school for young ladies. Pupils prepared for Local examinations) Craig Ian, Eskdaill terrace

Sculptors and Monumental Masons.

Robson, Robert, Bridge st
Stenhouse, Robert. Bridge st

Seedsmen—see Corn Merchants and also Nurserymen, &c.

Skinners.

Elliott, James, 8 Buccleuch st
Rutherford, Thomas, Rosevale cottages

Slaters—see also Plumbers, &c.
Miller, J. & Son (and plumber, &c.) 1 O'Connell st—see adv

Solicitors and Notaries Public.

Grier & Campbell, 3 Oliver place
Haddon & Turnbull, High st
Laing & Barrie, 77 High st
Oliver, G. & J., Tower knowe
Oliver, John, 2 Oliver place
Oliver, William, Bridge st
Paton, John, 4 Oliver place
Purdom, Thomas & Sons, (Solicitors and Town Clerks, and agents for National Bank), High street

Spirit Dealers.

Barclay, John (Royal Bar), 1 Drumlanrig square
Dalton, John, 9 Kirk style
Dodds, Mrs., 11 Green ter
Graham, John, 7 Drumlanrig square
Kyle, J. H., 9 Sandbed
Morrison, A., Drumlanrig square
Nodwell, S., Orrock place
Park, Francis, 56 High st
Richardson, Robert, Wilton place
Robertson, A. J., 14 Ladylaw place

Rutherford, Wm., 32 High st
Shiel, David (wholesale), 13 Teviot crescent
Shiel, James, 3 Loan
Turnbull, James, (wholesale), 51 High st

Tailors and Clothiers.

Cochrane, Andrew, 59 High st
Davidson, Wm. M., 7 Tower knowe
Dryden, P., 4 Drumlanrig sq
Gourley, S., 18 Bridge st
Hepworth & Co., Ltd., 61 High st
Kerr & Mackenzie, 80 High st
Mitchell, J., 4 Mill port
Moncur, Charles, 4 Wilton path
Notman, Wm., 4 Wilton crescent
Oliver, John, 2 Oliver place
Robison, Thomas, 17 Bourtree place
Scott, A., 7 Bridge st
Scott, E., 8 Howgate
Turnbull, Mrs., 56 High st
Waugh, Andrew, 38 High st
Wilkinson, S., Exchange arcade
Willet, Alexander, 21 Garfield st
Wright, Joseph, 7 Bourtree place

Tobacconists.

Lothian, Miss, 9a Oliver place
Rutherford, Mrs., 60 High st
Symington R., 17 High st
Walker, M., 3 Tower Knowe

Toy and Fancy Goods Merchants.

Deayell, Miss, Sandbed
Gilroy, Mrs., 7 Howgate
Huggan, John, 9 Oliver place
Nisbet, W., 6 O'Connell st
Oliver, Mrs., 76 High st
Park, D. S., 19 High st

Tweed Manufacturers.

Blenkhorn, Richardson & Co., Ld., Eastfield mills
Crosby & Co., Trow mills
Davidson, Wm., 5 Oliver crescent
Dicksons & Laings, Wilton mills
Greenwood, Watt & Co., Howlands mills
Grieve & Laidlaw, Stonefield mills
Henderson, J. Graham Weensforth mills
Kedie, Wm. & Co., Riversdale mills
Laidlaw, Wm. & Sons, Teviot crescent mills
Noble, R. & Co., Glebe mills
Scoon & Barrie, Teviotdale mills
Sime, Williamson, & Co., Weensland
Tait, B. & Co., Waverley mills
Watson, W. & Sons, Dangerfield mills
Wilson & Glenny, Ltd., Ladylaw mills
Wilson, Scott, & Co., Albert mills
Wilson, Walter & Sons Weensland

Tweed Merchants.

Affleck, John, 6 Northcote st
Currie Lee, & Gawn, Commercial rd
Finlay, Wm., 11 Melgund pl
Holmes, Hugh, 14 Bourtree pl
Innes, Chalmers, & Co. Commercial road
Jardine, James, 14 Croft rd
Knox Cowe F. & Co. 1 Mansfield cr
Lawson R. & Co., Hawick
M'Leod, George, & Sons, Oliver pl
White, John, Dovecote st

Umbrella Makers.

Fisher Thomas & Son, (Umbrella Manufacturers), Dovecote street
M'Leod, George & Sons, Oliver pl

Veterinary Surgeons.

Manuel, P., 6 Sandbed
Scott, Robert, 1 Oliver Crescent & Cauldmill

Watchmakers and Jewellers.

Gaylor, David, 59 High st
Gibson, Robert, 4 Buccleuch st
Lawson, Alexander S., 1 Sandbed
Murray, Gavin P., 70 High st
Murray, Tom G., 15 Bourtree pl
Ruthorford, F. E., 1 Oliver place

Wool Agents.

Fisher, Alexander, The Anchorage
Hunter, James Y., 18 Bourtree pl

Yarn Spinners.

Laidlaw & Sons, Lynnwood mills
Weensland Spinning Coy., Litd.,

Weensland

Miscellaneous.

Bill Poster—S. H. Munro, Bridge st
Coach Builder—John Bell, 54 High street
Cooper—J. R. Douglas, 3 Bourtree place
Dairymen—Teviotdale Dairy Co., Bridge st
Dentist—Wm. Edwards, Tower knowe
Glazier and Glass Merchant—Robt. Mitchell, 5 Oliver crescent
India Rubber Merchants—South of Scotland Rubber Co., 5 Bridge st
Iron Merchant—J. Douglas, 18 Oliver crescent
Letter File Manufacturers—A. & G. Donaldson, Waverley terrace
Pawnbroker—E. Gilligan, 6 Kirk style
Rope Maker-Adam Munro, 14 Bourtree place
Wood Merchant—Wm. Robson, 17 Havelock st
Yarns and Trimming Merchants—W. H. Potter & Co, 3 Dovemount place

HEITON—SEE KELSO.

HOWNAM—SEE JEDBURGH.

JEDBURGH,

Including BEDRULE, CRAILING, HOWNAM, OXNAM, and SOUTHDEAN.

JEDBURGH is a royal burgh, the seat of a presbytery, the capital of its parish, and the county town; 46 miles S.E. from Edinburgh, 10 S. by W. from Kelso, and 10 N. by E. from Hawick. The lords judiciary hold courts here for the south circuit (which includes the counties of Roxburgh, Berwick, and Selkirk), in April and September; and the Sheriff holds a court on Mondays and Thursdays for the dispatch of civil business, and a small debt court and the ordinary sheriff court every Thursday. The justice of peace hold their court on the first Tuesday of every month; and here also the court of general quarter session sits. The manufacture of tweeds, blankets, plaidings, &c., is carried on to a large extent, and in the neighbourhood are many corn mills. The market is held on Tuesday. Jedburgh parish comprises an area of 52,535 acres. Population 3,397.

BEDRULE is a parish in the centre of the county, and is distant from Jedburgh about four miles. Acreage, 3,917.

CRAILING is a parish situated 3½ milet from Jedburgh and 6½ from Kelso There are two small villages in the parish, CRAILING and NISBET. The North British Railway has a station ot Nisbet. Acreage, 5,966.

HOWMAN is a parish situated among the Cheviot Hills. The village of Hownam is distant from Jedburgh about 9 miles, and from Kelso about 12 miles. Acreage 15,075.

OXNAM is a parish on the borders of Northumberland. The village of Oxnam is 4 miles from Jedburgh, which is the nearest town and railway station. Acreage, 21,160.

SOUTHDEAN is a large parish in the southern part of Teviotdale. Acreage, 27,929.

Business Directory.

Agricultural Implement Maker.

Smail, Thomas (and Horse Shoer), Lanton

Auctioneers and Cattle Salesmen.

Mabon, William, Over Wells
Wilson, Alexander, Hudalee

Bakers and Confectioners.

Scott, James K. (Bread, Biscuit, and Pastry Baker and Confectioner), 10 High st
Veitch, Thomas, 49 Canongate
Young, Wm., 19 Canongate

Banks.

Bank of Scotland, 27 High st
British Linen Co, Bank, High st
Commercial Bank, Ld., Exchange st
National Bank, Ltd., High st
Royal Bank of Scotland, High st—R. B. & C. W. Anderson, agents

Blacksmiths.

Anderson, John, Bedrule
Dodds, Henry, Abbey place
Hall, George, 14 High st
Hume, John, Bonjedward
Murray, Elliot, Southdean
Oliver, Walter, Oxnam
Smail, Thomas (Horse Shoer, & Agricultural Implement Maker Lanton
Storie, T. & W. (and Implement Makers), Lanton
White, George, Crailing
Young, Adam, Nisbet
Young, James, Hundalee
Young, William, Mossburnford

Booksellers, Stationers, Newsagents and Printers.

Easton, Andrew & W., 18 High st
Easton, Walter, 9 Market pl
Geddes, Alexander, 41 High st
Smail, Thomas, 16 High st

Boot and Shoe Makers.

Gray, J. & Co., 5 Market pl
Irving, Robert (& Clogmaker), 8 Market place
Michie, George, 6, 8 Canongate
Phaup, William, 15 Canongate
Sylvester, Richard, 41 Canongate
Taylor, J., 5 Castlegate
Webb, William, Castlegate
Wood, Alex. & Co., 23 High st
Young, A. & Son, 7 High st

Builders and Masons.

Bell, Walter, Hindhousefield
Brunton, W. & Son., 20 New Bongate
Laidlaw, George, 71 High st

Cabinetmakers, Upholsterers, and Undertakers—see Joiners &c.

Cartwrights—see Joiners.

Chemists and Druggists.

Strachan, John, 30 High st
Walker, Alexander, 4 High st

Coal and Lime Merchants.

Burn, William, Anna house
Stewart, Robert, 44 High st

Confectioners and Fruiterers.

Crozier, Thomas, 15 Castlegate

Curle, J., 4 Exchange, st
Turnbull, M, J., 45 High st

Dentist.

Pringle. Robert (at Mr Strachan) 30 High st—see advt

Drapers Milliners Dressmakers and Clothiers.

Beattie, George, 11 Canongate
Hislop & Oliver, 8 High st
Phaup, James, 8 Market place
Simpson, H., 9 Exchange st
Thomson & Dodds, 12 & 14 High st

Dressmakers—see also Drapers &c.
Rutherford, Misses, 3 Canongate

Engineers and Millwrights.

Michie & Hardie, (General Engineers), Allaslay
Storrie, William, Bongate Engineering Works

Farmers—see end of Directory.

Fishmongers, Game and Poultry Dealers.

Miller, H., 7 Castlegate
Scott, Bros., 33 High st

Fleshers.

Sword, William D., 3 High st
Veitch, Archibald, 8 Exchange st
Wight, A. & Son, 13 High st

Grocers and General Merchants.

Balfour, G. & Son, 15 High st
Brown, William, 11 Castlegate
Guy, George W., 40 Castlegate
Halliburton, James, 9 High st
Halliburton, T. C., 9 Canongate
Jedburgh Co-operative Store Coy., Ltd., Exchange st
Murray, R., New Bongate
Noble, Robert, 12 Canongate
Reid, Robert, 59 Canongate
Sword John, (Licensed), 10 Market place
Telfer, A. R., 12 Market place
Telfer, R., 31 High st

Horse Breaker.

Fox, William. Langton, (Breakes to Saddle and Harness, by a new and humane method.

Hotels Inns and Posting Houses.

Caledonian, Canongate, — Charles Donaldson, proprietor
Davidson, Henry, Castlegate
Exchange Hotel — Henry Cleek, proprietor, 8 Exchange st
Hair, A., Townfoot
Railway Tavern Townfoot,— Thomas Danks, proprietor
Royal Hotel, (Bus meets all Trains),—Alexander Wilson, proprietor, Canongate
Rutherford, Robert, Castlegate
Rutherford, Samuel, Abbey place
Spread Eagle — John W. Scott, High st

Ironmongers and Hardwaremen.

Fair, Robert & Son, (and Ironfounders), 4 Canongate
Robertson, James, 1 Market place

Joiners, Cabinetmakers Upholsterers and Undertakers.
Marked 'e' are also Cartwrights.

e Amos, Gilbert, Dovesford
e Amos, Walter, Southdean
e Bell, Mark, Lanton
Brown, George, Bonjedward
e Brown, James, Nisbet
e Clark, John C., 16 Canongate
Cranston & Carruthers, (joiners, cabinetmakers, upholsterers, and undertakers), 33 Castlegate
e Fairbairn, W., 21 New Bongate
Haliday, Robert, 33 Canongate
Harkness, J. & Son, 28 High st
Hislop, Thomas, Bridgend
Inglis, A. & Sons, 34 & 36 High st
Mitchell, Ebenezer, New Bongate
Oliver, Alexander, Queen st
e Romanes, William, Crailing

Manufacturers.

Boyd, James & Son, New-Bongate
Hislop. J. & W., Bongate mills
Laidlaw, Bros., Allars, mills

Miller, Dobson, & Co., Abbey mills
Scott, & Co., Old Bridgend

Millers.

Elliot, James, Ferniehirst mill
Tully, Messrs, New mill
Wilson, Alexander, Hundalee mill
Young, William, Bonjedward mill

Milliners—see Drapers &c.

Newspapers.

Jedburgh Gazette—Walter Easton, publisher, 9 Market place
Teviotdale Record and Jedburgh Advertiser—A. & W. Easton, publishers, 18 High st

Nurserymen and Seedsmen.

Irvine, Charles, 2 Canongate
Neil, William, 5 High st

Painters and Decorators.

Russell, R. C., Abbey place
Waugh & Brown, 56 High st
Wright, J., 32 High st

Photographer.

Jack, R., Bongate

Plumbers, Gasfitters, and Slaters.

Charters, Geo. & Son, (Registered Plumbers and Sanitary Engineers), 19 Exchange st
Oliver, Andrew, (Plumber and Gasfitter), 9 Market place
Purdie, James, 49 High st
Waugh, W. & A., Exchange st

Printers—see Booksellers.

Saddlers and Harness Makers.

Main, William, 17 High st
Veitch, Alexander, 19 High st

Saw Mill Proprietors and Wood Merchants.

Farmer. William, Station Sawmills
Hislop, William, Mossburnfoot
Yellowlees, Andrew, Bongate

Skinners and Wool Merchants.

Collins, Edwin, Queen st
Veitch, William, Canongate

Solicitors and Notaries

Anderson, Charles & R. B., (and agents for the Royal Bank of Scotland), 38 High st
Elliot, William, (and Sheriff Clerk), County Buildings
Hilson, George, 9 High st
Riddock, James, High st
Stedman, James, County Buildings
Stevenson, J. C., County Buildings
Thomson, William & Robert, High st
Turnbull, Simon & Sturrock, Exchange street

Spirit Dealers—see Hotels and Inns.

Surgeons.

Blair, William, Abbey green
Hume, John, Friars st
Hume, Walter, 24 Castlegate
Jeffrey, William, Castlegate
M'Gregor, Donald, Spring Mount
Sturrock, Peter, High st

Tailors and Clothiers.

See also under Heading of Drapers.

Greig, D. J., Castlegate
Turnbull, John, 1 Castlegate
Wilson, Robert, 24 High st

Tanners and Curriers.

Guthrie, J. & Sons, Townfoot

Temperance Hotels.

Abbey Restaurant—William Henderson, Market place
Elliot, Mrs., High st

Veterinary Surgeons.

Hume, Thomas, 15 Cannongate
Pow, James, Castlegate

Watchmakers and Jewellers

Dodds, W., 11 High st
MacIvor, John, 19 High st
Rule, Walter, 1 High st

Wood Merchants—see Saw mill Proprietors.

Wool Merchants—see Skinners.

Miscellaneous.

Brewer—David Keddie, Friarsburn
Coachbuilder—T. Moore, 55 High st
Cooper—William Sinton, 33 High st
Fancy Dealers—Bell & Miller, 22 High st
Hairdresser—G. Hoare, 33 High st
Plasterers—Lauder & Bell, 3 Richmond Row
Taxidermist—Robert Hope, 6 Abbey place
Tobacconist—Francis Rutherford, 14 Cannongate

KELSO,

Including ECKFORD, EDNAM, HEITON, MAKERSTOUN, NENTHORN, ROXBURGH, SMAILHOLM, SPROUSTON, and STITCHEL.

KELSO is a burgh of barony, a market town, and the capital of its parish, 42 miles S.E. from Edinburgh, 10 N. from Jedburgh, and 23 S.W. from Berwick-upon-Tweed. It is connected with the North British and the Newcastle and Berwick Railways by branches. The weekly market, chiefly for corn, is held on Friday, and from October to June a market for cattle and sheep is held once a fortnight, on Monday. An annual fair also takes place on the 5th of August. Acreage of the parish, 5,384. Population, 4,184.

EDNAM is a small village and parish about 2½ miles north from Kelso. Acreage of the parish, 3, 849.

MAKERSTOUN is a small parish on the North bank of the river Tweed, 5 miles distant from Kelso. The nearest railway stations are Rutherford and Roxburgh. Acreage, 2,865.

NENTHORN is a parish in Berwickshire about 4 miles from Kelso. Acreage, 3,454.

ROXBURGH is a small village and parish, 3 miles from Kelso, and is a station on the North British Railway. Acreage, 7,781.

SMAILHOLM is a small village and parish 6 miles from Kelso. The nearest railway (for goods), is at Fans Loanend, about 4 miles from the village. Acreage, 4,104.

SPROUSTON is a parish and village, 2½ miles from Kelso. The North British Railway has a station here. Acreage, 8,635.

STITCHEL is a small village and parish 3 miles from Kelso. Acreage, 6,898.

Business Directory.

Auctioneers and Valuators.

Clow, D. & J., (and Cabinetmakers and Upholsterers), 18 Square
Forsyth, & Lillie, Border Auction Mart
Penny & Kay, 3 Square

Bakers and Confectioners.

Brooks, John, 66 Horse market
Donaldson, Robert, 39 Roxburgh st
Graham, William, 15 Horse market
Rae, W. & Son, 15 Roxburgh st
Sanderson, A., 8 Coal market
Scott, J. & E., (and Grocers and Corn and Meal Dealers), Maxwellheugh
Scott, John, 8 Roxburgh st
Turner, J. G., 14 Coal market
Watson, D. M. W., 55 Roxburgh st

Banks.

Bank of Scotland, Wood market
British Linen Co. Bank, Square
Commercial Bank Ltd., Square
Kelso Savings' Bank, Square
National Bank, Ltd., Square

Bill Poster.

Rodgers, John R., 93 Roxburgh st

Blacksmiths.

Aitken, George, Roxburgh
Aitken, George, Hume, by Stitchel
Cairns, George, Lempitlaw
Chalmers, John H., 10 Horse market
Davidson, Adam, Sheddon Park rd
Fairbairn, Edward, Ednam
Fox, James, Nenthorn
Hermiston, George, Stichel
Hewit, John, Heiton
Hope, J. & J., 51 Horse market
M'Kenzie, Alexander, Simon's Square
Rutherford, George, Smailholm
Rutherford, Robert, Rose lane
Rutherford, William, Makerstoun
Smail John, Huntershall near Kelso
Smith, Andrew, Haddon
Trotter, Thomas, Sprouston road
Walker, Thomas, Sprouston
Wilson, Andrew, Westfield, Smailholm
Wood, William, Eckford

Booksellers, Stationers, and Newsagents.

Clow, I. & J., 29 Square
M'Donald, John, Square
M'Donald, J., 11 Wood market
Mills, N. J., 21 Bridge st
Rutherford, Jn. & J. H., 20 Square
Stewart, R. & Son, 16 Bridge st
Wilson, Elizabeth, 43 Square

Boot and Shoe Makers.

Brown & Dick, 26 Roxburgh st
Davidson, Mrs., 28 Wood market
Douglas, James, 26 Wood market
Gibson, James, 77 Roxburgh st
Gray, John & Co., 19 Roxburgh st
Hardie, W., 35 Horse market
Kennan, J. & Son, 19 Bridge st
Leitch, Isaac, Post Office, Hume
M'Cutcheon, Anth., 4 Coal market
Murray, John, 27 Roxburgh st
Paterson, Robert, Stitchel
Taylor, J., 11 Horse market
Walker, Geo. & Son, 31 Bridge st
Young & Co., 7 Roxburgh st

Cabinetmakers, Upholsterers, and Undertakers.

Clow, D. & J. (& Auctioneers & Valuators), 18 Square
Frazer & Wright (& Appraisers), Crawford st

Carting Contractors.

Dods, Thomas (and Dairyman), Roxburgh st
Douglas, John, 31 Bowmont street

Eckford, John, 99 Roxburgh st
Temple, David, Hume

Chemists and Druggists.
Alexander, W. M., 34 Square
Massey, J. M., 17 Square
Maxton, William M., The Abbey

China and Glass Merchants.
Douglas, David, Cross st
Macpherson, Miss J., 32 Roxburgh street
Strathearn, James, 32, 34, Horse market
Wood, James, 66 Roxburgh st

Coach Builders.
Brown, Thomas, 5 E Bowmont st
Croall, P. & Sons, Bridge st
Maxwell, D. & Son, Crawford st

Coal Merchants and Agents.
Clark, William, Sprouston
Dodds, James, Railway statn, and 35 Bowmont st
Hendry, Charles, Roxburgh
Hume, Peter, Maxwellheugh
Jamieson, Walter, 68 Horse market
Slight, Mrs. Thos., 16 Woodmarket

Confectioners.
Bennett, W. & Co. (wholesale Fruit Merchants, Confectioners, Drysalters & Commission Agents) Wood Market
Reid, John, 28 Bridge st
Reid & Co. (wholesale), 41 Square
Tully, E. M., 21 Wood market

Copper and Tin Smiths.
Cook, James, 27 Horse market
Rae, D., Horse market

Corn, Grain, and Meal Merchants.
Dunn, Andrew, & Sons, Railway station
Hogarth, John, Heiton, Maxwellheugh, and Wooden Mills, Maxwellheugh
Robertson, James, (and Grocer), Maxwellheugh
Scott, J. & E. (& bakers & grocers), Maxwellheugh

Cycle Agents.
Alexander, George, 49 Square
Swan, Robert, Roxburgh st

Dairymen.
Dods, Thomas, (& Carting Contractor), Roxburgh st
Hood, John, Cross st

Dentists.
Vernon, W. Fred. (Resident Dental Surgeon, Gold Medalist of the College of Dentists), Bowmont house
Wilson, James B., 2 Bowmont st, and at 19 Laurieston place, Edinburgh

Drapers and Clothiers.
Brown, S., 26 Square
Donaldson & Evans, 8 Wood market
Glendinnen, Charles E, 2 Roxburgh street
Johnston, Miss E., Heiton
Lugton & Porteous, Bridge st
Mitchell, John, 16 Square
Muirhead & Purves, 36 Bridge st
Neil, James, Victoria buildings Horse market
Neil, James, 25 Roxburgh st
Redpath, William, 25 Square
Young, E., 40 Bridge st

Engineers, Ironfounders,, and Millwrights.
Cockburn, Alexander, Bowmont st
Hogarth, J. & R., Sheddon park
Ritchie, John, Bowmont st

Fancy Goods Merchants.
Bennett, Mrs., 105 Roxburgh st
Brown & Dick (and wool), 26 Roxburgh st
Carson, Alexander, 31 Roxburgh st
Ross & Son, 5 Roxburgh st
Smith, Robert, 47 Horse market
Thomson, Miss, 12 Bridge st
Young, E., 40 Bridge st

Farmers—see end of Directory.

Fishing Rod and Tackle Makers.

Forrest & Son, 35 Square
Redpath & Co., Roxburgh st
Wright, James, Sprouston

Fishmongers, Poulterers, and Game Dealers.

Hall, James, 24 Roxburgh st
Steel, Archibald, 11 Bridge street

Fleshers.

Allen, William, 21 Roxburgh st
Henry, M., 25 Square
Liddle, Andrew, 14 Roxburgh st
Mitchell, John, 77 Roxburgh st
Plummer, H., Shedden Park rd
Scoon, Mrs., 1 Roxburgh st
Simpson, Peter, 2 Horse market
Thomson, Ralph, 27 Horse market
White, John & Thomas, 19 Horse market
Young, Andrew, 2 Bridge st

Grocers and General Merchants.

Beveridge George & Son, 28 Square
Brotherston, And., 16 Roxburgh st
Chisholm, Miss Jane, Roxburgh
Clark, J., 135 Roxburgh st
Clark, Mrs. J., Post Office, Ednam
Co-operative Stores, Union st
Fairbairn, K., 80 Roxburgh st
Ferguson, W. K., 62 Wood market
Glen, M., 60 Horse market
Gow, Jn. & Sons, 119 Roxburgh st
Grieve, Andrew, Post Office, Smailholm
Hogg, John, 13 Square
Holmes, Alexander (licensed), 11 Coal market
Hume, Isa., Horse market
Inglis, S. E., 5 Bowmont st
Johnston, Thomas & Co., 11 Roxburgh st
Leitch, Isaac, Post Office, Hume
Mitchell, Wm., 75 Roxburgh st
Neil, John, 18 Bridge st
Paterson, Andrew, Post Office, Makerstoun
Paterson, Hugh, Ednam
Paterson, Mrs. Agnes, Sprouston
Plummer, James, 101 Roxburgh st
Rae, Robert, 12 Horse market
Rae, William, Sprouston
Reid, Thomas, Lempitlaw
Robertson, James (and Corn and Grain Merchant), Maxwellheugh
Robertson, John Smailholm
Rutherford, T., 49 Horse market
Scott, John, 17 Bridge st
Scott, J. & E. (and Bakers and Corn, Grain, & Meal Merchants), Maxwellheugh
Smith, William, 21 Square
Steele, J., Horse market
Torrie, Mrs. F. E., 31 Square
Walker, J., 109 Roxburgh st
Wilson, William, 155 Roxburgh st
Wood, Ellen, Post Office, Eckford
Wright, Robert, 10 Roxburgh st

Hairdressers and Perfumers.

Henry, T., 8 Bridge st
Thomson, George, 16 Horse market

Hardware Merchants and Jewellers.

Brown & Dick, 26 Roxburgh st

Horse Hiring and Posting Establishments.

Rathie & Co., 12 Bowmont st—Telephone No. 809

Hotels and Inns.

Black Swan (Tents and Marquees lent on hire), Robert Rodgers 5 Horse market
Commercial—Charles Hunt, Bowmont st
Cross Keys—Thos. Keddie, Square
Hume, Mrs. Annie, Crawford st
Queen's Head—John Hill, Bridgest
Robertson, John, Wood market
Spread Eagle Hotel—First-Class Commercial Hotel. Tents, Marquees, and all Table Requisites lent on hire. Billiards and Stabling —Robert M'Kenzie, proprietor, Bridge st
Waggon Inn (Good Stabling), Robert Lamont, Coal market
Weigh house — Thomas Murray, Bridge st

Insurance Companies.

Prudential Assurance Co. Limited—Thomas W. Crozier, Assistant Superintendent, 38 Shedden Park road

Ironmongers and Hardwaremen.

Blake, James, Square
Brown & Dick, 26 Roxburgh st
Hooper & Co., 6 Roxburgh st
M'Dougall, James, 7 Wood market
Stewart, James, 6 Wood market

Joiners, Builders, and Stonemasons.

Aitchison, William, Mellowlees
Bennie, Thomas, Bowmont st
Black, William, Huntershall
Black, William, Stitchel
Bruce & Son, 2 E. Bowmont st
Bulman, Andrew, Coal market
Carfrae, George, Smailholm
Carfrae, Wm. Westfield, Smail-holm
Campbell, William, Roxburgh
Dickison, B. & Co., Rose lane
Dodds, Robert, Heiton
Gray, William, Roxburgh
Hogarth, Andrew, Smailholm
Hogg, William, Roxburgh
Hunter, George, Ednam
Kinghorn, George, Stitchel
Leitch, Adam, Hume
Oliver, James, Makerstoun
Scott, John, Roxburgh st
Sheriff, Alexander, Lempitlaw
Sheriff, James, Haddon
Tate, Peter, Kalemouth, Eckford
Trotter, Thomas, Sprouston
Yule, George, Nenthorn

Millers.

Cessford, George, Ednam
Dunn, Andrew & Sons, Kelso mills
Hogarth, John, Heiton, Maxwellheugh, and Wooden mills, Maxwellheugh
Kinghorn, John, Mellerstain mills
Rutherford, A. & Son, East Ednam mill, Ednam
Wilson, George, Banff mill

Milliners and Dressmakers.

Halliwell, Mrs., Edenside rd
Henderson, Miss, 44 Bridge st
Maxwell, Miss, Roxburgh
Millar, Miss, 40 Wood market
Neil, James, Victoria buildings, Horse market
Oliver, Miss Helen, Makerstoun
Robertson, Jane S., 47 Roxburgh st
Smith, Miss A., Shedden Park rd
Taylor, J., 62 Roxburgh st
Watson, Miss M. M)illiner), 41 Roxburgh st

Monumental and Stonemasons and Builders—see Joiners and Builders.

Music Teachers.

Tansley, Alfred, The Terrace
Vernon, Miss, Bowmont house

Newspapers, Publishers, & Printers

"Kelso Chronicle," John M'Arthur Wood market
"Kelso Mail," John Smith, 12 Bridge st

Nurserymen and Seedsmen.

Laing & Mather, 8 Horse market
Stuart & Mein, 21 Wood market

Painters and Decorators.

Black, Walter, 51 Square
Hogarth, A. & Son, 15 Wood market
Russell, T. & A., 33 Square

Photographers.

Macintosh & Co., 27 Bridge st
Simpson, W. H., 18 Roxburgh st

Plumbers and Gasfitters.

Allan, John R., 79 Roxburgh st
Burns, Alexander R., Union st
Erskine, Andrew, 70 Horse market

Pork Curers.

Plummer, James, 101 Roxburgh st
Smith & Son, 11 Oven wynd

Printers.

Rutherford & Craig, 2 Cross st
Rutherford, J. & J. H., Square

Saddlers and Harness Makers.
Johnston, J. & J., 1 Bridge st
Ker, George, 42 Wood market

Schools—Boarding and Day.
Duff, Misses, Charlesfield
Kelso High School—John Kemp, M.A., Headmaster

Seed Merchants.—see Nurserymen, &c.

Slaters and Plasterers.
Johnston, James, Bowmont st
Michie, John, junr. & Co., Platers, Glaziers, & Roof Plumbers, 9 Coal Market
Rae, William, Sprouston

Solicitors and Notaries.
Darling, Patrick S., Wood market
Dove, T. B., Square
Faulds, Robert, Wood market
Guthrie, Robert, 52 Wood market
Main, A. W., Wood market
Robson & Smith, 64 Wood market
Stevenson, A. P., Bridge st
Tait, J. & D. W. R., Square

Surgeons.
Fleming, Alexander, D., Abbey row
Hamilton, Thomas, 81 Roxburgh st
Rutherford, Thomas, 2 Abbey row
Turnbull, George H., Bridge st
Wright, J. H., Forrest Fields

Tailors and Clothiers.
Affleck, Robert, Heiton
Bell, Robert, Roxburgh
Biggar, Thomas, Heiton
Cairns, John D., 56 Wood market
Donaldson & Evans, The Square
Gray, Henry, Sprouston
Tully, William, L., Edman
Melrose, G. & Son, 48 Square
Paulin, John, 23 Horse market
Purves, William, Stitchel
Rutherford, Robert, Square
Rutherford, Robert, Eckford

Walker, Alexander, Sprouston

Taxidermist.
Chisholm, James, Sheddon Park rd

Temperance Hotels.
Crown Temperance Hotel 13 Roxburgh st. William Mercer, Proprietor
The Border Temperance Hotel—Mrs Thomas Slight, 14 Wood market

Timber Merchants and Sawmill Owners.
Hay, William, Sharpit Law, near Sprouston
Romanes, Andrew, Kalemouth, Eckford
Trotter, Thomas, Sprouston road

Tobacconists.
Davis, William, Square
Lane, William, 4 Bridge st
Stewart, R. & Son, 16 Bridge st

Veterinary Surgeons.
Hutton, John, Bowmont st
Tully, A. B., Wood market

Watchmakers and Jewellers
Brown, T., 54 Square
Clark James H., 34 Wood market
Falconer, Robert, 6 Bridge st
Laing, Thomas, 2 Wood market

Miscellaneous.
Iron Merchant—George Henderson, Horse market
Refreshment Rooms—Mrs Middlemiss, 21 Horse market
Rope & Sheep Net Maker—Mrs C. Smith, Bowmont st
Wine & Spirit Merchants—The Border Whisky Co., (wholesale), 15 Wood market

KIRKTOWN—SEE HAWICK.

LEMPITLAW—SEE KELSO.

LILLIESLEAF, BOWDEN, AND MIDLEM.

LILLIESLEAF is a village and parish, the former 10 miles from Galashiels, 10 from Jedburgh, and 8 from Hawick, on the North British Railway. Acreage of the parish, 6,673.

BOWDEN village is 2½ miles from Melrose, and 1½ miles from St. Boswells Railway station.

MIDLEM village is 2 miles from Lilliesleaf. Acreage of Bowden parish, 7,667.

Business Directory.

Blacksmith.
Falla, William, Lilliesleaf

Boot and Shoe Makers.
Park, John, Lilliesleaf
Redpath, Charles, Bowden

Draper.
Hood, James, Lilliesleaf

Farmers—see end of Directory.

Grocers and General Merchants.
Fairbairn, Mrs., Midlem
Grant, Helen, Bowden
Mitchell, James, Lilliesleaf
Nicol, Mrs., Bowden
Redford, James, Lilliesleaf
Steele, Walter, Lilliesleaf
Thomson, George, Bowden
Turnbull, Miss, Lilliesleaf

Hotels and Inns.
Cross Keys, Lilliesleaf, W. Fairgrieve
Plough—Lilliesleaf—J. Pringle

Joiners and Wrights.
Bonnington, George, Bowden
Hardy, John, Bowden
Harvey, Andrew, Midlem
Riddell, William, Lilliesleaf

Tailors and Clothiers.
Borthwick, John, Lilliesleaf
Clark, Peter, Bowden
Hume, John, Lilliesleaf
Hume, Walter, Midlem
Redford, James, Lilliesleaf

LONGNEWTON—SEE ANCRUM.

MELROSE,
Including the Villages of NEWSTEAD, GATTONSIDE, DARNICK, and Neighbourhood.

MELROSE is a parish and free burgh of barony. The town is 36 miles S. by E. from Edinburgh, 12 S.W. from Jedburgh, 7 N.E. from Selkirk, and 4 S.E. from Galashiels, and on the line of the North British Railway. Acreage of the parish, 25,794. Population, 1432.

The village of GATTONSIDE stands on the north bank of the Tweed, in the parish of Melrose.

DARNICK is a small village in Melrose parish.

Business Directory.

Ærated Water Manufacturers.

Simson & MacPherson, Limited, (and Brewers), Abbey Brewery—see advt

Bakers.

Curle, William, High st
M'Laren, Andrew, Market place
Scott, Thomas, Market place

Banks.

British Linen Co. Bank, market pl
Commercial Bank, Ltd., Melrose
Royal Bank of Scotland, High st

Blacksmiths.

Adamson, John, High st
Dodds, John, Gattonside
Fairbairn, William, (and Cycle Agent, High st
Scott, John, Station gate
Waldie, James, Darnwick

Booksellers and Stationers.

Johnstone, D. H., High st
MacBean, Robert W., Market pl
Wilson, W., High st

Boot and Shoe Makers.

Beveridge, Thomas, Buccleuch st
Scott, Walter, High st
Tait, Robert, Market place

Brewers.

Simson & MacPherson, Limited(Aerated Water Manufacturers) Abbey Brewery—see advt

Cabinetmakers and Upholsterers.

M'Donald, David, Buccleuch st
Stevenson, William, High st

Chemists and Druggists.

Bogie, Thomas S., Market place
Johnstone, D. H., High st

Coal and Lime Merchants.

Kirkman, J. N., Railway station
Purdie, William, Darnick
Redpath, William, Newstead
Tait, James, Railway station

Confectioners.

Greig, J,, Abbey st
Mathieson, J., High st
Riddell, R., High st

Cycle Agent.

Fairbairn, William, High st

Drapers and Haberdashers.

Aitchison, J. (dressmaker), High st
Davidson, James, West end
Russell, Thomas, Market square
Sinclair, William, Market place

Farmers—see end of Directory

Fleshers.

Bowers, T. C., Darnick
Bunyan, James, Buccleuch st
Charles, James, Darnick
M'Laren, Andrew, Market place
Riddell, John, Market place
Sanderson, Thomas, High street

Grocers and General Merchants.

Beveridge, Thomas, Buccleuch st
Galloway, Margaret, Darnick
Graham, Miss, Post Office, Darnick
Hutchison. M., Darnick
Lawrie, Thomas, Abbey st
MacLean & Co. (licensed), High st
Milne, A., Darnick

Mitchell, James, Gattonside
Paterson, Thomas & Sons (and wine and spirit merchants), Market place
Redpath, James, Darnick
Wallace, George, Market place

Hotels and Posting Houses.

Abbey Hotel — George Hamilton, proprietor, Abbey gate
Anderson's Temperance — Market place
George and Abbotsford Hotels—George Hamilton, proprietor, High st
King's Arms Hotel—High st
Ship Hotel—W. Bow, Market sq
Station Hotel—Station gate
Waverley Hydropathic — Skirmish hill
Waverley Hotel--Station gate

Ironmongers and China and Glass Dealers.

Dick, William, High st
Jardine, C., Abbey st
Johnstone, John & Co., High st

Joiners, Wrights, and Builders.

Brown, Thomas & Son, East port
Dodds, Andrew, Little Fordell
Fairbairn, D. & J., Weirhill place
Milne, Adam, Darnick

Nurserymen, Seedsmen, & Florists.

Johnstone, John, High st
Mercer, Bros, Abbey St Nurseries
Ormiston, & Renwick, Market pl

Painters and Decorators.

M'Dowall, C., Galashiels road
Mercer, George, Station gate
Wilson, Thomas, (House Painter), Market place

Plumbers and Gasfitters.

Jardine, John, Buccleuch st
M'Gregor, Henry, Rosebank

School—Boarding and Day.

Hamilton, J. B., (Gentleman's), St. Mary's School

Surgeons.

Boyd, A., (Veterinary), High st
Calvert, W. H., Melrose

Tailors and Clothiers.

Cockburn, A. P., High st
Holmes, Wm., Market place
Tait, John B., High st
Turnbull, Richard, Darnick
Wishart, Alexander, High st

Watchmakers.

Hart, William, High st
Millar, G. L., Abbey st

Wine and Spirit Merchants.

Paterson, Thomas & Sons, (Sole Proprietors of the Dews O' Eildon Scotch Whisky), Melrose

Miscellaneous.

Coach Builder—Alex. Roy, Darnick
Dairyman—Wm. Thompson, Darnick
Fancy Dealer—Mrs Kerr, Anderson, Market square
Fishing Tackle Maker — John Veitch High st
Hairdresser—E. Robertson, Buccleuch st
Saddler—R. Butler, Buccleuch st
Stay Makers—Misses Cramond, Melrose

MAKERSTOUN—SEE KELSO.
MAXTON—SEE ST. BOSWELLS.
MERTOUN--SEE ST. BOSWELLS.
MIDLEM—SEE LILLIESLEAF.
MINTO—SEE HAWICK.
MOREBATTLE—SEE YETHOLM.
NENTHORN—SEE KELSO.

NEW CASTLETON.

A Village in a mountainous parish, is situated 26 miles from Jedburgh, and 20 S.E. from Hawick The parish is 18 miles in length and has an acreage of 67,858. Population, 924.

Business Directory.

Drapers and Clothiers.
Beattie, J., Hermitage st
Fraser, William, Douglas square
Little, Arthur, Douglas square
Murray, M. & A., Douglas square
Oliver, Murray, Hermitage st

Farmers—see end of Directory.

Grocers and General Merchants.
Marked e are also Spirit Dealers.
Benson, William, Douglas square
e Davidson, Thomas Douglas square
Edgar, James, Douglas square
Gordon, Thomas, Hermitage st
Grieve, Miss, Douglas square
Milligan, Henry, Hermitage st

Hotels and Inns.
Commercial Inn, Douglas square
Grapes Inn, Douglas square

Joiners and Wrights.
Inglis, James, Douglas square
Scott, Archibald, Hermitage st
Veevers, Robert, Winchester st

NEWSTEAD—SEE MELROSE.
NEWTOWN ST. BOSWELLS—SEE ST. BOSWELLS.
OXNAM—SEE JEDBURGH.
ROBERTON—SEE HAWICK.
ROXBURGH—SEE KELSO.

ST. BOSWELLS,

Including MAXTON. NEWTOWN. ST. BOSWELLS, AND MERTOUN.

ST. BOSWELLS is a village in the parish of its name, 10 miles W. from Kelso, 9 N. from Jedburgh, and 4 E. from Melrose, and about 1 mile from St. Boswells station on the North British Railway. Acreage of the parish, 3,155. Population, 959.

The parish of MAXTON is about four miles in length. Acreage, 4,442.

NEWTOWN ST. BOSWELLS is a village in the parish of Melrose, one mile from St. Boswells. Population, 481.

MERTOUN is a parish extending 6 miles along the banks of the Tweed. CLINTMAINS is a village in the parish, and 2 miles from St. Boswells village. Acreage, 6,374.

Business-Directory.

Bakers and Confectioners.
Brown, C. H., Newtown
Quarry, W. & J., St. Boswells

Banks.
Commercial Bank, Ld., Newtown
Royal Bank of Scotland, Newtown

Blacksmiths.
Aldcorn, John, Newtown
Fairbairn, John, Maxton

Boot and Shoe Makers.
Aitken, T., Newtown
Bowman, James, Newtown
Brown, Robert, St Boswells
Greerson, Alexander, Newtown
Quarry, William, St Boswells

Builders.
Grieve, Robert, Maxton
Lockie, J. & R., Newtown
Simpson, William, St Boswells

Carrier.
Thompson, James ('Bus to Station) St Boswells

Carting Contractor.
Hair, John, Newtown

Chemist and Druggist.
Robertson, James, St. Boswells

Coal Merchants and Agents.
Little, H. M., Newtown
Porteous, Ronald, Newtown
Stewart, T., Newtown

Corn, Grain, Seed, and Manure Merchants.
Douglas, G. & Son., Newtown
Hogarth, & Son, Newtown
Smith, W. & Son, Newtown
Wight, & Co., Newtown

Drapers and Haberdashers.
Ballantyne, Miss M., St. Boswells
Richardson, Miss, (Milliner), Newtown
Stirling, Stuart E., St. Boswells
Thomson, A. & J., St. Boswells

Farmers.—see end of Directory.

Fleshers.
Laing, Andrew, St. Boswells
Wood, Robert, St. Boswells

Grocers and General Merchants.
Marked 'e' are also Spirit Dealers.
Ballantyne, W. & Son, (Grocers, Provision and Wine Merchants), St. Boswells—see advt
e Cochrane, David, (licensed), St. Boswells
Dickson, Archibald, Eildon
Dickson, James, Newtown
Galashiels Co-operative Store, Ld., Newtown
Grieve, Robert, Maxton
Hunter, Benjamin, St. Boswells
Kerr, Thomas, (and Ironmonmonger), Newtown
Lamb, Charles, St. Boswells
Lamb, Helen, St. Boswells
Lockie, E. & M., Newtown
Richardson, Andrew, St. Boswells

Hotels, Inns, and Posting Houses.
Dryburgh Arms—James Graham, Newtown
Buccleuch Arms, St. Boswells
Railway Hotel—Mrs. Brydon, Newtown—see advt
Scott, William, St. Boswell st
Temperance Hotel—Robert Brown, Newtown
Wright, G,, Newtown

Ironmongers and Hardwaremen.
Ballantyne, W. & Son, (and Grocers), St. Boswells—see advt
Ker, Thomas, Newtown
Nichol, Jonathan, R,, (& Saddler), St. Boswells

Joiners and Wrights.
Anderson, William, Mertoun
Grant, James. W, Newtown
Henderson, William, Mertoun
Ker, Andrew, Newtown
Nicol, William, St. Boswells
Oliver, Robert, Dryburgh
Thomson, John Y., St. Boswells
Wood, James. St. Boswells

Plasterers and Slaters.
Common, R. & Sons, (& Plumbers), St. Boswell
Stewart, T., Newtown

Saddler,
Nichol, Jonathan R., (and Ironmonger), St. Boswells

Stationers.
Ballantyne, W. & Son, St. Boswells
Brown, Andrew, St. Boswells

Tailors and Clothiers.
Cochrane, James, (and Hatter), St. Boswells
Dickson, David, St. Boswell
Grierson, A. T., Newtown
Inglis, James W., (and Hatter), Newtown
Melrose, George, St. Boswell
Middlemas, Walter, St. Boswell
Robertson, Robert, Newtown

Miscellaneous.
Cabinetmaker—James Turnbull, St. Boswells
Fishing Rod Maker and Joiner—Joseph Thompson: St. Boswell
Watchmaker—G. L., Millar, St. Boswell
Woollen Spinners—A. Hall & Sons, Newtown

SMAILHOLM—SEE KELSO.
SOUTHDEAN—SEE JEDBURGH.
SPROUSTON—SEE KELSO.
STITCHEL—SEE KELSO
TEVIOT-HEAD—SEE HAWICK.
WILTON—SEE HAWICK.

YETHOLM, LINTON, AND MOREBATTLE.

YETHOLM is a parish. The village is 8 miles from Kelso. Acreage of parish, 5,960. Population, 746.

LINTON is a parish. Acreage, 6,393.

MOREBATTLE is a parish and village. The village is 7½ miles from Kelso and 18 from Jedburgh. Acreage of parish, 22,334.

Business Directory.

Bakers and Confectioners.
Cowe, R., Kirk-Yetholm
Scott, William, Morebattle
Tice, George, Yetholm

Blacksmiths.
Gladstone, Archibald, Yetholm
Lees, Robert, Yetholm
Purves, Alexander, Morebattle
Stenhouse, J., Linton Downs

Boot and Shoe Makers.

Hogarth, James, Yetholm
Laidlaw, John, Morebattle
Lyon, James, Yetholm
Ovens, Thomas, Morebattle
Rutherford, W., Yetholm
Turnbull, James, Yetholm
Whellans, John, Morebattle

Drapers and Clothiers.

Cairns, James R., (& Tailor), Yetholm
Cuthbertson, Walter, Morebattle
Leishman, J., Morebattle
Thomson, Mabel, Morebattle

Farmers—see end of Directory.

Fleshers.

Currie, John, Morebattle
Simpson, Thomas, Yetholm
Young, Andrew, Yetholm

Florists.

Scott, H. & Sons, Yetholm

Grocers and General Merchants.

Bell, George, (Licensed), Yetholm
Cuthbertson, Walter, Morebattle
Davidson, Henry T., Yetholm
Grahamslaw, Thomas, Yetholm
Hardie, John, Heiton
Handyside, J., Morebattle
Holiday, Mrs., Morebattle
Hunter, Ann, Morebattle
Laidlaw. James S., Yetholm
Leishman, J., Morebattle
Oliver, Jessie, Yetholm
Stenhouse, J., Yetholm
Stephen, James, Yetholm
Watt, John, Kirk-Yetholm
Young, William, Yetholm

Joiners and Wrights.

Black, Thomas, Yetholm
Christie, William, Yetholm
Fox, John, Yetholm
Herbert, John, (Builder), Yetholm
Hogg, Andrew, Yetholm
Hume, James, Linton Downs
Ker, John, Yetholm
Renwick, John, Morebattle

Millers.

Bell, Wm., Linton Corn Mills, Yetholm
White, Thomas, Yetholm Corn Mills

Saddlers and Harness Makers.

Allan, Robert, Yetholm
Lees, Robert, Morebattle

Spirit Dealers.

Brown, George, Yetholm
Reid, John, Morebattle
Renilson, Thomas, Kirk Yetholm
Turnbull, James, Yetholm

Tailors and Clothiers.

Cairns James R., Yetholm
Cairns, T., Morebattle
Scott, W., Morebattle
Wood, James, Yetholm

Watchmakers.

Chalmers, Robert, Yetholm
Young, J., (Jeweller), Morebattle

Miscellaneous.

Fancy Dealer—Miss Janette Storie, Yetholm
Manufacturers—Cairns Brothers, Yetholm
Millright—Thomas Kennedy, Yetholm
Refreshment Rooms—Matthew Douglas, Kirk-Yetholm
Surgeon—Dr. Hodge. Yetholm

SELKIRKSHIRE.

THIS County lies in the south of Scotland, bounded by Roxburghshire on the east and south-east, on the west by the counties of Dumfries and Peebles, and on the south and south-west by Dumfriesshire. The county extends 27 miles from south-west to north-east, and is 17½ miles in breadth. Its area is 260 square miles, or 166,524 acres, of which 1997 acres are under water. In size the county stands as the twenty-fourth, and in population the twenty-seventh of the counties of Scotland. The principal mountains, with their altitudes, are—Blackhouse Hills, 2,370 feet; Windlestrae Law, 2,295; Law Kneis, 1,900; the Three Brethren, 1,978; Black Andrew, 1,966; Peatlaw, 1,964; Wardlaw, 1,900; Minchmoor, 1,877; Hangingshaw Law, 1,780; and Peatlaw, 1,557.

The county is well watered by the Ettrick, the Yarrow, and the Tweed; the latter valuable river, after draining Peebles-shire, intersects the northern extremity of Selkirkshire from west to east, during the placid course in a deep channel of nine miles, when it is joined by the Ettrick, and receiving the Gala, passes on to Roxburghshire and Berwick on Tweed, where it empties itself into the German Ocean.

The Manufactures of this county consists of woollens, tweeds, tartans, shawls, and hosiery, together with the tanning of leather and the dressing of sheep and lamb skins. There are also several engineering and machine making establishments.

The principal railway line with which this county is connected is the North British, and the chief town that lies in its route is Galashiels, and a branch from the main line runs to Selkirk.

The county of Selkirk contains only three complete parishes, namely Ettrick, Stow, and Kirkhope, but has proportions of seven other parochial divisions. The only towns are those of Selkirk and Galashiels—the former a royal burgh. This county joins with Peeblesshire in returning one member to Parliament, the present representative being Walter Thorburn, Esq. The lord-lieutenant is Lord Polwarth. Population, 27, 762.

ASHKIRK—SEE SELKIRK.
CADDONFOOT—SEE GALASHIELS.
CLOVENFORDS - SEE GALASHIELS.
ETTRICK—SEE SELKIRK.

GALASHIELS,

With CADDONFOOT, CLOVENFORDS, and Neighbourhoods.

GALASHIELS is a parliamentary burgh, a manufacturing and market town, 31 miles S.S.E. from Edinburgh, 18 E. from Peebles, 6 N. from Selkirk, 4 N.W. from Melrose, and 30 S. by W. from Berwick, partly in the parish of Galashiels and partly in that of Melrose, situated on both sides of the Gala, about one mile above the confluence of that river with the Tweed. It lies on the North British Railway, for which line there is a station in the town; there is also a line to Selkirk, and to Edinburgh, Innerleithen, and Peebles. Galashiels has enjoyed an envied distinction in the manufacture of Tweeds. A grain market is held on the Tuesday, a fair on the third Wednesday of March, and a live stock sale is every alternate Wednesday. The parish of Galishiels comprises an acreage of 8,440. Population 17,252.

CADDONFOOT is a *quoad sacra* parish (presbytery of Selkirk) in the north-eastern division of the county. It is partly in the civil parish of Yarrow, and partly in those of Galashiels and Stow, and the hamlet of Clovenfords, 3 miles west from Galashiels, being in the latter. Here is a station on the Peebles branch of the North British Railway.

Business Directory.

Accountants and House Agents.
Houston, Samuel, 65 Magdala ter
Thomson, J. Lamb., 38 High st

Ærated Water Manufacturers and Bottlers.
Anderson, E., 26 St. John st
Gray, William, Market st
Gray, Wm, C. & Son, 37 Channel st
Imrie, William, Channel st
Middlemass, J. (G. W. Scott agent) Wilderhaugh st
Murray W & A, Brewery buildings
Sheal, William, Hunter square

Architects and Surveyors.
Black Andrew, (and Valuator) 52 High st
Hall, J. & J., (and Builders and Contractors), Ladhope Vale
Stirling, William (and Valuator and Burgh Assessor) Market st

Auctioneers and Valuators,
Chadwick, J. & Co., (and Furniture Dealers), Bridge place
Forsyth, F. S., Galabrig
King, George, W., Mill House

Baby Linen, Ladies Underclothing, Fancy & Berlin Wool Repositorier.
Aitken, H., 111 High st
Bolton, Mrs. J., 28 Bank st
Cornish, James, Balmoral place
Fisher, Mrs., High st
Fleming, Miss, 43 High Buckholmside
Hood, Miss, High st
Hunter, Mrs., Kirkbrae
Joyce, Miss., 13 Scott street
Mirtle, Agnes, 94 Channel st
Ritchie, Mrs. W., 65 High st
Scott, Mrs.. Greenbank st
Scott, J., 13A King st
Stewart, Mrs., 17 Bank st
Turnbull, Mrs. H., 68 High st

Bakers and Confectioners.
Broad, W., Market st
Brown, Joseph, 1 Market st
Dobson, & Co., (& Restaurant), Bank st
Fairley, Gideon, 3 Bank st
Gala Store Co., Roxburgh st
Gibson, P., 15 Bank st
Grant, James, Market st
Grieve, J., 7 High st
Hodg, W., 41 Island st
Kennedy, H. Overhaugh st
Redpath, James, 88 High st
Robertson, John, 72 Croft st
Scott, John, 34 Magdala terrace
Scott, John, 8a King st
Smith, J., 201 Galapark road
Turnbull John S., Arcade buildings Channell st
Wilkie, John, 14 Island st

Banks.
Bank of Scotland, Channel st
British Linen Co., 46 High st
Commercial Bank, Ltd., 79 High st
National Bank, Ltd., Bank st
Royal Bank of Scotland, High st
Trustees Savings Bank, High st

Bicycle and Cycle Makers and Agents.
Boyd, James, Market square
Hall, Robert, 101 High st
Leishman & Son, (Furniture Dealers), Meigle st
M'Nish, K. F., Island st
Milligan, James W., Gala Forge, Hunter square
Rutter, John W., 23 Elm row, see advt
Strachan, Andrew, Channel st

Bill Posters.
Robertson, Andrew, 44 Bank street
Taylor, Chris., 29 Albert place

Blacksmiths.
Aikman, R., Galaside
Fairbairn, G., Galaside
Hepburn, James, (& Ironmonger), Sime place
Herbert, Robert, Union st
Milligan, James W., Gala Forge, Hunter square
Mitchell, A., Market square
Purves, Adam. Damside

Booksellers, Stationers and Newsagents.
Cornish, J., Balmoral place
Craighead, D., Ladhope vale
Dawson, R. & Son, 40 High st
Frier, R., (& Tobacconist), High st
Grant, John, 92 High st
Haig. William, (& Tobacconist), Market st
Hay, R., High Buckholmside
Liddle, James T., (& Tobacconist), 9 High st
MacPhail, M., (& Musicsellers), High st
MacQueen, John, Channel st
Melrose. John, (& Tobacconist), 57 High Buckholmside
Scott, R., 18 Island st
Somerville, R., (& Tobacconist), 84 Channel st
Walker, A. & Son, (& Printers), 113 High st
Walker, Mrs R., 56 Bank st

Boot and Shoe Makers.

Ainslie, J., 12 aKing st
Boot Repairing Co., Bank Close
Brown, J., 119 High Buckholmside
Cowan, J., 17 King st
Douglas, John, Island st
Dove, James, 21 Bank st
Dundee Equitable Coy., 56 Bank st
Drummond, George, 191 Gala Park rd
Gass, William, 157 Holliburton pl
Gray, Thomas A., Channel st
Hall, George, 2 High st
Healey, J., 22 Channel st
Heugh, A., King st
Hogarth, C., Overhaugh st
Lauder, W., 10 Bank st
Mirtle & Son, 74 High st
Morton, N., Market st
Pringle, George, 67 High st
Richardson, D., 76 Scott st
Stead & Simpson, Ltd., 70 High st
Steele, W., 22 Livingstone place
Stewart, John, 785 Magdala terrace
Turner, J., 288 Gala Park rd
Tyler, H. P., Bank st

Builders and Contractors.

Dalgleish, P. & D., Roxburgh place
Hall, R. & Co., Island st
Hall, J., & J., (Builders & Contractors, Architects and Surveyors), Ladhope vale
Herbertson, A. & Son, Albert place
Johnstone, J., 263 Gala Park rd
Park, G. & Son, Gala terrace
Sanderson, Hugh, 58 St. Andrew st
Wood, W. & J., (& Joiners), Galapark road

Cabinetmakers, Upholsterers, and Undertakers.

Brydon, William (& Joiner), Botany lane
Fairbairn & Tait, Bridge street
Goodsir, Thomas, 99 Albert place
Hepburn, P., 1 Bridge st
Lees, Andrew, Elm row
Lynn, Francis, Galapark road
Rankine, J. & Son & (House agents), High st
Scott, William, 23 High st

Chemists and Druggists.

Alexander, J. G., 45 Bank st
Cartwright, B., High st
Noble, Alevander, Island st
Poustie, J. H., 176 Galapark rd
Ross, W., Bank st
Wilkie, A. L., 25 High st

Chimney Sweep.

Kerr, Robert (& Mason), 9 Green st

Glass and China Merchants.

Clerk, James, 58 High st
Connell, John, 23 Low Buckholmside
Fleming, J. & W., 6 Market st
M'Leod, Alexander, Bank st
Robertson, Thomas, Overhaugh st
Sword, E., 63 Channel st

Clog and Pattern Makers.

Haugh Joseph, 77 Overhaugh st
Irvine John, Overhaugh st

Coach Builders.

Darnley, James, Clovenfords
Notman Bros, The Galashiels Carriage Works, Magdala terrace —see adt

Coal Merchants and Agents.

Dalgleish, Wm., 46 Livingstone pl
Erskine, D. S., 7 Station & Bank st
Henderson, J. T., 2 Station
Hume J. H., 6 Station
Lennox, L, 29 High Buckholmside
Lillie, T., 10 Station
Lothian Coal Co., Station
Mulholland, J., 173 Scott st
Skillen, W., Green st
Smail Alexander, 104 St Andrew st
Whyte, James, Station
Wilson Robert, 8 St Andrew st

Confectioners and Fruiterers.

Boyd Amelia, 60 Bank st
Curran, P. 4 High st
Fofey P. Overhaugh st
Fyfe Janet, 1 High st
Graham, Mrs. E., 73 High st
Grant, Mrs. T., 3 Island st
Kerr, Jane, 103 St. Andrews st
Lindsay, M. A., Bank st
Murray, H., Bank st

Murray, J. L., Ladhope Bank
Scott, J. & A., 56 High st
Scott, J. W., Island st
Tait, James, 119 High st
Watt, Alexander, Gala terrace

Contractors.

Brown, Robert, Scott street
Hogarth, James, 189 Galapark road
Hume, J. H., 4 St Andrew street
Logan, George, 29 Church street

Corn and Grain Merchants.

Gladstone, John (Grain Merchant), Station Brea sec adv
Hogarth, James, Market st

Dentist.

Bain, A. H., L. D. S., 1 Bank st

Drapers, Dressmakers, Millners, and Clothiers.

Ainslie, Mrs. Sarah, 12a King st
Ballantyne George, B., 108 High st
Beveridge, Thomas, 37 Bank st
Church, Adam, 55 High st
Cochrane, John, Victoria Buildings
Cornish, James, Balmoral place
Cunningham, Robert F., 20 Market st
Gordon, C. F., 100 High st
Graham, Mrs., 10 St John st
Grand Colosseum Warehouse Co., Ltd., 11 High st
Haggart, D., 56 St Andrew st
Muir, James, 18 High st
Scott, James, 47, 48 Bank st
Scott, William, 75 Channel st
Thomson Brothers, 47 High st

Dressmakers and Milliners—see also Drapers

Gilles, Miss (Dressmaking on the Anglo-Parisian System), 124 Croft st
Mullen, B. T., 59 Bank st
Rankin, Miss M. (Dress and Mantle Maker), 20 Island st—see advt
Walker, Miss (Milliner), 107 High street

Drysalters and Mill Furnishers

Adam, Robert P., 9 Roxburgh st
Watson, A. & Son, Market st
Waverley Mill Furnishing Co., Roxburgh st
Young, John, 4 Roxburgh st

Dyers and Cloth Finishers.

Brownlee, James, Paton st
Gray, Ballatyne & Co., Plumtree
Kemp, Blair, & Co., Gala Dye Works

Egg Merchants.

Barrie, A (& Fish) Chapel st
Hislop, William, Queen st
Michie, William (and Fish) Stirling place
Scott, A., Scott st
Wilson, A., Island st

Electrical Engineers.

National Telephone Co., Ltd., 72 High st
Tweedie, Brownlee & Co., Bank st

Engineers and Millwrights.

Aimers, T. & Sons, Waverley Iron works
Burns, George & Sons (and Woollen Machine Makers), Roxburgh st

Farmers—see end of Directory.

Firewood Merchants.

Cunningham, J., Park st
Maguire, J., Hunter square
Mercor, John, Galashiels Steam Fire wood Factory, Halliburton pl
Thomson, T., 240 Scott st

Fishmongers, Poulterers, and Game Dealers.

Barrie, J. (and Egg Merchant), 309 Galapark rd
Bolton, John R. (Fish, Poulterer and Licensed Game Dealer), Bank st—see advt
Carss, T. T. (poulterer) Bridge st
Haig, D., High Buckholmside
Hislop, William, 33 Queen st
Michie, William, Stirling place

M'Laren, J., 185 Glendining ter
Noble, James, 121 High st
Robertson, B., 13 Channel st
Tait, A., (and Egg Merchant), 233 Galapark rd
Thomson, J., 95 Lintburn st

Fishing Tackle Makers

Boyd, J., Market st
Cochrane, John, Island st
Gray, L., 26 High st
Hall, Robert, 101 High st
Hay, R., 111 High Buckholmside
Lumsden, J. (and Tobacconist), 61 Bank st
Wilson, A., 59 Island st

Fleshers.

Barth, C. (pork), High st
Clapperton, John, High st
Cleghorn, Alexander, 31 Bank st
Finlay, T. J., 117 High Buckholmside
Kerr, J., Paton st
Oliver, George, Galapark road
Peden, P., 21 High st
Tait, J. & A., 50 King st
Wilkie Bros., 236 Galapark rd

Furriers.

Cochrane, John, Victoria buildings
Thomson Bros., 47 High st

Grocers and General Merchants.
Marked *e* are Spirit Dealers.

Archibald, James (and Egg), 54 St. Andrew st
Archibald, Miss J., Galapark rd
Bain, A., Wilderhaugh
Ballantyne, F. P., Island st
e Bell Mrs M. (Licensed), 38 Halliburton place
e Bennie, M. (Licensed), 76 Croft st
e Beveridge, James, 44 Market st
e **Blake, James** (and Wine and Spirit Merchant), 104 High st
Blake, E., 273 Galapark rd
e Boyd, William, 24 King st
Brown, Mrs M., Woodside place
e Campbell, Peter, 222 Halliburton place
Carruthers, G., Bridge place
Clapperton, G., Overhaugh st
e Clapperton, John, Princes st
Clark, R., Elm row
Currie, John, 155 Magdala terrace
Dalgleish, J. C. (provision), Bank st
Dalgleish, W., 51 Wood st
Dobson, George, Island st
Donald, V., Tweed place
Ferguson, R., 305 Galapark rd
Galashiels Co-operative Co., High st
Gray, William (Licensed), Market st
Grant, William, 162 Croft st
Haggart, D., 56 St Andrew st
Hardie, Mrs. A., 23 Stanley st
Hay, Mrs. E., 28 St John st
Henry, George, Victoria st
Henry, M., 16 High st
Henry, M. & G., 150 St Andrew st
Hoole, Walter, 59 High Buckholmside
Hume, Andrew C., 30 Bank st
Hume, Mrs J., Overhaugh st
Inglis, George, Clovenfords
Inglis, John, 11 Market st
Irvine, C., 51 Scott st
Keddie, Alexander, 8 Bank st
Kerr, W., 186 High Buckholmside
Lauder, W., Galapark rd
Latta, Mrs., Dale st
Lipton, Thos. J. (and provision), 20 High st
e Leithead, Mrs W., 40 Island st
London, &c., Tea Co., 16 Channel st
e Marshall, John (and Wine and Spirit Merchant), Magdala ter
Messer, W., 61 Scott st
Milne, J., 79 Halliburton place
Nisbet, J., 74 Croft st
Nixon, Mrs J., Magdala terrace
Paterson, J., Thornbank st
e Riddle, H. & Co., Channel st
Robertson, John, Dale st
Scott, A., 91 High Buckholmside
Scott, J. W., 8 Island st
Smith, Mrs P., Huddersfield st
Sutherland, B., 92 Scott st
e **Taket, Mrs J.** (and Wine and Spirit Merchant), Market sq
Thomson, J. (and Fruit, &c.), 95 High st
Turnbull, Thomas, 94 High st

Waverley Co-operative Co., Channel st
Welsh, R., Galapark rd
Wilson, Mrs., 2 Croft st
Wilson, Miss A., Island st
e Wright, Mrs James, Bridge st
Young, D., Overhaugh st

Hairdressers.

Aitken, William, (& Tobacconist), Market Square
Brown, George. High st
Dalgleish, Adam, 39 Channel st
Dobson, J., 5 High st
Elliot F,, 6 Island st
Hay R., High Buckholmside
Meiklejohn, J., Overhaugh st
Milne, W., 31 High st
Roseburgh, J., Market st

Hatters and Hosiers.

Cochrane, John, Channel st
Dillon, Mrs T., Lintburn st
Fulton, J. R., 51 High st
Hogg, John A., Bank zt
M'Nish, R. F., High st

Heddle and Reed Makers.

Baron & Hogarth, Bank close
Hume, Mrs Robert, St John st
Neilson & Son, Roxburgh st
Scott Robert & Co., 28 Overhaugh st

Horse and Carriage Hirers.

Flynn, James, 23 Victoria st
Oliver, R., 37 Queen st
Stewart, J., Channel st

Hosiery Manufacturers.

Cunningham, Robert F., 20 Market st
Currie, John, Ladhope vale, and 8 High st
Greenock Hosiery Stores, Victoria buildings
Henderson, Mrs John, 14 Union st
Lees, Mrs, 31 Scott st
M'Laughlan, Mrs, 228 Galapark rd
Melrose, J., 307 Galapark rd
Scott, W., Channel st
Young, Mrs R., 4 Roxburgh st

Hotels Inns & Posting Establishments

Abbotsford Arms—Adam Swanson, Stirling st
Bridge Inn—W Balmer Island st
Commercial—S. Maxwell, Bridge st
Donaldson, J., Bank st
Douglas Family and Commercial Hotel—D. M'Lagan Channel st, proprietor
Graham, W., Waverley House
Harrow Inn, R. M'Intyre, 22 High street
Ladhope Inn, J. Hair, High Buckholmside
Railway Hotel—William Wilson, proprietor, Market st
Royal—Sam Gillon, Channel st
Salmon Inn—George Walker, 53 Bank st
Temperance — George W. King, Market st
Town's Arms Inn—Mrs J. Michie, 37 High st
Victoria and Volunteer Arms — Archibald Wilson, Market st
Waverley Temperance—Mrs Rankine, Market st
Young, Andrew (spirit merchant), 57 Bank st

House and Property Agents.—see also Accountants, &c.

Clark, J., Magdala terrace
Scott, William, 23 High st
Thom, William, Galapark rd

Iron and Brass Founders.

Aimers, T. & Sons, Waverley Iron works
M'Laren, Thomas & Sons, Victoria foundry

Ironmongers and Hardwaremen.

Hall, Robert, 101 High st
Hogg, Walter, 41 Bank st
Milne, William, 31 High st
Thripland, Robert, Channel st
Yellowlees, A., Bank st

Joiners and Wrights—see also Cabinetmakers.

Brydon, William (& Cabinetmaker, &c.), Botany lane

Donald, Hugh, Wilderhaugh
Gladstone, A. & Son, Channel st
Hislop, George (and Hand Loom Maker), Channel st
Hogarth, W., Union st
Kennedy, Thomas, High Buckholmside
Ramage, James, Galaside
Reid, Robert, High st
Whitie, William, Market square

Laundries.

Hogg, W., 1 High st
Nicholson, W. A., Wilderhaugh st

Manufacturers.

Abbotsford Tweed Co, Ladhope vale
Anderson, George, 78 Lintburn st
Anderson, Peter (Tweed), Bridge mills, Roxburgh st—see ad
Ballantyne, W., 51 Lintburn st
Boothroyd, J. & Son, Albert place
Brown Brothers, Buckholm mills
Brown, W. & Sons, Wilderbank mill
Christie, A., Stirling st
Clark Brothers, Ladhope vale
Cochrane, Adam, L. & Bros. (Limited), Netherdale mills
Cochrane, J. & W., Mid mill
Currie, M'Dougall, & Scott, Langhaugh mills
Dickson, A. & Co, Wheatlands mill
Dorward, J. & J. C, Waulkrigg mill
Graham, J., 26 Roxburgh place
Hunter, William, 6 Bridge st
Irving, Adam, Galapark rd
Keddie, Gordon, & Co., Rosebank mill
Lennox, L. (Tweed Manufacturer), 29 Buckholmside
Lees, George & Co., Galabank mill
Lees, R., Huddersfield st
M'Crirrick, Thomas (tweed) Lawyer's brae
M'Laren, P., Market st
Ovens, Hunter & Co., Abbots mills
Park, Thomas, Bristol terrace
Paterson, Geo. & Co., Huddersfield mill
Roberts, Somerville & Co., Ladhope vale
Roberts, W. & Co., Victoria mill
Roberts, J. & W., Waverley mill
Sanderson, Hugh & Son, Comely bank mill
Sanderson, P. & R., Tweed mill
Sanderson, R. & A. & Co., Gala mills
Scott, R. & Co., Overhaugh st
Shaw, James, & Brothers, Nether mill
Sime, Sanderson, & Co., Botany mill
Wood, Thomas, 8 Tweed place

Manure Merchants.

Dun, John & Co., Island st
Thomson, Wm. & Sons, Limited (and Nurserymen), Clovenfords, by Galashiels—see advt

Mill Furnishers—see Drysalters, &c

Music Teachers.

Bairstow, J. A., Gala terrace
Blackwood, William, Stirling place—see advt
Burns, William, Damside
Cousins, Thomas (Organist and Music Teacher), 264 Scott st
Hislop, T., Galapark road
M'Laren, W. (violin), Meigle st
Mitchell, Miss, St John st
Moore, Thomas, Plumtree cottage
Morris, W. R., Fernbank
Prentice, W. T., Curwen house
Sime, Misses, The Moat House
Simpson, W. G., 108 Magdala ter
Strachan, A. (violin), Channel st
Thomson, Misses, High st
Townley, Joseph, F.C.C.G. (Professor of Music), 14 Bridge st

Music and Musical Instrument Sellers.

Strachan, Andrew, 20 Channel st
Wightman & Son, High st

Newspapers, Printers, and Publishers.

Border Advertiser—D. Craighead, Ladhope vale
Scottish Border Record — John M'Queen, Channel st

Nurserymen.

Thomson, Wm. & Sons, Limited (& manure merchants) Clovenfords by Galashiels—see ad

Painters and Decorators.

Balmer, William, 6 Sime pl
Bell, James M., 117 High st
Hislop, T., Ladhope bank
Lindsay, J. G., Lawyer's brae
Melville, John S., 40 Market st
Mill, John, 50 Island st
Tait Brothers, 60 High st
Watt, Gavin & Son, 15 Bridge st

Paviors.

Dalgleish, James, 79 Halliburton pl
Hutchison, Peter, 4 Chapel st

Photographers.

Clapperton, John, Albert place
Macnair, J. B., Gala terrace
Parisian Photographic Co., Bank st

Plasterers—see Slaters and Plasterers

Plumders, Gasfitters, and Tinsmiths

Bell, J. & P., 105 High st
Davidson, Thomas, Bank st
Hutton & Co. (Registered Plumbers, &c.), Lawyer's brae
Ruthven, Baillie, 44 Island st
Scott, John, Bank st
Thomson, A., Albert place
Tweedie, John & Son (and Bell-hangers), 80 High st

Printers.—see Newspapers Publishers and Printers

Saddlers and Harness Makers.

Cowan, Adam, 97 High st
Mercer, J., Channel st

Sculptor.

Sutherland, George, Albert place

Seed Merchants.

Dun, John & Co. (Seed Manure and Wool Merchants) Island st

Servants Registry Offices.

Bolton, Mrs. J. 28 Bank st
Mirtle, Agnes, 94 Channel st

Slaters and Plasterers.

Gibb, Joseph, 13 St. Andrew st
Hogg, George, (and Roofing Plumber), 34 Stirling st
Heatlie, Robert, 186 Scott st
Johnstone, J. & Son, Stirling st
M'Laren, Lawrence, 81 Channel st
Mason, John, 121 High st
Robertson, A., 76 St. Andrew st

Solicitors and Notaries Public.

Cramond, G. D., 17 Bridge st
Fairbairn, & Co., Sime place
Lees, Richard, Bridge place
Peebles, J. K., 72 High st
Pike & Chapman, Bank st
Robson, A. D., High st
Rutherford, W. A. & F. Channel st
Stalker, J. & D. G., High st

Surgeons.

Doig, William, Roxburgh st
Menzies, James, Park villa
Murray, William, Hy., 9 Church st
Somerville, James, Wm., Abbotsford road
Somerville, Robert, Abbotsford rd
Stevenson Nathaniel Rutland house
Tyrrell, Edward M., Round Tree House

Spirit Dealers—see Hotels and Inns

Tailors and Clothiers.

Bain, Alexander, Island st
Ballantyne, James, Galapark rd
Bell, James, 27 High st
Brown, C., Greenbank st
Brownlee, G., 112 Galapark rd
Cossar Robert, High Buckholmside
Currie, John N., Overhaugh st
Fisher, D., School close
Forsyth, John, 100 Channel st
Fulton, J., Arcade buildings
Grossart, A., Woodside place
Johnstone, James, 69 High st
Laidlaw & Clark, 9 Bank st
Mack, Thomas, 89 Channel st
Mathie, Thomas, 144 Scott st

Melrose, Alexander, 48 Glendining terrace
Mercer, T. & Sons, Gala Park rd
Mercer, T., 39 King st
Millar, F., 250 Scott st
Oven, Brothers, 15 High st
Robertson, Wm., 281 Galapark rd
Robertson, A., Magdala terrace
Sinclair, L., 5 Rosebank place
Taylor, John, Wilderhaugh st
Tait, J., Wilderhaugh
Temple, W., Queen st
Thomson Brothers, 47 High st

Taxidernist.

Chisholm, James, 9 Sheddon Park road, Kelso

Timber Merchants and Sawmill Proprietors.

Paterson, A. & Co. (& Bone Millers) Low Buckholmside
Romanis, W. & A., Station

Tobacconists and Fancy Goods Merchants.

Connacher, R., Channel st
Crossbie. Miss, 154 Magdala terrace
Gilmartin, J., Channel st
Leitch. L., 1 Green st
Lumsden, Miss J., Bank st
Pirrie, Alexander, Green st
Reid, R., 104 High st
Scott, Miss, Bank st
Thorburn, R., Market st

Tweed Merchants.

Chisholm & Co., 49½ High st
Gow, Geo. & Co., Huddersfield st
Graham, Andrew, Overhaugh st
Hume, Mrs Robert, St John st
Lennox, L., 29 High Buckholmside
Lowe, Sons, & Co., Station brae
Morrison, J. & R., Station brae
Schulze, W. & Co., Channel st

Valuator.

Black, Andrew (and Architect and Surveyor), 52 High st

Veterinary Surgeon.

Connochie, T. D., Gala terrace

Vine and Plant Growers.

Thomson, Wm. & Sons, Limited, Tweed Vineyards, Clovenfords, by Galashiels — see advt

Waste Merchants.

Ellis, S., Wilderhaugh — Joseph Attack, agent
Kivlichan, Mrs Hugh, 16 Magdala terrace
Scott, J., 99 Queen st
Wood, D., 4 Bridge st

Watchmakers and Jewellers.

Boyd, George, 17 Market st
Dilger, D., 3 Johnstone's close
Guntert, Louis, & Son, 46 Market st
Hepburn, J., Sime place
Hogg, Robert, 119 St. Andrew st
Miller, Charles, 17 High st
Ross, D., 23 Bank st

Wool Agents.

Bathgate, G., 4 Market st
Bowie, James, 163 Magdala ter
Currie, A. M., 8 Station
Dunn, W. H., Market st
Gilfillan, Alfred, 4 Station
Gill, A. P., 3 Station
Smith, T., 3 St. Andrew st
Thomson, R., Abbots place

Wool Merchants.

Dun, John & Co., (and Seed and Manure Merchants), Island st
M'Caig, J. & Co., Ladhope vale
Sanderson & Murray, Ltd., (Skinners), Roxburgh st
Wood, James, High st

Woollen Machine Makers.

Burns, George & Sons, (and Engineers, &c.,) Roxburgh st

Yarn Merchants and Agents.

Boyd, R. & Co., 43 Bank st
Laidlaw & Fairgrieve, (Spinners), Ladhope Mill

Miscellaneous.

Basketmaker—Mrs J. Murray, Gala Park road

Cooper and Shuttle Maker—John Scott, 21 Albert place

Gilder—James Rankin, 22 Bank st

Lathsplitter—J. Ross, 58 Meigle st

Wine & Spirit Merchants,(wholesale)—Laidlaw. & Sandeman, 43 High st

HEATHERLIE—SEE SELKIRK.

KIRKHOPE—SEE SELKIRK.

LINDEAN—SEE SELKIRK.

SELKIRK,

Including the parishes of ASHKIRK, ETTRICK, HEATHERLIE, KIRKHOPE, LINDEAN and YARROW.

SELKIRK is an ancient, town, a royal burgh, the seat of a presbytery, and the capital of its county and parish ; 38 miles S.S.E. from Edinburgh, 22 E. by S. from Peebles, 12 N.N.W. from Hawick, 8 S.W. from Melrose, and 6 S. from Galashiels. The principle manufactnres carried on consist of various discriptions of woollen goods—tweeds, tartans, plaids, and shawls, and wool spinning, and tanning. A Railway to Galashiels, where it joinis the Waverley line of the North British system. The sheriff's court is held on Friday. The market is held on Wednesday. Acreage of the parish, 22,559. Population, 6,397.

ETTRICK is a parish situated in the south-west of Selkirkshire, bordering on Dumfriesshire ; is 19 miles S. W. from Selkirk. Acreage, 42,386.

KIRKHOPE parish is in the presbytery of Selkirk. ETTRICK BRIDGE END a small village in Kirkhope, 7 miles S.W. from Selkirk. Acreage, 22,724.

LINDEAN it a parish 2 miles N.E. of Selkirk, a station on the North British Railway.

YARROW is a parish in the presbytery of Selkirk, lying south-west from that town. Acreage, 41,046.

ASHBANK is a parish. The village is 5½ miles from Hawick its post town and 6½ from Selkirk, on the river Ale, a tributary of the Teviot. Acreage, 11,708.

Business Directory.

Bakers and Confectioners.

Douglas, Robert, Market place
Heatlie, J. J., Market place
Hope, Robert. High st
Scott, Thomas, High st

Baby Linen, Berlin Wool, & Fancy Goods Dealers.

Hutchison, Mrs. J.. west port
Inglis, Mrs R., (and Milliner), High st
Little, Miss, West port
Taylor, Misses, (and Dressmakers), High st

Banks.

British Linen Co., Market place
Commercial Bank, Ltd., High st
National Bank, Ltd., West port

Billposters.

Douglas, James, 10 Heatherlie ter
Emond, James, Kirk wynd

Blacksmiths.

Brotherstone, W. & Co., Back row
Brown, James, Halidays park
Keddie, T. & R., Heatherlie
Kennedy James; Ettrick bridge end
Laidlaw, Robert, Tower st
Mabon, J., Chapel st
Mitchell, Alex., Mitchell's close
Scott, Adam, Yarrow
Scott, James, Lindean
Shankie, Andrew, Ettrick
Thomson, Robert, Back row
Whitelaw, George, Ashkirk

Booksellers, Stationers, and News-agents.

Crichton, Wm., Buccleuch buildgs
Douglas, Andrew, Ettrick terrace
Johnstone, Archibald, Market pl
Lewis, James, High st
Thomson, Walter, (and Printer), High st
Younger, Adam, (and Tobacconist), West Port

Boot and Shoe Makers.

Coutts, Wm. & Son, Market place
Dickson, Thomas, High st
Guthrie, Archibald, High st
Henderson, Daniel, High st
Ingles, Robert, High st
Inglis, Walter, Chapel st
Irvine, B. (clogger), Scott's place

Builders and Contractors.

Dickson & Inglis, Mill st
Grieve, John, Glebe
Linton, Walter, Glebe
Smith, George, Forest terrace

Cabinetmakers, Upholsterers, and Undertakers.

Leithhead, James, Chapel st
Little, Thomas (and Auctioneer), Fleshmarket st
Mitchell, John (and Fishing Rod Maker), Buccleuch road

Chemists and Druggists.

Borthwick, A. J., Market place
Dunn, Thomas, High st
Stavert, Walter, High st

China and Glass Merchants.

Allan, Mrs Maria, West port
Bateman, Charles, High st
Bourke, Patrick, Kirk wynd
Oliver, Mrs., Tower st

Cloth Board Manufacturers.

Mitchell, D. & Sons, Philiphaugh Saw mills

Coal, Brick, and Tile Merchants, and Agents.

Brydon, James, Scott's place
Dickson, Thomas, Parkside
Harper, J. J., Tower st
Mitchell, William, The Green
Pringle, John, Heatherlie
Strain, John, Heatherlie terrace
Weatherstone, John, West port

Confectioners and Fruiterers.
Anderson, John, High st
Ballantyne, Robert, High st
Currie, James, Market place
Dryden, J. & M., Buccleuch bdgs
Hall, James, Market place
Johnstone, Jane, West port
Mackay, Alexander, High st
Scott, J. N., Market place
Stroh, P. H., West port

Contractors.
Brown, Walter, The Glebe
Robertson, A. & Sons, Ettrick place

Drapers, Dressmakers, Milliners, and Clothiers.
Brown, A. S. (draper and hosier), Heatherlie
Brown, Andrew, High st
Cunningham, G., High st
Lidderdale, P. H., Market place
Muir, Michael, Market place
M'Neil, George, High st
Penman, R., West port
Scott, James, West port

Dressmakers and Milliners—see also Drapers, &c.
Coutts, Miss, Market place
Lamb, Misses, Chapel place
Macaulay, Misses, West port

Dyers.
Cochrane, Smith, & Co., Cheviot mills
Kemp, Ninian & Co., Ettrick mills

Engineers.
Burns, George & Sons, Selkirk

Farmers—see end of Directory.

Fishmongers, Game and Poultry Dealers.
Hall, George, Market place
Hislop, D., High st
Lindsay, Bros., Market place

Fleshers.
Blair, John, Tower st
Emond, Robert, High st
Forsyth, Robert, West Port
Ritchie, Cosmo, Heatherlie
Turnbull, Robert, (Family Butcher), 14A Market place

Grocers and General Merchants.
Marked 'e' are also Spirit Dealers.
Anderson, John, High st
e Blair, John, (Licensed), Market place
e Chalmers, Miss, (Licensed), 46 Back row
e Christie, J., Market place
Currie, Helen, Dunsdalehaugh
e Doughty, Thomas, West Port
e Downie, George B., 6 West Port
e Elliot, Henry, Tower st
Elliot, James, Market place
Equitable Store, Union Hall bdgs
e Hamilton, John, 16 Tower st
e Johnstone, Archibald, 11 High st
Linton, William, Sloethorn Bank
Muldoon, A., Kirk wynd
Nichol, William, Curror st
e Park, Wm., 28 Buccleuch road
Reekie, C., Mill st
Rodgers, D., Cannon st
Scott, John, 18 West Port
Selkirk, Store Co., Ltd., 52 High st
Turnbull, M. & G., Heatherlie ter
Veitch, J. A., Cannon st
Wallace, Wm., 28 Kirk wynd
e Waugh, J. T. S., 27 High st
Wood, John, Back row
Young, John, Back row

Hairdressers.
Anderson, Andrew, (and Fishing Tackle Maker), High st
Connel, James, Heatherlie
Cowan, James, West port
Lamb, Robert, High st
Lawrie, Wm., (and Tobacconist), High st

Heddle and Reed Makers.
Baron, & Hogarth, Mill st
Neilson & Son, Mill st

Hosiery Manufacturers.
Brown, Andrew, Tait's hill
Currie, Robert, Millburn
Ramsay, Samuel, Back row

Scott, William, Castle st
Thomson, Robert, South port

Hotels, Inns, and Posting Establishments.

Abbotsford Temperance, Market place—Mrs. Conn
Amos, Thomas, Ettrick
Armour, Robert, West Port
Beattie, Walter, Yarrow
County—James Mercer, Market pl
Cross Keys, Market place—J. A. Scarborough
Fleece, Market place—Jas Maculay
Johnstone, Andrew, Market place
Richardson, Robert, Ettrick Bridge end
Rodono—R. M., Chisholm Yarrow
Station Hotel—J Charles Dorn Proprietor

Ironmongers and Hardwaremen.

Laurie, Robert, 19 Market place
Thomson, George, 1 Back row
Yellowlees, John, 11 West port

Joiners and Wrights.

Ballantyne, James, Buccleuch road
Brodie, Charles, Chapel st
Cleghorn, Andrew, Back row
Falla, John, Dunsdale cottage
Gray, George, Lindean
Hall, Thomas, High st
Mitchell, D. & Sons, (joiners, cartwrights, & wood merchants), Philiphaugh Saw mills
Nichol, John, Tower st
Reid, John, Yarrow terrace
Robertson, Gideon, The Green
Smith, John & Sons, Scott's pl
Watson, John, Tower st

Laundry.

Miller, John, Heatherlie

Manufacturers.

Anderson, P. & R., Tweed mills
Brown, Allan & Co. (and Dyers & Spinners), Riverside mills
Brown & Clarke, Ettrick mills
Gardiner, E. & Sons, Tweed mill
Gibson & Lumgair, St Mary's mills
Hogg Bros., Muthag st
Little, William, Kilncroft
Mitchell, D. & Sons (cloth boards) Philiphaugh saw mills
Roberts, G. & Co., Forest mills
Robson, W. H. & Co., Muthay st
Russell, J. & R. W., Ettrickbank mill
Sanderson Bros., Linglie mill
Scott, Bell, & Co., Cheviot mill
Scotch Tweed Society, Ltd., Ettrick mills
Sim & Co., Bridgehaugh mills
Waddel & Turnbull, Dunsdale mill

Millers.

Douglas, James, Lindean
Ewing, William, Corn mill
Hogg, D., Deuchar mill

Music Teachers.

Colledge, G. R., Elm Cottage
Colledge, Adam, Rosemount
Colquhoun, Miss E., Marion cres
D'Agrosa, Sgr., Kirk wynd
Johnstone. Miss, Market place
Reekie, C., Mill st
Stavert, A., Castle st
Walker, W. H., Maple cottage

Newspapers, Publishers, and Printers.

Selkirk Advertiser — W. Crichton, Buccleuch buildings
Southern Reporter—G. Lewis & Co., High st

Nurserymen and Seedsmen.

Bowie, John, Philiphaugh
Cockburn, William, Thorniehall
Currie, James, Market place
Linton, Wm., Old Bridge st
Macaulay, William, The Glebe

Painters and Decorators.

Nichol, William, Tower st
Scott, N. Francis, High st
Towns, David, Market place
Welsh, William, High st

Photographers.

Clapperton, J. & R., Meadow cot
Edwards, A. R., Tower st

Plumbers, Gasfitters, and Tinsmiths
Ruthven, Peter, West Port
Smith, J. & T., Tower st
Turnbull, & Taylor, Mill st
Watson, Adam, West Port

Plasterers and Slaters.
Clapperton, & Sons Halliday's park
Hogg, William, Kirk wynd
Johnstone, John, Forest road
Leithead, John, Back row
Smith, John, Castle st
Smith, John, junr., Back row

Printers—see Newspaper Publishers, &c.

Saddlers and Harness Makers.
Johnstone, Robert, Market place
Weir, Alexander, Market place

Schools—Ladies.
Brown, Miss M. T., Hermitage
Colquhoun, Miss, Baptist Church Hall

Sculptors—Monumental
Boyd, Bros., Buccleuch rd
Grieve, Adam, The Glebe

Seeasmen—see Nurserymen.

Sick Nurse.
M'Danald, Mrs., 9 Chapel st—see advt

Slaters—see Plasterers.

Solicitors and Notaries Public.
Alexander, D. C. & C., West port
Pollock, John, (P.F.), County bdgs
Rodger P & G & Chalmers, High st
Steedman, John, S.S.C., Market
Tosh, Andrew, S.S.C., High st

Spirit Dealers—see Hotels and Inns

Surgeons.
Muir, John S., Thorncroft
Reid, Charles, The Glebe
Thomas, James, Kirkbrea

Surveyors.
Bartie, James, Alva cottage
Pritty, John, Heath park

Tailors and Clothiers.
Brown, J. H., 31 Kirk brae
Dobson, W. D., Tower st
Douglas, Thomas, Kilncroft
Gray, D., High st
Hardie, John, Tower st
Hardie, Robert. Tower st
Hope, George, Heatherlie terrace
Johsntone, Alexander, West port
Johnstone, James, South port
Lothian, James, The Green
Linton, Alexander, High st
Lees, William, Market place
Lyon, Walter, Yarrow feus
Miller, G. & J., High st
Scott, Thomas, High st
Scott, John, Back row
Simpson, John, 19 Buccleuch rd
Stoddart, Simon, West port
Watson, Adam, Mill st

Timber Merchants and Sawmill Proprietors.
Mitchell D. & Sons (joiners & wood merchants—fencing done wood or wire, and manufacturers of cloth boards) Philiphaugh Saw Mill
Yellowlees, Robert, Whinfield

Tobacconist.
Brown, Miss S., West port
Douglas, James (and Newsagent), Tower st

Veterinary Surgeons.
Connochie, W. D., 47 High st
Connochie, W. D. jun., 47 High st
Robertson, W. O., M.R.C.V.S Ettrick place

Watchmakers and Jewellers
Brown, John, High st
Henderson, Andrew, Market place
Millar, James, Tower st

Wine and Spirit Merchants—Wholesale.
Scott, Gideon T., (& aerated water

manufacturer), High
Turnbull, Thomas, Market place

Woollen Yarn Spinners.

Anderson, George & Co., Ettrick Vale mills
Craig-Brown, T. & Co., Yarrow mills
Cunningham & Hall, Burn mill
Wright, David, Ettrick mills
Wright, Pennel, & Co., Bridgehaugh mill

Miscellaneous.

Drysalter—Wm, Douglas, Dunsdale road
Fishing Tackle Maker—John Simpson, Kirk wynd
Mill Furnisher—Jn. Burns, Chapel street
Sheriff-Officer — John Thomson County buildings
Skinner—Wm. Forrest, Mill st
Tweed Merchant—James Chisholm, 8 Ettrick terrace

YARROW—see SELKIRK.

PEEBLESSHIRE.

PEEBLESSHIRE (or TWEEDALE), a county in the southern part of Scotland, is bounded on the north and north-east by Edinburghshire on the east and south-east by Selkirkshire, on the south by Dumfriesshire, and by the county of Lanark for almost the whole extent of its western border. In length, from its southern border to its extreme northern apex, it measures fully thirty miles; from east to west, including the parts on the latter boundary that mingle with Selkirkshire, its breadth is upwards of twenty miles, whilst in other parts it varies from ten to fifteen miles. Its form is exceedingly irregular, and it comprehends an area of 356 square miles, or 227,869 acres. In size, Peebles is the twenty-third, and in population the thirtieth of the counties of Scotland.

The following are among the most conspicious in height above the level of the sea—Hartfell, 2,916; Broad Law, 2,850; Dollar Law, 2,840; Scrape, 2,560; Gums Cleugh, 2,200: Dundreich, Pykestane, and Hell's Cleugh, each 2,100; Cardon, 2,000; Cairn Hill, 1,800: Broughton Heights 1,483; and Meigle, 1,480.

At Peebles, Innerleithen, and Walkerburn, there are mills for the manufacture of tweeds.

The principal river is the Tweed, distinguished as the fourth of Scottish streams: the upper sources of this beautiful water are found in the parish of Tweedsmuir, in this county; it is enriched by many tributaries, and after passing the ancient town of Berwick, falls into the German Ocean. The other rivers are the Lyne, the Leithen, and the Manor, all of which are subsidiary to the Tweed, and the Meggett, which runs into St. Mary's Loch, in Selkirkshire. In the rivers and small lakes there are abundance of salmon and trout, and a lake, called the West Water Loch, is noted for the quantity of eels with which it swarms. The railway from Peebles to Edinburgh is the North British, the one from Symington to Peebles, the Caledonian. There is also a railway to Innerleithen, and a line from thence to Galashiels, and a railway to Linton (properly called West Linton), to distinguish it from East Linton, in Haddingtonshire.

The shire now comprises fourteen parishes, and two parts of parishes; it contains one royal burgh—Peebles—but possesses no representative burgh; the county, in conjunction with Selkirkshire, returns one Member to Parliament, the present member being Walter Thorhurn, Esq. Population, 14,279.

BROUGHTON—SEE PEEBLES
CARLOPS—SEE WEST LINTON
DRUMMELZIER—SEE PEEBLES
EDDLESTON—SEE PEEBLES
GLENHOLM—SEE PEEBLES

INNELEITHEN, WALKERBURN, AND TRAQUAIR.

INNERLEITHEN is a parish and village—is 28 miles S from Edinburgh 16 N.W. from Selkirk, 12 W. from Galashiels, and 6 E. from Peebles, situated near the month of the Leithen, within a quarter of a mile of the left bank of the Tweed. There are several large woollen manufactories. The parish has an area of 23,981 acres. Population, 2501.

WALKERBURN, 1½ mile distant, is a village in the above parish.

TRAQUAIR is a parish on the south side of the Tweed, with an areage of 15,327 acres.

Business Directory.

Aerated Water Manufacturers.

Pearce, W. Morning side
St. Ronans Well Co. Ltd., St. Ronans Well

Bakers and Confectioners.

Dalgleish, Robert, High st
Lennie, Robert, High st
Tait, John, Chapel st
Whitson, Thomas, High st
Williamson, Silas, High st

Billiard Rooms.

Scott, Walter, (and Tobacconist), Millar st

Blacksmiths.

Burns, James, Traquair
Grieve, James, Station road
Shiell, James, Morningside
Whitson, John, High st

Booksellers, Stationers, Newsagents, and Printers.

Smail, Robert, High st
Smith, Robert, High st
Tait, John K., High st
Winter, A., Walkerburn

Boot and Shoe Makers.

Aitchison, James, Chapel st
Baillie, P., Millar st
Campbell, John, St Ronans place
Einnan, Andrew, High st
Harvey, James, High st

Builders and Contractors.

Brodie, Charles, Leithen road
Dalgleish, Adam, Princes st
Graham, George, Millar st
Watt, Adam (& joiner), Morningside

Cabinetmakers and Upholsterers.

Aitken, J. R., Morningside
Anderson, John R. (and General House Furnisher and Cycle Agent), High st

Chemists and Druggists.
Mathieson, Robert, High st
Rennie, J. C., High st

China and Glass Dealers.
Hogg, Helen, Morningside
Lees, John, Walkerburn

Coal Merchants and Agents.
Nicol, R., High st
Ramsay, William (and contractor), Walkerburn

Confectioners—see Bakers, &c.

Contractors.
Ramsay, William (and Coal Merchant), Walkerburn

Cycle Agent.
Anderson, John, High st

Dairies.
Hay, J., Chapel st
Tennant, J., High st

Drapers, Dressmakers, Milliners, and Clothiers.
Craig, J. N., High st
Docharty, John, High st
Fleming, W. M., High st
Lees, Miss (milliner), High st
Rutherford, Miss, St Ronans place
Wood, Andrew, High st

Farmers—see end of Directory.

Fleshers.
Brydon, Adam, Millar st
Pearce, F. W., High st

Grocers and General Merchants.
Anderson, M. & Co., Millar st
Baptie, William, Greenhead
Beattie, John, Walkerburn
Binnie, William, High st
Co-operative Co., Ld., Walkerburn
Co-operative Co., Ld., Chapel st
Dickson, Andrew, St. Ronans place
Ferguson, John, Chapel st
Ferguson, William, High st
Hills, Andrew, High st
Hogg, Henry, Isle croft
Hogg, J., Strand
Mathieson, Mrs E., High st
Paul, John, Bridge end
Ruthven, John, High st
Temple, William, High st
Thomson, A., Millar st

Hairdressers.
Arcari & Persichini, Millar st
Ingram, D. A., High st

Hotels, Inns, and Posting Houses.
St. Ronans' — Alex. Lennie, High st
Temperance—John Tait, Chapel st
Traquair Arms—Graham Macpherson, Station road
Volunteer Arms — R. Robertson, High st

Joiners and Wrights.
Dalgleish, William (Joiner, Carpenter, and Undertaker), Bridge end
Hope, Thomas, Station road
Little, Queen, Walkerburn
Watt, Adam (Joiner, Builder, Undertaker, Cart and Wheel Wright; Estab. 1784)– Workshop Morningside

Manufacturers.
Ballantyne Bros., Waverley mills
Ballantyne & Sons, Walkerburn
Ballantyne, J. J. & H., Damside
Beckett & Robertson, St Ronan's
Birnie, Thomas, Morningside
Colquhoun, A., St Ronan's
Dalziel, James, & Co., Walkerburn
Smail, Walter, & Son, Leithen mills
Thomson, G., The Strand

Painters and Decorators.
Bennett, T., Peebles road
Campbell & Sons, Leithenside
Tait Brothers, Peebles road
Storie, Robert, High st

Plumbers, Gasfitters, and Tinsmiths.
Euman, John, & Co., High st
Scott, John, Leithen crescent

Saddlers and Harness Makers.
Ferguson, W., Chapel st
Scott, John, High st (West-end)

Surgeons.
Cameron, John, M.B., Leithen cres
Wishart, James, Hillend

Solicitor.
Stobie, William, High st

Tailors and Clothiers.
Archibald, Robert, Devon pl
Euman, Robert, High st
Hope, Thomas, High st
Johnstone, Robert, Chapel st
Russell, Kenneth, Chapel st
Scott, Thomas, High st

Tweed Warehousemen.
•Melrose, T., 8 High st
Euman Brothers, High st

Watchmakers and Jewellers.
Eaton, Arthur, High st
Loughty, Alexander, High st

Wood Merchant.
Stewart, William. Morningside

Wrights—see Builders, Joiners, and Wrights.

Miscellaneous.
Florist—John Gardner, High st
Photographer—T. H. M. Colledge, The Studio

KILBUCHO—SEE PEEBLES.
KIRKURD—SEE PEEBLES.
LYNE—SEE PEEBLES.
MANOR—SEE PEEBLES.
MEGGET | SEE PEEBLES.
NEWLANDS—SEE WEST LINTON.
NOBLEHOUSE—SEE WEST LINTON.

PEEBLES,

Including the Parishes and Villages of EDDLESTON, BROUGHTON, GLENHOLM and KILBUCHO, DRUMMELZIER, KIRKURD, LYNE and MEGGET MANOR, SHIRLING, STOBO, TWEEDSMUIR, and Neighbourhoods.

PEEBLES is a royal burgh and manufacturing town, the capital of its county and parish, and the seat of a presbytery, 22 miles S. from Edinburgh, 22 W. by N. from Selkirk, 54 N.N.E. from Dumfries. and 47 E. by S. from Glasgow. A Sheriff court is held on Tuesday and Thursday. and a sheriff small debt court every Friday. The market is held on Tuesday. The parish of Peebles has an acreage of 16,597. Population, 4,704.

EDDLESTON is a parish and village, the latter 4 miles north from Peebles situated on both sides of the Eddleston water. Acreage, 18,490.

BROUGHTON, GLENHOLM, and KILBUCHO are parishes. The village of Broughton stands on the road from Edinburgh to Dumfries, and from

Peebles to Biggar. A branch of the Caledonian Railway from Symington to Peebles passes through the parish. Acreage, 18,065.

DRUMMELZIER is a parish in the south-western part of the county. Acreage, 17,948.

KIRKURD parish lies on the western confines of the county. Acreage, 5,967.

LYNE and MEGGET are two parishes. Acreage, 17,227.

MANOR parish is bounded by Peebles, and from which the new water supply for Peebles is taken. Acreage, 16,622.

SKIRLING is a small parish and village, 2½ miles N.W. from Broughton. Acreage, 3,423.

STOBO is a parish in the western part of the county. Acreage, 10,302.

TWEEDSMUIR parish lies in the south-western corner of the county, with Lanarkshire for its western border. Acreage, 23,469.

Business Directory.

Architects and Surveyors.

Anderson, R. S. (Civil Engineer and County Road Surveyor), County bnildings

Wilkie, George (Architect, Builder and Contractor), Damdale and at Caledonian station

Auctioneers and Valuators.

Cairns, John Eshiels
Smith, J. & J., 29 Northgate

Bakers and Confectioners.

Brodie, Alexander, High st
Craig, Charles, Young st
Goodburn, John H., Northgate
Howitt, Mrs S., 23 Northgate
M'Intyre, J., Eastgate
Mitchell, D. R. & Son, High st
Oldham, John, High st
Scott, William, Eastgate

Banks.

Bank of Scotland, High st—Robert Thorburn, agent
British Linen Co. Bank, High st
Commercial Bank of Scotland, Ld., High st—J. & W. Buchan, agents

Blacksmiths.

Amos, Walter, Temple Bar, near Eddleston
Anderson, Gabriel, Stobo
Bruce, John, White bridge
Brydon, James, Tweedgreen
Ferguson, John. Northgate
Hislop, James F., Glenholm
Horsburgh, Adam, Kirkton manor
Ker, Charles T., Northgate
Ker, Robert, Winkston
Ritchie, William, Broughton
Scott, William, Skirling
Smith, John (and implement maker) Hall Lyne, Stobo
Wallace, T. & Son (Engineers) Bridgegate
White, W. R., Eddleston

Booksellers, Stationers, and Newsagents.

Davidson, Thomas D., 73 High st
Ker, J. A. (printer), Northgate
Redpath, Adam, High st
Watson, James, High st

Boot and Shoe Makers.

Baptie, John, Waterside
M'Kenzie, A., Northgate
Mackenzie, Alexander, Dean park
Mason, James, Eastgate
Mitchell, W., 47 Northgate
Oldham, Matthew, Northgate
Smith, Agnes, Eastgate
Somerville, J., 25 Eastgate
Somerville, Robert, Broughton
Stavert, James, Old town
Walker, William, High st
Whitie, James, 57 High st
Williamson, James, Caledonian Boot and Shoe Warehouse 3 Northgate
Wilson, William, Tweedsmuir

Builders and Contractors.

Blackstocks, James, Drummelzier
Bryden, Adam, Broughton
Murray, J. & D. (and joiners), Murrayfield
Ramsay, Wm. (Builder and Joiner) Deanpark
Tod, William (Builder and Sculptor), March st
Wilkie, George (Builder, Contractor, and Architect), Damdale and at Caledonian station

Cabinetmakers, Upholsterers, and Undertakers.

Black, J., Tweedgreen
Smith, J. & M., Eastgate

Cart and Plough Wrights—see Joiners and Wrights.

Chemists and Druggists.

Lindsay, Robert, High st
Morison, George, High st
Sanderson, William J., High st

China, Glass, &c., Merchants.

Aitchison, A., 23 Northgate
Brockie, Wm. J., Tweedgreen
Morrison, E. & M., High st

Coal Merchants and Agents.

Dyer, James, N.B. Station
Hamilton, John, N.B. Station
Kelly, Thomas (and manure), Lyne
M'Farlane, Duncan, Cal. Station
Millar, William, Cal. Station
Noble, William, Broughton

Confectioners and Fruiterers.

Hanaghan, T., Northgate
Kirk, A., Bridgend
M'Intyre, John, Eastgate
Montgomerie, A. & B., 43 High st
Spalding, T. & Co. (& nurserymen), High st
Watson, Miss, 44 High st

Dentist.

Watson, William, 12 Gregory place —see advt

Drapers, Dressmakers, Milliners, and Clothiers.

Anderson, George, Old Town
Duthie, Alexander, Old Town
Goodburn, Miss, Northgate
Green, John, 42 High st
Ker & Rennilson (and Clothiers and Outfitters), 86 High st
Low, Andrew, High st
M'Lean, J., Old Town
Melrose & Co., High st
Mill, J. & Co., High st
Noble, Miss (Milliner, &c.) Broughton station
Sanderson, C. W., Stewartfield
Veitch, G. & Sons, High st
Veitch, Robert, 2 High st

Fancy Goods Repositories.

Phillips, R., High st
Spalding, M. & M., 27 Eastgate

Farmers—see end of Directory.

Fishmongers, Game Dealers, and Poulterers.

Thomson, John, Northgate
Wood, William, 19 Northgate

Fleshers.

Bridges, G. & A., High st
Horsbrough, Thomas, Elcho st brae
Hunter, A. T., Elcho st brae
Laidlaw, John, 1 Northgate
M'Kenna, James, Eastgate
Turnbull, James (and game dealer), High st

Fruiterers—see Confectioners, &c.

Grocers, General Merchants, and Spirit Dealers.

Anderson, George, High st
Ball, Charles (Licensed Grocer), Young st—see adv
Ballantyne, Mrs J., Post Office, Eddleston
Blackstocks, James, Drummelzier
Brockie, Thomas, High st
Brown, George, Northgate
Calvert, Margaret, Eddleston
Clapperton. John, Eastgate
Goodwillie, John, Northgate
Grainger, S. & E., Stobe
Greenshields, Miss E., Broughton
Harris, J., (and Flesher), 1 Montgomerie place
Howitt, Thomas, Eddleston
Hush, John, Bridgegate
Hush, Robert, Young st
Hush, Thomas, High st
Irvine, Alexander, 5, 7 Northgate
Lockhart, M., Northgate
Little, Christina, Eastgate
Meldrum, John, Old Town
Miller, J., Old town
Morris, B., Rosetta road
M'Innes, Samuel, High st
Newbiggings, Rich. R., Broughton
Noble, Alex., Skirling, by Biggar
Pairman, James, High st
Peden, Thomas, High st
Peebles Co-operative Society, Litd., Greenside
Robertson, James E. (& ironmonger) High st
Russell, Robert, Greenside
Russell, James S., 33 High st
Shiel, Alexander, Old town

Hairdressers.

Affleck, R., 8 High st
Swanson, W., Northgate

Horse Hiring and Posting Establishments.

Fraser, W. D., Cross Keys Hotel, Northgate, Telephone No. 410
Halliday, R., Ellerslee stables
M'Pherson, Duncan, High st

Hotels and Posting Houses—see also Temperance Hotels.

Commercial, High st—Wm. Gordon
Cross Keys Hotel & Posting Establishment—W. D. Fraser, proprietor, Northgate Telephone No. 410
Crown—J. Young, High st
Green Tree Hotel—William Mathieson, proprietor, Eastgate
Tontine, Hotel, High st

Hydropathic Establishment.

Peebles Hydropathic (The largest and finest in Scotland within a mile of Peebles), Robert Rimmer, manager

Insurance Companies and Agents.

Insurance Co. of Scotland Robert, Thorburn, High st
Standard Life—Robert Thorburn, High st

Ironmongers and Hardwaremen.

Grieve, James M., (and Registered Plumber, &c), 6 & 10 Old Town
Moffat, W. & R.; 60 High st
Scott Brothers, 50 High st
Thomson, John, (& Fishing Tackle Warehouse), Eastgate

Joiners and Wrights.

Those Marked 'e' are Timber Merchants.

Gilchrist, Wm., Gladstone place
Henderson, Archibald, Broughton
Mathison, R. & Sons, (& Builders), Northgate
Milne. Alexander, Stobo
M'Culloch, Thomas, Elcho st brae
Proudfoot, William, Skirling
Ramsay, William, (and Builder), Deanpark
Renwick & Weir, Elcho st
Scott, J. W., Portmore, Eddleston
Stewart, W., Lyne
Veitch, William & John, Drummelzier
Watson, Adam & Son, Old Town

Laundries.

Tweedside Steam Laun-

dry, Greenside—Alx M'Culloch, proprietor
Wilson, G. E., March st

Millers.

Clarkson, Alexander, Skirling
Minto, David, Eddleston
Veitch, John, Drummelzier

Milliners and Dressmakers—see Drapers, &c.

Music Teachers.

Barton, Leonard, (and Organist of St. Peter's Church, Peebles), 24 Deanpark
Finlay, James J., F.Sc. (Lond), (Teacher of Music and Chemistry) Bonnington Park School, (Organist and Choirmaster Parish Church), Denbrae
Tait, J., (and Organist), Springfield

Painters and Decorators.

Hamilton, Archibald, High st
Mitchell, D. & A. (and Paperhangers), 71 High st—see adv
Steel, Adam, Eastgate

Photographers.

M'Knaught, J. & Son, High st
Robertson, Mrs. (Portrait & Landscape), The Studio, Blinkbonny, March st, and at West Linton

Plasterers and Slaters.

Fairbairn, William, Damdale
Grandison, L., Kerfield road

Plumbers, Gasfitters, and Tinsmiths

Clark, David, 84 High st
Edgar, Andrew, Old town
Grieve, James M. (Registered Plumber), 8 and 10 Old town
Runciman, Charles (Registered Plumber), Northgate
Thomson, John, Eastgate

Refreshment Rooms.

Peebles Public Coffee & Reading Rooms, 20 Northgate
Rankine, Robert, Northgate

Saddlers and Harness Makers.

Adams, W., 67 High st
Weatherston, W., High st

Schools.

(School Board.)

Burgh and County High School, Bonnington road
English School, Tweed green
Halyrude School, Elcho st
William Lyon, Clerk to Peebles School Board

(Day and Boarding)

Burgh and County High School, Bonnington road — George C. Pringle, Head Master
Dixon, Miss, School brae
Jowatt, Miss, Innerleithen road
St. Joseph's (Roman Catholic) School, Rosetta Road — Miss Biggar, School Mistress

Solicitors and Notaries.

Blackwood & Smith, High street
Brown, Andrew, 3 Northgate
Buchan, John & William, High st
Lyon, William (of Thorburn & Lyon—Clerk to Peebles School Board), High st
Ogilvie, John (sheriff-clerk) County buildings
Thorburn & Lyon, High st
Thorburn, Robert (of Thorburn & Lyon—Agent for Bank of Scotland. Distributor & Collector of Stamps and Taxes for the Counties of Peebles and Selkirk, and Secretary and Treasurer to the Gas Co.), High st

Spirit Dealers.

Cameron, Robert, Neidpath Inn, Old Town
Gunn, John, Tweedsmuir
Gray, Alexander, Port brae
Hope, George, Northgate

Surgeons.

Connel, John, Northgate
Gunn, Clement B., Old Town

Kirkland, Dr., Crosland crescent

Tailors and Clothiers.
Brown, A. W., 40 High st
Cranston, James, 33 Eastgate—see advt
Dalling, Peter, Northgate
Ferguson, A., Old Town
Jones, James, George st
Ker, Alexander, Old Town
Ker, Charles, High st
Ker & Rennilson, (Drapers, Clothiers, and Outfitters), 86 High st
Pirie, W., Northgate
Sanderson, C. W., (and Tweed and Hosiery Merchant), Stewartfield
Shaw, Angus, Young st
Walker, James, 3 Elcho st
Williamson, Robert, 61 High st
Wilson, James, Eddleston

Tanners and Curriers.
Hume, & Thompson, Old Town

Temperance Hotels.
Lossocks Temperance Hotel, High st—see advt
Newbigging, William, Broughton
Niven's Temperance Hotel, High st

Timber Merchants and Saw Millers.
see also Joiners, &c.
Douglas, Robert, N.B. Railway stn
Dyer, James, Station
Yellowlees, John, Old Station

Tobacconists.
Ferguson, A. J., 27 Eastgate
Johnston, John, Bridgegate
M'Kay, J. & J., High st
Pride, Miss J. (and Fishing Tackle Maker), Northgate

Veterinary Surgeons.
Johnston, John C., M.R.C.VS.. Montgomery place
Ker, John, Northgate

Watchmakers and Jewellers.
Hislop, Robert, 28 High st
Taylor, George C., Northgate

Woollen Merchants & Manufacturers
Ballantyne, D. & Co., March st
Black, James, & Co., Peebles
Lowe, Donald, & Co., North British station
Marshall & Chalmers, Damcroft
Sanderson, C. W. (Tweed and Hosiery Merchant), Stewartfield
Thorburn, Walt. & Bros., Damdale
Thorburn & Co., Tweedside

Miscellaneous.
Coach Builders—J. & M. Smith, Dovecot
Printers—Watson & Smith, *Peeblesshire Advertiser*, Bridgegate
Pianoforte Tuner—John Hope, Old Town

ROMANNO BRIDGE—SEE WEST LINTON.
SKIRLING—SEE PEEBLES.
STOBO—SEE PEEBLES.
TRAQUAIR—SEE INNERLEITHEN.
TWEEDSMUIR—SEE PEEBLES.
WALKERBURN—SEE INNERLEITHEN.

WEST LINTON,
Including NEWLANDS, NOBLE HOUSE, ROMANNO BRIDGE, CARLOPS, and Neighbourhoods.

WEST LINTON is a parish and village, the latter 16 miles S.S.W. from Edinburgh, 14 N.W. from Peebles, and 11 N.N.E. from Biggar. The parish has an area of 23,256 acres. Population, 434.

NEWLANDS is a parish lying between West Linton and Eddleston. Acreage of the parish, 12,518.

NOBLEHOUSE is in Newlands parish.

CARLOPS, in West Linton parish, is a small village 3 miles from West Linton

Business Directory.

Agents.

Alexander, John (Insurance), West Linton
Saunderson, Robert (House), West Linton
Thompson, Thomas (Estate), West Linton

Bakers and Confectioners.

Drysdale, Andrew, West Linton
Jackson, William, West Linton

Banks.

Bank of Scotland, West Linton
Savings Bank, West Linton

Blacksmiths.

Burns, James (& implement maker), Blyth bridge
Clarke, William, Newlands
Graham, Chancellor, Romanno bridge
Johnson, William, West Linton

Boot and Shoe Makers.

Bain, Archibald, West Linton
Bain, John, West Linton
Borthwick & Rodger, West Linton

Builders and Masons.

Cameron, Robert, West Linton
Melrose, William, West Linton
Veitch, Adam, West Linton

Carting Contractor.

Marshall, William, West Linton

Drapers and Dressmakers, &c.

Aitken, Mrs., West Linton
Laidlaw, Miss M., West Linton
Somerville, Miss Agnes, West Linton

Farmers—see end of Directory.

Flesher.

Alexander, Robert, West Linton

Grocers and General Merchants.

Alexander, John, Post Office, West Linton
Fraser, Richard, Noblehouse
M'Call, Mrs., West Linton
M'Laughlan, Mrs. Catherine, Romanno bridge
Noble, J. & M., Post Office, Blyth bridge
Paterson, David, West Linton
Ramsay, Adam, Post Office Carlops
Watson, H., West Linton

Hotels—see also Temperance Hotels.

Allan Ramsay, Carlops, Mrs Veitch
Linton Hotel (and Posting House), Alexander Gordon, West Linton
Mowbray, Thomas, West Linton
Thomson, Alexander S. (and Posting House), Leadburn

Joiners and Wrights.

Alexander, John, West Linton
Moubray, Thomas, West Linton
Proudfoot, Robert, Blyth bridge
Ramsay, Adam, Carlops
Sligh, David R. (Joiner and Cabinetmaker), Romanno bridge
Wilson, C. & A. F, Romanno bridge

Wilson, George, Stoneyknow, Lamancha

Millers.

Lewis, Alexander, Newlands
Proudfoot, Robert. Knocknowes

Photographer.

Robetrson, Mrs., West Linton, and March st, Peebles

Plumber.

Walter, Richard, West Linton

Posting Establishments.

Gordon, Alexander, Linton Hotel, West Linton
Thomson, Alexander, S. Leadburn
Watson, Robert, West Linton

School.

Episcopal Church School—Miss A. Syme, School Mistress, West Linton

Slater and Plasterer.

Paterson, William, West Linton

Surgeon and Physician.

Clark, Duncan, West Linton

Tailors and Clothiers.

Gordon, James, (and Stationer and Newsagent), West Linton
Rodger, John, West Linton

Temperance Hotels.

Dickson, Gavin, Romanno Bridge
M'Gill, William, Carlops

Woollen Manufacturer.

Dickson, Gavin, Romanno mill

Miscellaneous.

Coal Merchant—William Laidlaw, West Linton
Nurseryman—William Millar West Linton
Timber Merchant — James Leslie, Railway Station

HADDINGTONSHIRE,

OR EAST LOTHIAN, lies in the south-eastern part of Scotland; bounded on the north by the Firth of Forth, on the east by that Strait, and also by the North Sea, on the south by Berwickshire, and on the west by Edinburghshire, Mid-Lothian; from east to west it extends twenty-six miles; from north to south, at the middle, sixteen—at the east end it is not more than ten miles across, and a the west end about twelve; its surface presents an area of about two hundred and eighty square miles, or 179,142 statute acres. In extent this is the twenty-fourth, and in population the twenty-third of the counties of Scotland.

The greatest elevations in East Lothian above the level of the sea are Traprain Law, 700 feet: North Berwick Law, 940 feet; Soutra Hill, 1230 feet; and Spartleton Hill, 1615 feet.

The manufactures of this county are unimportant, and are carried on but to a limited extent. There are woollen mills in the neighbourhood of the county town, whilst in other parts of the shire are brick and tile works, agricultural implement works, and breweries. Salt is manufactured in the vicinity ot Prestonpans, coal also being extensively wrought here aud at Tranent, Ormiston, and Pencaitland. The climate in the Lowlands is on the whole genial and favourable for agriculture, whilst in Lammermoor district it is colder, and more liable to falls of rain and snow.

Several streams intersect the county, but none of them merit the title of river except the Tyne, which, passing Haddington, falls into the sea at Tynninghame, where it forms a bay. The shire is destitute of natural lakes, but this deficiency seems no way injurious to the district, and is amply made up by the Frith of Forth, which yields a large supply of fish. The North British Railway passes through the county, and possesses stations in all the principal towns; there are also one or two branches diverging from it.

Haddingtonshire comprises twenty-three complete parishes and two parts of parishes, and three royal burghs—Haddington, Dunbar, and North Berwick. The present member for the county is R. B. Haldane, Esq., Q.C. The Lord-lieutenant of the county is the Earl of Haddington, Population of the county, 37,491.

ABERLADY AND NEIGHBOURHOOD.

THE parish of ABERLADY lies S.E. of the south coast of the mouth of the Frith of Forth. The village is situated 15 miles W. from Edinburgh, 5½ W.N.W. from Haddington, and 4½ S. from Dirleton. Acreage, 4319. Population of the parish, 1063, of the village, 501.

Business Directory.

Bakers.
Guy, Robert, Aberlady
Smith, G. & J., Post Office, Aberlady

Drapers.
Bird, Thomas, Aberlady
Scott, Jane, Aberlady

Farmers—see end of Directory.

Horse Hiring and Posting Establishment.
Dalgleish, William, Aberlady
Pincott, John, Aberlady

Joiners and Wrights.
Brown, Peter, Aberlady
Cuthbert, Walter, Aberlady
Miller, John, Aberlady

Spirit Dealers.
Clark, John, Aberlady
Welch, Henry, Aberlady

Miscellaneous.
Blacksmith—John Anderson, Aberlady
Bootmaker—John Amos, Aberlady
Flesher—William Eeles, Aberlady
Golf Club Maker — T. Waggot, Aberlady
Grocer Jane Welch, Aberlady
Maltsters—Bernard & Co, Aberlady
Market Gardener — J. M'Laren, Ballencrieff
Mason—A. Fraser, Aberlady
Plumber — H. Rutherford, Aberlady
Slater—J. Lambert, Aberlady
Temperance Hotel—Mrs J. Hunter, Aberlady

ATHELSTANEFORD AND DREM.

ATHELSTANEFORD parish lies on the north-east boundary of Haddington, and is separated on the north by Dirleton from the mouth of the Forth ; the small village lies within 5½ miles S.E. from North Berwick, 5. S.E. from Aberlady, and 3 N.E. from Haddington.

DREM, 2½ miles distant, is a station on the North British line. It is a village in this parish, the acreage of which is 5,077. Population 745.

Business Directory.

Blacksmiths.
Carrick, Alex., Athelstaneford
Cowan, George, Drem
Robertson, John, Fenton barns

Farmers—see end of Directory.

Grocers and General Merchants.
Binnie, John (& baker), Athelstaneford
Grierson, Thomas, Athelstaneford

Joiners and Wrights.
Bertram, James, Drem
Neilson, Adam, Athelstaneford

Maltster.
Watt, James Wm., Athelstaneford

Miscellaneous.
Bootmaker — Alex. Tait, Athelstaneford
Market Gardener—Robert Sinclair, Drem
Stationer—Mrs. E. Robertson, Post Office, Athelstaneford

BARO—SEE EAST LINTON.
BELHAVEN—SEE DUNBAR.
BLACKSHIELS—SEE FALA.
BOLTON—SEE HADDINGTON.
COCKENZIE—SEE PRESTONPANS.

DIRLETON,

With GULLANE, FENTON, KINGSTON, and Neighbourhoods.

DIRLETON village is 20 miles E.N.E. of Edinburgh, 7 N. of Haddington 4½ N.E. from Aberlady, and nearly 3 from North Berwick. The parish embraces 9,146 acres. Besides Dirleton, the parish contains three other villages, namely GULLANE, FENTON, and KINGSTON. Population of the parish, 1,445.

GULLANE is a village, 2 miles south-west of Dirleton. The Links of Gullane have become a favourite resort of the lovers of the ancient game of golf, and it is also rising into importance as a resort for summer visitors.

Business Directory.

Bakers and Confectioners.
Oliver, Robert, Gullane
Tulloch, John, Gullane—see advt

Blacksmiths.
Cowan, David, Kingston
Darg, John & Alexander, Gullane

Ferguson, William, Dirleton
Lilley, John, Kingston

Farmers—see end of Directory.

Grocers and General Merchants.
Edington, M. & A., Gullane
Erskine, Alexander, Kingston
Gibb, Christina, Dirleton
Tulloch, John (Licensed Grocer, and Baker and Confectioner), Gullane—see advt
Yule, Thomas, Dirleton

Horse Hiring and Posting Establishments.
Clarkson, John, Gullane
Gillam, William, Gullane
Pincott, William (and 'Bus proprietor, 'Bus to Station), Gullane

Hotels and Posting Houses.
Dirleton Castle—Peter Cathie, Dirleton
Golf—Wm. K. Smith, Gullane
New Hotel (late Royal Hotel)—Jas Bisset, Gullane

Joiners and Wrights.
Erskine, Alexander, Kingston
Urquhart, William, Dirleton

Market Gardeners.
Plenderleigh, G., Rockville
Robertson, Wm., Dirleton
Shiells, John, Dirleton

Miscellaneous.
Bootmaker—Francis Morrison, Gullane
Carriers and Contractors—J. Brotherson & Sons, Gullane
Flesher—William Eeles, Gullane
Fruiterer—Wm Robertson, Gullane
Golf Club Maker—Alexander Aitken, Gullane
Masons—P. & J. Scott, Gullane
Tailor—George Hamilton, Dirleton
Tobacconist—W. Robertson, Gullane
Refreshment Rooms—Mrs. J. Ellis, Gullane

DREM—SEE ATHELSTANEFORD.

DUNBAR,

With BELHAVEN, EAST BARNS, WEST BARNS, SPOTT, and Neighbourhoods.

DUNBAR is a royal burgh and seaport, the seat of a presbytery, and the capital of its parish, and of the eastern part of the district of East Lothian: 28 miles E. from Edinburgh, 11 E. from Haddington, and 30 N.N.W. from Berwick-upon-Tweed. The manufactures of Dunbar are fish-curing, comprising several extensive concerns. The parish of Dunbar embraces an area of 7,497 acres. The market is held on Tuesdays.

There are two annual fairs, one on the first Tuesday after the 26th May, the other on the first Tuesday after the 22nd November. The entire parish contains 5,210, a population of which number 3,746 were given for the town, including that portion comprised in Belhaven for which 427 were returned.

BELHAVEN is a village included within the jurisdiction of the burgh of Dunbar, situated about 1 mile from that town,

EAST BARNS is a village in Dunbar parish, about 3 miles south-east from that town.

WEST BARNS another part of the royalty of Dunbar, is about half a mile from Belhaven. Population 648.

SPOTT is a village in the parish of that name, situated 2 miles south from Dunbar. The parish contains an acreage of 7,583. Population of 472.

Business Directory.

Bakers and Confectioners.

Brown, John, 139 High st
Bruce, John, 66 High st
Gibb, John, 117 High st
Graham, John G., 84 High st
Huntly, Robert (Baker and Confectioner), Post Office, West Barns
Smith, William, 120 High st
White, John, 65 High st

Banks.

Bank of Scotland, High st
British Linen Co., Delisle
Commercial Bank Ld., 105 High st

Blacksmiths.

Browning, John (and Farrier and Cycle Agent and Repairer), 8 Colvin st
Donald, Henry, Pinkerton
Dunn, Walter, Broxburn
Duncanson, H. & W. (and Farriers) Lawson pl & 113 Highst
Gray, William, Burnhead, Spott
Hadden, William, Spott
Lillie, Andrew, Pitcox
Lindsay, John, Beltonford
Paxton, Robert, East Barns
Robertson, Wm. (Lock), 73 High st
Smith, James, Gateside

Booksellers, Stationers, and Newsagents.

Downie, Mrs. J. (and House agent), 56 High st
Knox, James, 64 High st
Knox, Thomas B. (and Printer), 62 High st

Boot and Shoe Makers.

Anderson, John, 149 High st
Clark, A , 17 West port
Donaldson, William, West port
Gray, John & Co., 2 West port
Heugh, R., 27 High st
Law, James, 54 High st
Mason, Joseph, 80 High st
Ramsay, James, 88 High st

Builders—see Joiners and Builders.

Cabinetmakers, Upholsterers, and Undertakers.

Clark, David, High st
Low, George, 67 High st
Purves, William B. & Son, George Hotel lane
Russell, William L , 86 High st

Chemists and Druggists

Purves, J. A., 25 High st
The Laboratory, 39 High st
Wilson, W. P. (and Aerated Water Manufacturer), 67 High st

China and Glass Merchants.

Graham, George, 99 High st
M'Laughlin, Mrs., 138 High st
Murray, Miss E., 31 High st
Reilly, Martin, 18 Castle st

Coach Builders.

Brown, D. & J., Belhaven

Coal Merchants and Agents.

Bell, John, 58 High st, & at Station
Blyth, Andrew, 129 High st—depot, Station

Deans & Moore, Beltonford
Polwart, Charles, 32 High st
White, Thomas, 40 High st

Confectioners—see also Bakers and Confectioners.

Mayne, William (and Temperance Refreshments), 146 High street
Sharp, John, West Barns
Thomson, M., 33 High st

Contractors—Carting.

Craik, James (and Dairyman), Friars croft
Nisbet, Alexander, 30 Castle street

Dairymen.

Amos, John, West port
Blackhall, James, West Barns
Cowan, Walter & Son (and Family Grocers, &c.), 157 High street
Craik, James (and Contractor) Friars croft

Drapers, Dressmakers, Milliners, and Clothiers.

Anderson, P. A., 3 Westport
Barr, J., 5 Westport
Black, W. & M., 126 High st
Edgar, Robert, 47 High st
Grahame, Alexander, 17 High st
Melville, Robert, 159 High st
Sanson, William, (and Tailor and Clothier), 109 High st
Smith, Daniel, 53 High st
Smith, John, 60 High st
Young, James, 104 High st

Dressmakers—see Milliners &c., and also Drapers.

Fancy Goods and Berlin Wool Repositories.

Bell, Margaret, 50 High st
Murray, Miss E., 31 High st
Paxton, N. & M., 131 High st
Scott, J. & M., 7 High st

Farmers—see end of Directory.

Fishcurers and Merchants.

Craig, Thomas, Victoria Harbour
Grahame, William, 133 High st
Hutchison, William, Woodbush
Robertson, A. & G., Woodbush
Robertson. Thomas, Victoria st and High st

Fleshers.

Shiel, R. C. & J., 103 High st
Tait, Brothers, 96 High st
Tait, George, (& Poulterer), 10 High st

Fruiterers and Florists.

Borthwick, A., 43 High st
Hunter, F., (& Dairy), Belhaven
Hynde, Elizabeth D., High st
Jenkinson, Mrs. A., 76 High st
Mayne, William, (Florist, Confectioner, and Temperance Refreshments), 146 High st
Smith, Alexander, 28 High st

Grocers and General Merchants.
Marked 'e' are also Spirit Merchants.

e Baillie, Alexander, 48 High st
e Boyd, Alexander, 2 Castle st
e Congdon, Samuel, (Licensed) 2 Vennel
Cowan, Walter & Son, Family Grocers and Dairymen), 157 High st
e Craigie. R. D., 20 Victoria st
e **Cunningham, Robert,** (Wine Merchant & Italian Warehouseman), 124 High st
Fairbairn, E., 14 Writers' court
e **Fraser, Thomas & Sons,** (Wine Merchants and Italian Warehousemen), 77 High st
Hynde, Elizabeth D., (& Fruiterer), 143 High st
Johnston, Miss M. (& Dressmaker), Spott
e Kerr, Archibald, Belhaven
e Malcolm, Alexander, (and Coal Merchant), 98 High street
e Malcolm, John, (Licensed), 49 High st
e Purves, James, (Licensed), West Barns
Raeburn, J., 50 Victoria st

e Riddell, Robert, 61 High st
Ritchie, Robert, 151 High st
Sanson, James, Broxburn
Smith, James H., 48 Victoria st
e Turner, Alison, Belhaven
West Barns Co-operative Society, Limited.
White, James A., 5 Victoria st
Wood, Alexander, (Licensed), 71 High st
e Wood, Alexander, Victoria st
Wood, W. M., 91 High st

Hairdresser and Perfumer.

Brown, Adam, (Ladies' and Gentlemen's Hairdressing and Shampooing Saloons), 6 High st

Horse Hiring and Posting Establishments.

Horne, Alfred (Job and Postmaster), St. George's Stables
Little, Thomas, West Barns
Watson, John, West Barns

Hotels and Inns—see also Temperance Hotels.

Black Bull—Tom Kyle, proprietor, 72 High st
Castle—A Macpherson, 163 High st
Denholm, John, West Barns
Eagle Hotel—Adam Robertson proprietor, 75 High st
Forester's Arms—Thomas Robertson, 6 Silver st
Jersey Arms—J. F. Borrowman, 25 Lamer st
Mason's Arms—Thomas Barbour, Castlegate
Mason's Arms—Isabella Clark, Belhaven
Old Ship—John M'Michan, Old Harbour
Railway—G. Milne, Station road
Redheugh House & Park View (Private) Hotel—George, Kerridge, proprietor
Royal Oak—John M'Intyre, proprietor, Victoria harbour
Royal—James Pettigrew, Dunbar
Roxburghe Marine Hotel, Limited, Dunbar
Volunteer Arms — C. Robertson, Victoria st
St. George's Hotel—Edmond Leach, proprietor, High st
Shepherd's Arms—Mrs. C. Bell, 2 Writer's court

House Agent.

Downie, Mrs. J., 56 High st

Ironmongers and Hardwaremen.

Bowhill, Archibald, 165 High st
Grahame, George (and Oil Merchant), 99 High st
Grahame, Janet, 135 High st
Melville, Andrew & Sons, 114 High street

Joiners and Wrights.

Angus, George, 1 Westgate
Bald, James, Beltonford
Bell, Thomas, Castle st
Blair, George (Builder), 161 High st
Cunningham, C., Dunbar
Cunningham. William (Joiner), Victoria st
Galbraith, George, West port
Gibson, Robert, Broxburn
Horsburgh, Thomas D., East Barns
Porter, James, Gateside
Manderson, John, 1 High st
Ritchie, Robert, Lamer st
Scott, George, Spott
White, Hugh, (Joiner, Cartwright, and Undertaker), Castle street

Maltsters.

British Malt Product Malt Co., West Barns
Hunter, Alexander, Beltonford

Milliners and Dressmakers—see also Drapers.

Moodie, Miss E., High st
Watson, J. & J., West port

Painters and Decorators.

Hunter, G. L. (Glazier), 112 High st
Laing, James, 59 High st
M'Kenzie, James, 2 High st

Plasterers—see Slaters and Plasterers.

Plumbers and Gasfitters.

Grahame, George, 99 High st
Melville, Andw. & Sons, 114 Highst

Potato Merchants.

Bowe, John H., 1 Bowmont villas
Cairns, Wm., Westgate end

Slaters and Plasterers.

Aitken, Archibald, 161 High st
Alder, Ralph, West port
Boyle, Thomas (Slater and Chimney Sweep), 31 High st
Gillies, James, High st

Solicitors.

Anderson, Wm. F. & Barlas, 17 High st
Ferme, Ferme, & Williamson, 21 High st and Haddington
Notman, Charles (Solicitor, Town Clerk, Clerk to the Eastern District of the County Council, and Clerk to the (Parish) School Board), High st
Sinclair, John Henry, 38 High st
White, Robert, West port

Spirit Dealers—see Hotels and Inns

Surgeons.

Black, James D., High st
M'Donald, William B., High st
Sinclair, G. T., 44 High st

Tailors and Clothiers—see also Drapers.

Kerse, G., 4 High st
Marshall & Scambler, Spott
Sanson, William, 109 High st
Simpson, A., West port
Wood, John, High st

Temperance Hotels.

Lorne—M. Huntly, 134 High st
Wilson's Temperance Family and Commercial **Hotel**—W. J. Wilson, proprietor, 95 High st

Tobacconists.

Andrew, James, 103 High st
Laing, James, 59 High st
M'Kenzie, James, 2 High st

Veterinary Surgeons.

Balfour, George W., M.R.C.V.S., West port
Russell, William, 90 High st

Watch and Clock Makers.

Anderson, Andrew, 113 High st
Fehrenbach & Hepting, 6 Westport
Gardner, Thomas J., 121 High st
Kinnach, William, 83 High st

Miscellaneous.

Auctioneers—Brand & Henderson, 30 High st
Brewers—Dudgeon & Co., Belhaven
Engineers—Thos. Sheriff & Co., West Barns
Golf Club Maker—Andrew Sommerville, Golf house
Land Surveyor — Thomas Black, Belhaven
Lime Burners — Mitchell & Son, Oxwell mains
Miller — Wm. Borthwick, Easter Broomhouse
Photographer—C. Spence, Station road
Quarrymaster — C. Cunningham, Broomhouse
Saddler—Wm. Main, 87 High st
Sculptor—James Denholm, 3 Westgate
School (Ladies' Boarding) — Mrs. Fish, Kirklands

EAST BARNS—see DUNBAR.

EAST LINTON in PRESTONHIRK,

Garvald and Baro, Stenton, Whitekirk and Tynninghame, and Whittinghame.

EAST LINTON is a burgh in the parish of Prestonkirk, 22 miles E. from Edinburgh, 6 S.S.E. from North Berwick, 6 W. from Dunbar, and 5 E. from Haddington. The parish of Prestonkirk comprises 7,058 acres. The North British line of railway passes through the village, and has a station here. A cattle market is held here annually, in October. March, May, and June. The parish of Prestonkirk contained a population of 1798.

Garvald and Baro, an united parish, is bounded by Morham and Whittinghame on the north and East, and by Gifford on the west. The village of Garvald is 22 miles E.S.E. from Edinburgh, 8½ S.W. from Dunbar, 5 S. from Linton, and nearly 6 S.E. from Haddington. Acreage, 13,442, The population of the parish is 600, and of the village 280.

Stenton is a parish and small village, the latter situated 4½ miles east from East Linton. The parish contained a population of 359 : it comprises an area of 7,676.

Whitekirk is a very small village in the united parish of Whitekirk and Tynninghame, 4 miles north from Linton.

Two miles from Linton and the same from Whitekirk, is Tynninghame village. Whitekirk and Tynninghame, the acreage of which is 6,195, contained a population of 933.

Whittinghame is an extensive parish, comprising 15,595 acres. The village, a very small one, is 3 miles south from the village of Linton, and 6 east from Haddington. Parish has a population of 485.

Business Directory.

Bakers and Confectioners.

Bridges, Hugh, Garval
Brown, Walter, Tynninghame Prestonkirk
Burns, William, East Linton
Cockburn, John, Stenton
Ferguson, William, Garvald
Muir, Thomas, East Linton
Murray, William, East Linton
Nisbet, Mrs., East Linton

Blacksmiths.

Brown, Thomas W., Hailes, East Linton

Burns, Richard, East Linton
Combe, James, Whittinghame
Durie, David, East Linton
Hogg, William, Merrylaws, Whitekirk
Horsburgh, George, East Linton
Lawrie, John, East Linton
Sked, John, Garvald
Thomson, Andrew, Tynninghame
Watt, Thomas, Stenton

Booksellers, Stationers, and Newsagents.

Ford, William, East Linton
Hally, Charles, East Linton

Boot and Shoe Makers.

Barrie, Alexander, East Linton
Craics, R. & A., East Linton
Mason, Alexander, East Linton

Builders and Masons.

Malcolm & Laing, East Linton
Pettigrew, James, East Linton

Coal Merchants.

Barrie, William, East Linton
Hardie, James, East Linton
Malcolm, Alexander, East Linton
Newar, R., East Linton
Watt, William, East Linton

Drapers, Milliners, and Clothiers.

Davidson, James, Stenton
Ferguson, William, Garvald
Galbraith, Samuel (Draper and Licensed Grocer), Stenton
Knox, R. & M., East Linton
Park, Agnes, B., East Linton
Smith, A. & E., East Linton

Engineers and Millwrights.

Pratt & Pringle (and General Mechanics and Bicycle Agents, and Manufacturers of Steam Traps for Tweed Mills, &c. and Dishorning Machines), East Linton and at North Berwick see adv

Farmers--see end of Directory.

Fleshers.

Cockburn, John, Stenton
Cowe, William, East Linton
Stewart, Alexander, East Linton

Fruiterers and Confectioners.

Gordon, John, East Linton
White, James, East Linton

Grocers and General Merchants.

Barrie, William, East Linton
Clapperton, Alexander (Licensed Grocer), East Linton
Davidson, James, Stenton
Ferguson, William (Licensed), Garvald
Galbraith, Samuel (Licensed Grocer and Draper), Stenton
Gordon, Mrs Ellen, East Linton
Hogg, Ann (Beer and Porter), East Linton
Howie, John, Garvald
Kerr, David, East Linton
Malcolm, Alexander (grocer and spirit merchant), East Linton
Tait, R., Tynninghame
Watt, James, East Linton
Young, Miss J., East Linton

Horse Hiring and Posting Establishments.

Lindsay, John (and Corn Dealer), East Linton
Menzies, James (Good Horses and Carriages), East Linton
Pond, William, Garvald Hotel, Garvald, Prestonkirk

Hotels and Inns.

Crown — Andrew Denholm, East Linton
Garvald Hotel & Posting House (Good Stabling)—Wm. Pond, proprietor, Garvald, Prestonkirk
Railway—John Heath, East Linton
Red Lion—James Clapperton, East Linton

Ironmongers, Plumbers, and Gasfitters.

Ford, William, East Linton
Lawrie, William, East Linton
Melville & Sons, East Linton

Joiners and Wrights.
Fraser, J. (and Sawmiller), East Linton
Halliday, William, Garvald
Lawrie, W., Tynninghame
White, Peter, Merrylaws, Whitekirk
Wilson, John, Stenton

Millers.
Duncan, John & James, Sandy's mill
Watt, William, East Linton

Plasterers—see Slaters and Plasterers.

Plumbers and Gasfitters—see Ironmongers.

Slaters and Plasterers.
Cameron, John, East Linton
Katchen, James, East Linton
Linton, John, Garvald

Poultry Breeder.
Brown. John (Prize Poultry Breeder), Garvald, Prestonkirk

Spirit Dealers— see Hotels and Inns

Surgeons.
Black, David B., East Linton
Gordon, James, East Linton
Storie, John junr (v.s.) East Linton

Tailors and Clothiers—see also Drapers.
Anderson, Robert M., East Linton
Bryson, George, East Linton
Johnston, Thomas, Post Office, Prestonkirk
M'Lean, William, Tynninghame
Walker, Peter, East Linton
Wilson, Robert, Stenton

Miscellaneous.
Aerated Water Manufacturer—Jas. Dunbar, East Linton
Bankers National Bank of Scotland, Limited, East Linton
Chemist — William Nicol, East Linton
Painter—James Sandie, East Linton
Saddler—Jas. Hardie, East Linton
Watchmaker—G. Joyner, East Linton

ELPHINSTONE—SEE TRANENT.

FALA AND SOUTRA, HUMBIE AND BLACKSHIELS.

FALA and SOUTRA is a united parish, the first of which is within the eastern border of Edinburghshire, the other in the county of Haddington. The villages of Fala and Fala-dam are situated on the road from Edinburgh to Lauder, about 14 miles from the former, and 11 from Hadington. Blackshiels is a village in this parish, the acreage of which is 6,064, its population, 248.

The parish of HUMBIE lies on the south-western part of Haddingtonshire; bounded by Salton and Ormiston on the north, part of Bolton and Gifford on the east, and Fala and Soutra on the west. The parish encloses an area of 9,316 acres, and contains a population of 907.

Business Directory.

Farmers—see end of Directory.

Grocers and General Merchants.
Archibald, Adam, Blackshiels
Brockie, Miss Helen, Fala-dam
Ketchin, Archibald, Fala

Joiners and Wrights.
Simpson, James, Fala-dam
Stoddart, Walter, Fala

Miscellaneous.
Baker—Adam Smeal, Fala
Blacksmith — Alexander Leitch, Woodcot
Registrar—James Duncan, Fala
Spirit Dealer—James Nichol, Juniper lea

FENTON—SEE DIRLETON.
GARVALD—SEE EAST LINTON.

GIFFORD AND NEIGHBOURHOOD.

GIFFORD is a village and the capital of the parish of Yester, 20 miles E.S.E. from Edinburgh, 9 S.E. from Tranent, and 4 S.E. from Haddington. Fairs are held here in March, June, and October. The population of the parish of Yester is 716, the acreage of which is 8,848, of which Gifford contains 305.

Business Directory.

Blacksmiths.
Cowan, T., Gifford
Gray, George, Longyester

Farmers—see end of Directory.

Fleshers.
Stewart, James, Gifford
Tait, Robert, Gifford

Grocers and General Merchants.
Baillie & Co., Gifford
Bisset, M., Gifford
Dodds, John, Gifford
Falconer, J. Gifford
King, Alexander, Gifford
Lawrie, Helen, Gifford
Ogilvie, William, Gifford
Redpath, Margaret, Gifford

Hotels and Inns.
The Tavern—William Simpson, (Wine & Spirit Merchant, Dinners & Teas, Stabling), Gifford
Tweeddale Arms—W. J. Whyte, Gifford

Joiners.
Bertram, George, Gifford
Logan, John, (& Undertaker), Gifford

Masons and Builders.
Logan, Peter, Gifford
Tait, Robert, Gifford

Miscellaneous.
Baker—Matthew M'Couch, Gifford
Bootmaker—Alexander Barrie, Gifford
Confectioner—J. Stuart, Gifford
Horse Hirer—James Wood, Gifford
Miller—Alexander Robertson, Gifford
Slater—Robert Dunlop, Gifford
Tailor—A. Paterson. Gifford

GLADSMUIR—SEE TRANENT.
GULLANE—SEE DIRLETON.

HADDINGTON,

With the Parishes of BOLTON and MORHAM, and Neighbourhoods.

HADDINGTON is a royal burgh, the seat of a presbytery, the county town of East Lothian, and the capital of the parish of its name, 17 miles E. from Edinburgh, 38 N.W. from Berwick-upon-Tweed, 11 W. from Dunbar, and 9½ S. from North Berwick, situated on the left bank of river Tyne, and is the terminus of a branch line from the North British Railway. The trade of Haddington consists principally in corn; on the market days immense quantities are brought for sale, and it is considered one of the leading grain marts in Scotland. The weekly market is held on Friday. A weekly auction for the sale of live stock is also held every Monday. A cattle fair is held in October, and the United East Lothian Agricultural Society hold their meetings here. Population of the burgh, 3,770.

BOLTON is a parish and village—the latter 3 miles S.W. from Haddington Acreage, 3,106. Population, 271.

MORHAM is a parish 3 miles S.E. from Haddington. Acreage, 2,087. Population, 199.

Business Directory.

Accountant.
Leslie, D. S. (Accountant and Sheriff-Officer), 3 Sidegate

Ærated Water Manufacturers.
Geddes & Co. 19 High st

Architects and Surveyors.
Farquharson, John (Architect, Builder, and Joiner), 31 Court st
Muat, J. H., Court st
Wilson, John, 28 Sidegate st

Bakers and Confectioners.
Black, Thomas, 9 Hardgate st
Co-operative Society, Limited, 49 Court st

Murdoch, C., Court st
Neil, William, 14 Market st
Smith, Mrs, 15 High st
Stewart, Duncan, 1 Market st
Teviotdale, Robert, 45 High street
Wilson, William, Nungate

Banks.

Bank of Scotland, Court st
British Linen Co., High st
Commercial Bank, Ltd., Court st
Royal Bank of Scotland, Court st

Bill Poster.

Sounness, Charles C., 8 Hardgate st

Blacksmiths.

Baillie, James, Bolton
Bertram, David, 42 Market st
Edmond, Wm., Samuelston
Millar, Robert, Blackmains
Neilson & Hardie, Brewery park
Nisbet, John, Court st
Oliver, Robert, Cockles
Tait, David F., Coldale, Morham
Tait, John, Morham

Booksellers, Stationers, and Printers.

Bruce, Charles, 22 Market st
Cowan, Thomas, 61 High st
Hutchison, John, 81 High st

Boot and Shoe Makers.

Barrie. Alexander, 71 High st, and at Gifford
Gray, John, & Co., 53 Court st
Ramsay, Alexander, 68 High st
Scottish Boot Co., 24 Market st
Smith, George, 1 Church st
Thomson, Thomas, 1 High st
Wood, Andrew, 18 Hardgate st

Brass Finisher.

Amos, Robert, 58 Hardgate st

Brewers and Maltsters.

Bernard & Co., Haddington maltings
Binnie, M. (and Ærated Water Manufacturer), Nungate
Hunter, Alexander, Brewery park
Montgomery, J. M., Sidegate st

Builders and Masons.

Arnott, Robert. Meadow park
Farquharson, John, 31 Court st
Grant, William, Hope park
Ormiston, Peter, & Son Church st—Yard, Sidegate st
Paterson, Alexander, Peffer's place

Cabinetmakers, Upholsterers, and Undertakers.

Brown, David, 9 Court st
Jardine, James, 34 Court st
Pringle, James, 11 Hardgate st
Stark, James, Nungate

Chemists and Druggists.

Gardiner, David, 36 Market st
Mather, John, 92 High st
Watt, James, 36 High st

Coachbuilders.

Amos & Son, Hardgate st
Cowan & Hazley, 12 Market st
Kennedy, A. D., Church st

Coal Merchant.

Beattie, James, Meadow park

Confectioners—see also Bakers and Confectioners.

Guthrie, E. (& smallware dealer), 75 High st
Paton, Elizabeth, 84 Market st
Robertson, Richd., 14 High st
Shaw, M., 49 Market st

Contractors and Carriers.

Dignan, John, Hardgate st
Paterson, George, 15 Sidegate st

Corn Merchants—see Millers and Corn Merchants.

Dairymen.

Prentice, Thomas, Newton port
Scott, George, Sidegate st
Watson, John, 90 High st
Wilson, James, Hardgate st

Dentists.

Fergie, W., Hardgate st

Findlay, W. A., Church st

Drapers, Milliners, Dressmakers, and Clothiers.

Brown & Shaw, 82 High st
Couper, Thomas C., 14 High st
Frier, William H., 9 High st
Gillie, W. S., 95 Hardgate st
Gracey, Mrs. (dressmaker), Market street
Kellie, R. & A., 30 Market st
Main, Alex. M., 17 Hardgate st
Muat, G. & J., St. Ann's place
Neilson, George & Co., 67 High st
Williamson & Spark, 60 Market st

Engineers, Iron Founders, and Millwrights.

Bridges, J. & A., Rose Hall
Dodds, Samuel, Sommerfield
Hunter, John & Sons, Sandersdean

Fancy Goods and Berlin Wool Repositories.

Gilchrist, A. & M., 43 High st
White, H. & S., 58 Court st

Farmers—see end of Directory.

Fishmongers and Poulterers.

Balloch, W., 33 High st
Johnson, James, 7 High st

Fleshers.

Dower, A. & Son, 26 High st
Kirk, J. & T., Market st
Pringle, George, 17 Market st
Tait, William, 10 Market st
Thomson, James, 11 High st

Glass, China, and Earthenware Dealers.

Allan, David S. (and Market Gardener), 55 Court st
Paton, William, 69 Hardgate st
Reilly, Cornelius, Nungate
Skirving, Robert (and Broker), 80 Market st
Thomson, E. & J., 31 High st

Grocers and General Merchants.

Amos, William, 69 High st
Barrie, William, Nungate
Bell, George, 89 High st
Black, G., Blackmains
Brass, A., 67 Hardgate st
Brook, John, 60 High st
Co-operative Society Limited, 49 Court st
Goodall, John, Nungate
Green, Charles E., 82 High st
Guy, George W. (licensed), 28 High street
Johnston, M. (licensed grocer), Nungate
M'Neill, Martin, 7 Sidegate
Maltman, William, 84 High st
Martin, James, 5 Church st
Matthew & Thompson, 27 Marketst
Oswald, Wm. (and Confectioner), 12 Brown st
Paterson, Thomas, 64 Hardgate st
Paul & Co. (Licensed) 65 Market st
Porteous, James, 22 High st
Smith, James (Licensed Grocer), 20 High st
Wilson & Co., 70 Hardgate st

Horse Hiring and Posting Establishments.

Black, George (Posting in all its branches), 11 Market st
Cleghorn, W., West port
Conquer, R. & Son, High st
Knox, Barbara, Hardgate st
Robertson, John, Newton port

Hotels and Inns.

Aitchison, Mrs J., 29 High st
Bay Horse—Mrs Dickson, 1 Courtst
Black Bull—George Richardson, 71 Market st
Commercial Hotel — P. M'Rorie, proprieter, 73 High st
Crown—Geo. Kemp, 70 Market st
Gardeners' Arms—J. Brown, Market st
George Hotel—James Stuart, proprietor, 91 High st—see adv
Golf Tavern—Philip Prentice, Nungate
Market Tavern—David Oswald, 46 Cours st
Plough Tavern—D. Sanderson. 6 Court st

Railway — E. H. Romannel, 30 Court st
Tyneside Tavern—Thomas Anderson, Poldrate
Wallace's Temperance, 61 Marketst

Ironmongers and Hardwaremen.
Bertram, David, 42 Market st
Brown & Murray, 7 Market st
Brown, Thomas, 79 High st
Davie, Wm. & Co., 40 Market st

Joiners and Wrights.
Cockburn, David, Court st
Farquharson, John, 21 Court st
Gilbert, W., Market st
Goodlet, William (and Cycle Agent), Flora bank
Hodgson, Robert (and Undertaker, Jobbing in all its branches promptly attended to—Estimates furnished), Brewery park
Inglis, John, Newton port
Orr, James, 45, 46 Market st
Paterson, Alexander, Peffer's place
Stark, John, Nungate
Thomson, George, Mitchell hall

Marine Store Dealer and Rag and Skin Merchant.
Gearie, Patrick, 33 Market st

Market Gardeners and Fruit Growers.
Baillie, William, Millfield
Cossar, Peter (and florist), 12 High street
Farmer, James, Nungate
Purves, William, Gourlay bank
Ritchie, Andrew, Clerkington
Scott, George, 1 Sidegate st
Turner, Richard (Fruit—Grapes—Vegetables, and Leeks), Byres
Wilson, Andrew, West port

Millers and Corn Merchants.
Chapman, R. & Sons, East mills
Golightly, Robert, Abbey mills
Hogarth, Alexander, Ginmers mill
Peffers Bros., Clerkington mills

Milliners and Dressmakers
—see Drapers.

Newspapers, Publishers, and Printers.
Haddingtonshire Advertiser and North Berwick Advertiser—Wm. Sinclair, 63 Market st
Haddingtonshire Courier—D. & J. Croal, 19 Market st

Painters and Decorators.
Cunningham, John, 18 High st
Main, William A., 39 High st
Taylor, Henry, 4 Market st

Photographer.
Gordon, James T. (Photography in all its branches, and Picture Framer, &c.), 48 Market street

Plumbers and Gasfitters.
Mitchell, James, 51 Court st
Ross, T. M., 32 High st
Runciman, Alexander, 34 Marketst
Watson, Alexander (R.P.), 68 High street

Printers—see Newspapers, Publishers, and also Booksellers, &c.

Saddlers and Harness Makers.
Allan & Husband, 87 High st
Main, William, 64 High st
Porteous, Robert, 77 High st

Seed Merchants.
Dods, Wm. & Son, 44 Court st
Roughhead & Park (& Sackmakers) High st

Sheriff-Officer.
Leslie, D. S. (and Accountant), 3 Sidegate st

Slaters and Glaziers.
Amos, William, 56 Court st
Cumming Charles, 59 Hardgate st
Whitehead, Hugh, Nungate

Solicitors.
Brook, Alexander (W.S.,

Solicitor and Joint-Agent of Bank of Scotland), Court st
Ferme, Ferme, & Williamson, High st, and at Dunbar
Main, R. Maxwell, Hardgate st
Rattray, George (Solicitor, Liberal Agent, and Agent to Scottish Trade Protection Society) 55 High st
Richardson & Gemmell, (w.s.) (W. Murray & A. S. Gray) (Factors for Letham Estate, &c., Agents for Sun Fire Insurance Co., and Secretaries Haddington Brewery Co.), High st
Stevenson, George H., Court st
Stirling, John, Court st
Todrick, T. & T. W., Court st
Watson, J. & J., Court st
Wood, Andrew (Solicitor, Clerk to Aberlady and Morham School Boards, Auditor Aberlady Gas Light Company, and Clerk to Haddington Court House Commissioners), 13 Market st

Spirit Dealers—see Hotels and Inns

Surgeons.

Howden, Robert, High st
Howden, Thomas, Maitlandfield
James, John D., Poldrate
Martin, W. Robert, Court st
Mather, John, 93 High st
Ronaldson, James B., Victoria rd

Surveyors—see Architects and Surveyors.

Tailors and Clothiers—see also Drapers, &c.

Bradford, William, 14 Hardgate st
Cunningham, Duncan (Clothier, Hatter, & Outfitter), 4 High st and West Salton
Gillies, J. & P., 37 High st
Milne Brothers, 17 High st
Spence, Thomas, 50 High st

Tallow Chandlers.

Sinclair, George, 20 Market st
Watson, John & Wm. 6 High st

Teacher.

Brown, George Brewster, Bolton by Haddington

Timber Merchants and Saw Millers.

Dewar, Alexander, Flora bank
Stevenson, Wm., Loanend, Samuelston

Tobacconists.

Those marked 'e' are Manufacturers
Falconer, Alexander, 43 High st
Lawrie, Robert, 24 High st
e Sinclair, George, 20 Market st
e Watson, John & Wm., 6 High st

Veterinary Surgeons.

Bannatyne, W., Station rd
Hume, Andrew, 16 Court st
Young, George, Brewery park

Watchmakers and Jewellers.

Gilchrist, John G., 40 High st
M Farlane, John, 85 High st
Rose, David T. M., 9 Market st
Wright, Alexander, 1 Hardgate st

Wool Merchants.

Coalston, H. & H. (and skinners & tanners), Tyneside tannery
Gankroger, George, 28 Hardgate st

Woollen Manufacturers.

Paterson, Adam, West mills
Robson & Co., Wauk mill

Miscellaneous.

Auctioneer—John Swan & Sons Ld. Court st
Fruiterer—E. Scott, 79 Market st
Hairdresser—T. C. Watson, High street
Laundry—Bernard Cullen, Bridge end
Refreshment Rooms—J. Beazley, 78 High st

HUMBIE—SEE FALA.

INNERWICK AND OLDHAMSTOCKS.

THE parish of INNERWICK is bounded by Oldhamstocks on the east, Spott and Dunbar on the west, the sea on the north, and Cranshaws and Longformacus (in Berwickshire) on the south, and embraces an areage of 13,157 acres. The village of Innerwick is 30 miles E. from Edinburgh, 14 E. from Haddington, and 4 S.E. from Dunbar. Population, 761.

OLDHAMSTOCKS parish includes an areage of 8,837 acres. The parish of Innerwick bounds it on the north-west, west, and part of the south, and Cockburnspath lies on its east. The village is 3 miles south-east from Innerwick. Population of the parish, 529.

Business Directory.

Baker and Confectioner.
Grieve, James, Innerwick

Blacksmiths.
Henry, Michael, Oldhamstocks
Watt, William, Innerwick

Farmers—see end of Directory.

Grocers and General Merchants.
Ford, G. & A., Innerwick
Ford, Mary, Oldhamstocks
Ford, Mrs James, Innerwick
Kilpatrick, David, Innerwick
Torry, Henry D., Innerwick
Tunnie, Miss J., Crow hill

Laundries.
Michael, M., Innerwick
Thornton Mill Steam Laundry, Thornton

Miscellaneous.
Bootmaker—Wm Henry, Innerwick
Draper and Tailor—Peter Laing, Innerwick
Joiner—James Manderson, Oldhamstocks

KINGSTON—SEE DIRLETON.
LONGYESTER—SEE GIFFORD.
LONGNIDDRY—SEE TRANENT.
MACMERRY—SEE TRANENT.
MORHAM—SEE HADDINGTON.
NORTH BERWICK AND NEIGHBOURHOOD.

NORTH BERWICK is a parish containing a royal burgh and seaport, and summer resort for visitors, 23 miles N.E. from Edinburgh, 11 N.W. from Dunbar, and 10 N. from Haddington; situated on a low sandy plain on the shore of the German Ocean, at the entrance of the Firth of Forth, and on a branch of the North British Railway. The chief trade of

Berwick is the export of potatoes, &c.; the imports are coal and bones for manure. The Sheriff's Small Debt Courts are held on the third Wednesday in January, and the second Wednesday in May, July, and October, and the Justice of Peace Courts when necessary. The area of the parish is 5,067 acres, and its populotion is 3038.

Business Directory.

Agent.

Mackechnie, R. M. (agent for for the leading Fire, Life, and Accident Insurance Offices, and agent for the Clydesdale Bank, Limited, High st

Bakers and Confectioners.

Brodie. James, Westgate and 9 High st
Divine, Helen, 8 High st
Fowler, George, 67 High st
Ramage, Marion. 61 High st
Wood, Archibald, Westgate

Banks.

British Linen Co. Bank, High st
The Clydesdale Bank Ltd. High st—R. M. M'Kechnie agent

Blacksmith.

Bell, James, Forth st

Booksellers, Stationers and Newsagents.

Brownlea, Mrs., 38 High st
Melville, William, (and Circulating Library), 69 High st
Murray, G. & D., (Printers), High street

Boot and Shoe Makers.

Horsburgh, David, High st
Mirrilees, Andrew, 53 High st
Walker, John, 16 High st
Watson, William, 1 High st

Builders—see Joiners and Builders.

Cab and Coach Proprietor.

Bruce, William, East road

Cabinetmakers, Upholsterers and Undertakers.

Himsworth, Thomas, (and Joiner), 103 High st
Sked, Alexander, East road

Carting Contractor.

Hunter, George, (and Coal Merchant), 7 Melbourne square

Coach Builder.

Milne James, (Coach and Carriage Work executed in all its branches), Quadrant

Coal Merchant,

Hunter, George, (and Carting Contractor), 7 Melbourne square

Confectioners and Fruiterers.

Lawrie, Alice, 44 High st
Taylor, James, Abbey Nurseries

Cycle Agents.

Pratt & Pringle, (& repairers), and Engineers, North Berwick and at East Linton—see advt

Dairymen.

Clark, John, Wamphray Dairy High st
Dalgleish, Robert, Forth st
Young, Adam, Forth st

Drapers, Milliners, Dressmakers, & Clothiers.

Balden Misses, E. & H., 41 High st
Henderson, Miss A., 19 High st
Mills, Fred, 31 High st
Sim George, (Draper & Tailor), 37 & 39 High st
Smellie, & Brown, 52 High st

Engineers.

Pratt & Pringle (Domestic Engineers, Cycle Agents, & Manufacturers of Steam Traps for Tweed Mills, and Dishorning Machines), North Berwick, and at East Linton—see advt

Farmers—see end of Directory.

Fishmongers, Poultry and Game Dealers.

Easson, Thomas, High st
Goodall, James (and Grocer and Spirit Merchant), Market pl

Fleshers.

Dickson, Frank, 47 High st
Eeles, Francis, 5 High st
Gillies, John, 97 High st
Scott, Alexander (Butcher and Poulterer), 75 High st
Sturth, William, High st

Golf Club and Ball Makers.

Hutchison, J. H., Links
Sayers, B., Links

Grocers and General Merchants.

Marked thus 'e' are also Wine and Spirit Dealers.

Dickson, James, High st
Dixon, James, High st and Forth street
Edington, M. & A., 91 High st
Goodall, James (Grocer, Spirit Dealer, Fishmonger, Poultry and Game Dealer), Market pl
e Moyes, James, 35 High st
e Shiel, George & Sons (Licensed), High st
Smith, Andrew H., 28 High st
Stewart, John K., Forth st
e Whitecross, John, High st
Whitecross, John R. (Family Grocer, Wine Merchant, and House Agent), West end—see ad

Hairdresser and Perfumer.

Coulter, George (and Tobacconist), 42 High st

Horse Hiring and Posting Establishments.

Bell, George A., 6 High st
Bruce, William (and Cab and Carriage Proprietor), East road
Burnett, James 64 High st
Fowler, George, Quality st
Gilbert, J., Quality st
Medcalf & Swinburn (Saddle Horses and Stabling), Quadrant
Runciman, David, Quadrant and at 28 Quality st

Hotels and Inns.

Astley's (Private) Hotel—West end
Auld Hoose—Thomas Clark, Forth st
Bradbury's (Private) Hotel—West Links
Canty Bay—J. Hendall, Canty Bay
Commercial—H. White, 6 High st
Dalrymple Arms Hotel & Posting Establishment — John M'Ainsh, proprietor, Quality st—see advt on back inside cover
Golf Restaurant—Simpson Henderson, High st
Imperial Hotel—Henry Imrie proprietor, Quality st
Lenhiem Park —James Bolton, Westgate
Marine—W. Niebecher West Links
Royal Hotel—Arthur George Holloway, proprietor West Links
Ship Tavern—Alexander Vass, 25 Quality st
Warrender (Private) Hotel—Robert Malcolmson, proprietor, adjoining the Golfing Links

House Agents.

Brodie, James, Westgate & High st

Shiel, George & Sons, High st
Whitecross, John R. (Register of furnished houses) West end

Ironmongers Plumbers, and Gasfitters.
Dickson, William, 62 High st
Grieve, John, 23 High st
Howie, Henry, High st
Kendall, James, Shore st
Mann, Alexander, 87 High st

Joiners and Builders.
Auld, William. High st
Glass, James, Dalrymple buildings
Himsworth, Thomas (Joiner, Cabinetmaker, Upholsterer, and Undertaker), 103 High st
Whitecross, Wm. R., Forth st
Whitecross & Son, High st

Laundry.
Morton, Hugh (Table Linen and General Finery), Auburn cottage, Clifford road

Library—Circulating.
Melville, William (and Bookseller, &c.), 69 High st

Painters and Decorators.
Hutchison, Alexander, (House Painter and Photographic Artist), 46 and 48 High st
Laing, W., 9 Quality st

Photographic Artist.
Hutchison, Alexander, (and House Painter), 46 and 48 High st
Ross, John, West Links

Plasterers and Slaters.
Arundel, J. W., 11 Melbourne sq
Arundel, T., Harbour st
M'Laren, Alexander, 27 High st

Poulterer—see also Fishmonger, &c.
Scott, Alexander (& Butcher) 65 High st

Plumbers and Gasfitters—see Ironmongers.

Printers—see Booksellers, &c.

Schools—Boarding and Day.
Dodd, Misses, Eldon house
Turpie, Mrs. D. M., West Links

Slaters—see Plasterers and Slaters.

Spirit Dealers—see Hotels and Inns

Solicitors and Notaries.
Jackson, Donald M., High st
Lyle & Wallace, East road
M'Culloch, David, High st
M'Culloch, Ferme & Williamson, High st

Surgeons.
Crombie, John, High st
Matheson, Angus, High st

Tailors and Clothiers.
Inglis, William, 13 Quality st
Little, J. & Son, High st
Sim, George, (Tailor & Draper) 37 and 39 High st
Slimmand, Robert, High st
Wilson, Thomas, 7 High st

Tobacconists.
Coulter, George, 42 High st
Fraser, L., High st
Turnbull, J., High st

Watchmakers and Jewellers.
Bennett, Edwin, 102 High st
Kellas, William, High st
Muat, James T., Dalrymple bdgs

Miscellaneous.
Auctioneer—J. W. Hardie, Ravensheugh
Berlin Wool & Fancy Repository—E. Brown, High st
Chemists & Aerated Water Manufacturers—Macintyre & Co., 33 High st
China & Glass Dealers — G. & D. Murray, High st
Saddler—Thomas Robb, Quality st

OLDHAMSTOCKS—SEE INNERWICK.
ORMISTON—SEE TRANENT.
PENCAITLAND—SEE SALTON.
PENSTON—SEE TRANENT.
PRESTON—SEE PRESTONPANS.
PRESTONKIRK—SEE EAST LINTON.

PRESTONPANS,

With the villages of PRESTON, COCKENZIE, and Neighbourhoods.

PRESTONPANS is a market and post town, and burgh of barony, 9 miles E. from Edinburgh, 14 S.W. from North Berwick, 9½ W.N.W. from Haddington, and 3 E. from Musselburgh: situated on the shore of the Firth of Forth; and the North British Railway passes about a half a mile to the south. It is much frequented during the bathing season by visitors from Edinburgh and different parts of the country. MEADOW HILL is a hamlet 1½ miles of Prestonpans. The market is held on Friday. The parish has an area of 1,291 acres, and its population is 2,659.

COCKENZIE is a fishing village in the parish of Tranent, 1 mile east from Prestonpans, situated on the road leading to North Berwick, and the shore of the Firth of Forth. A fair is held here on the first Thursday in November. Population, 1,612.

Business Directory.

Bakers and Confectioners.

Cooper, George, Prestonpans
Donaldson, John, Cockenzie
Ferguson, Andrew, Cockenzie
Rennie, James & T., Prestonpans
Rennie, William, Prestonpans
Thomson, John & William, Lorimer place, and High st, Cockenzie

Blacksmiths.

Allan, John Cockenzie
Brownlee, Alexander, Brestonpans
Fortune, Richard, Preston Links
Hardie, Andrew, Cockenzie
Merrylees, Thomas, Prestonpans

Boot and Shoe Makers.

Bryce, James, Prestonpans
Donaldson, Archibald, Cockenzie
Hay, George, Prestonpans
Stewart, Agnes, Cockenzie
Watt, James, Prestonpans

Coal Masters and Fire Brick Manufacturers

Luke & Co., Prestonpans
Summerlee and Mossend Iron and Steel Co., Prestonpans

Dairyman.

Robertson, James (and Horse Hirer), Cockenzie

Drapers and Clothiers.

Borland, John, Prestonpans
Fraser, James, Prestonpans
Richardson, John, Prestonpans
Thomson, John & William, Lorimer place, and High st, Cockenzie
Turnbull, Isabella, Prestonpans
Wilson, William, Prestonpans

Earthenware Manufacturers.

Belfield & Co., Prestonpans

Farmers—see end of Directory.

Fleshers.

Belford, William, Cockenzie
Herriot, John, Prestonpans
Instant, Alexander, Prestonpans
Pow, Archibald, Prestonpans
Stevenson, Robert, (Flesher and Poulterer), Shipping supplied Prestonpans

Grocers and Spirit Dealers.
Marked 'e' are Grocers only.

e Baillie, A. & Son, Cockenzie
Buchanan, Daniel, Cockenzie
e Buchanan, Robert, Prestonpans
e Campbell, W., Prestonpans
e Co-operative Store, Cockenzie
e Co-operative Soc. Ld. Prestonpans
Duncan, William, (Family Grocer, Wine & Spirit Merchant. and Agent for Melroses Teas), Prestonpans
e Dunn, William, Prestonpans
Duns, Wm., Prestonpans
Drysdale, Catherine, C., (Licensed Grocer), Prestonpans
Grandison, A., Prestonpans
e Greig, Mary, Prestonpans
e Harkes, Alexander, Cockenzie
Hume, Brothers, Prestonpans
Hunter, James, Prestonpans
e Inglis, Catherine, Prestonpans
Kay, John, Cockenzie
Purdie, William, Prestonpans
Ross, Helen, Cockenzie
Thomson John & William, (Grocers, Wine and Spirit Merchants, Bakers Drapers, and Ironmongers), Lorimer Place, & High Street, Cockenzie

Horse Hiring Establishments.

Robertson, James, ('Bus to Railway Station), Cockenzie

Hotels and Inns.

Black Bull Inn—David Adams, Prestonpans
Queen's—James Grant, Prestonpans
Railway—James Beech Prestonpans
Thorn Tree, (General Accommodation for Cycles), —Clement Lamb, Port Seton, Cockenzie
Wemyss Arms Hotel, and Posting House (First-Class accommodation for Cyclists &c.), John Sinclair, proprietor, Cockenzie

Joiners and Wrights.

Cooper, Thomas, Prestonpans
Hare, William, Cockenzie
Hunter, George, Prestonpans
Reekie, James, Cockenzie
Weatherhead, William, Cockenzie

Laundry.

Henderson, William, Prestonpans

Market Gardeners & Fruit Growers.

Aitken, James H., Northfield mains
Barrie, Robert, Cockenzie
Bathgate, Robert, Seton Gardens, near Prestonpans
Greenfield, Archibald, Prestonpans
Henderson, John, Prestonpans
Inglis, A., (trus of), Prestonpans
Sibbald, William, Prestonpans

Plumbers and Gasfitters.

Monro, Andrew, Prestonpans
Sandilands, John, Prestonpans

Poulterer.

Stevenson, Robert, (and Flesher), Shipping supplied, Prestonpans

Salt Manufacturers.

Forman, Peter & Chas., Cockenzie
Scottish Salt Co. Ltd., Prestonpans

Spirit Dealers—see Hotels and Inns

Surgeons.

Fraser, James, Prestonpans
M'Ewan, William, Prestonpans

Tailors and Clothiers—see also Drapers and Clothiers.

Burns, John, Prestonpans

Miscellaneous.

Bankers—Royal Bank, Prestonpans
Booksellers—Mrs E. H. Thompson, Prestonpans
Brewers—John Fowler & Co. Ld., Prestonpans
Chemist—Robert Stenhouse, Prestonpans
Coal Merchant—J. Anderson, Prestonpans
Contractor—Wm. Rodger, Prestonpans
Fruiterer—George Bell, Prestonpans
Lime Factors—R. & C. H. Luke, & Co., Prestonpans
Rope and Sail Makers—R. & J. Clark, Prestonpans
Soap Makers—Mellis & Co., Prestonpans
Watchmaker—Mrs. M. Henderson, Cockenzie

SALTON (EAST AND WEST), PENCAITLAND, and Neighbourhoods.

SALTON Parish lies on the north side of the Lammermoor hills. The village of EAST SALTON is situated 15 miles E. from Edinburgh, 5 S.W. from Haddington, and 5 S.E. from Tranent.

WEST SALTON, in the same parish, is about half a mile from East Salton. The population of the parish, which embraces an area of 3,812 statute acres, is 497.

PENCAITLAND is a village and parish, the former is 2½ miles N.W. from East Salton. The population of the parish is 1,125, and contains 5,075 acres.

Business Directory.

Agricultural Implement Maker.

Chirnside, George (& Blacksmith), Pencaitland

Blacksmiths.

Anderson, James, East Salton
Chirnside, George (& Agricultural Implement Maker), Pencaitland
Jeffrey, Alexander, West Salton
Murray, Charles, Nisbet Loanhead, Pencaitland

Booksellers, Stationers, and Newsagents.

Cossar, Peter, Pencaitland
Ford, Thomas, Post Office, Pencaitland

Boot and Shoe Makers.

Cockburn, David, Pencaitland
Hastie, James, Pencaitland (Boots and Shoes of every description kept in stock or made to order, at lowest possible prices for cash)

Polson, John, East Salton

Distillers and Maltsters.

The Glen-Kinchie Distillery Co., Limited—William Cockburn, Secy., Pencaitland

Farmers—see end of Directory.

Fruiterer.

Taylor, Andrew, The Cross, Pencaitland

Grocers and General Merchants.

Binnie, Alexander, (and Baker and Horse Hirer), Pencaitland
Cameron, Daniel, East Salton
Gordon, James W., (& Baker), Pencaitland
Herriot, Mrs E., Pencaitland
Lawrie, Mrs. Christina, West Salton
Paterson, John, (Licensed, and Draper), West Salton
Taylor, Andrew, (and Fruiterer), Pencaitland

Innkeeper.

Salton Inn, (Good Stabling)—Robert Henderson, Pencaitland, East Salton

Joiners and Wrights.

Harkes, George, (Joiner, Undertaker, and Repairer of Agricultural Implements), East Salton
Morgan, J. H., Pencaitland
Porteous, John, (Joiner, Undertaker, Wheelwright and General Household Repairs), Pencaitland

Miller.

Staig, David, Barley Mill, West Salton

Tailors and Clothiers.

Cunningham, Duncan, (Clothier, Hatter, and Outfitter), West Salton and Haddington
Plain, Alexander, (and Outfitter), Pencaitland

Miscellaneous.

Baker—George Bathgate, East Salton
Slater—Peter Dunlop, Pencaitland

SAMUELSTON—SEE HADDINGTON.

SOUTRA—SEE FALA.

SPOTT—SEE DUNBAR.

STENTON—SEE EAST LINTON.

TRANENT,

ELPHINSTONE, GLADSMUIR, LONGNIDDRY, MACMERRY, PENSTON AND ORMISTON.

TRANENT, a town in the parish of its name, is 10 miles E. from Edinburgh, 18 W. from Dunbar, and 7 W. from Haddington. The North British Railway has a station here. Acreage of the parish, 5,919. Population, 5,470.

ELPHINSTONE is a village 2 miles S. from Tranent.

GLADSMUIR is a parish. The population of this parish is 1,604, and the acreage is 7,043.

LONGNIDDRY is a village in the parish of Gladsmuir. Population 246.

ORMISTON is a parish. The village is 2½ miles N. of Tranent. Acreage of the parish, 3,444. Population, 1,178.

Business Directory.

Bakers and Confectioners.

Forsyth, John, High st
Innes, James P. (Baker and Confectioner), High st—see advt
Johnston, David, Ormiston
Smith, Mary, Church st
Wood, James, Bridge st

Blacksmiths.

Fiddes, George, High st
Hadden, James, Longniddry
Hepburn, Thomas, Ormiston
Mitchell, William, Gladsmuir
Renton, Archibald, Seton, Longniddry
Renton, John, Elphinstone
Smith, William (V.S.), Bridge st
Watters, John, Macmerry, near Tranent

Booksellers, Stationers, and Newsagents.

Beale, David (& Printer), High st
Black, James, High st
Gibson, Mrs J., Bridge st
Naysmith, David, Post Office, Ormiston

Boot and Shoe Makers.

Baptie William C., Winton pl
Charles, John, Bridge st
Egan, James, High st

Builders and Contractors.

M'Walter, Thomas, Bridge st
Wilson, John, Church st

China, Glass, and Earthenware Dealers.

Bradley, Edward, Elder st
Goldie, Mrs M., Church st
Neilson, A., High st

Coal Masters.

Deans & Moore, Penston & Winston
Durie, R. & J., Elphinstone
Ormiston Coal Co., Ld., Ormiston
Waldie, James & Son, High st
White, Andrew, Ormiston

Drapers, Milliners, Dressmakers, and Clothiers.

Marked 'e' are Milliners and Dressmakers only.

Beale, Robert, Bridge st
Carlisle, T. R., High st
e Grieve, Beatrice, High st
e Hood, Miss A., Church st
Johnston, John, Ormiston
Kirsopp, Edward, High st
Laidlaw, James, High st
e Lees, Agnes, New row
Millar, W. & G. (and Tailors and Clothiers), High st

Engineers, Millwrights, and Ironfounders.

Kirkwood, James, Tranent
Learmouth, William, Church st

Farmers—see end of Directory.

Fleshers.

Bald, Robert C. H., Ormiston
Dickson, David, High st
Pow, Archibald, High st

Fruiterers and Confectioners.

Mingle, John, High st
Young, Adam, Church st

Grocers and General Merchants.
Marked 'e' are also Spirit Dealers.

Allan, James (Grocer, Ale and Porter Merchant), Macmerry
Baillie, Robert (& Dairy) Macmerry
Chirnside, Andrew (Family Grocer), Longniddry
Colgan. William, Church st
Co-operative Soc. Ld., Bridge st
e Fortune, Thomas, Elphinstone
e Fraser, A. & Co., High st
Gowans, R. & J., High st
e Hunter, Jane, Church st
Johnstone, G. C., High st
Kay Brothers, High st
Lawrence, Robert, Elphinstone
e **Leslie, Peter & Sons** (Licensed). High st
e Leslie, William, Ormiston
Mitchell, Wm., Post Office, Gladsmuir
Naysmith, David, Post Office, Ormiston
Nicholson, Ramsay, Church st
e Scott, George, New Winton
e Simpson, William, Church st
Young, George, Church st

Horse Hiring and Posting Establishment.

Scott, James, Crown Hotel

Hotels and Inns.

Cross Keys Inn—Robert Malcolm, Bridge st
Crown Hotel and Posting House—Mrs. M. F. Duncan, High st
Forbes, Henry, Church st
Hopetoun Arms—A. W. Jackson, Ormiston
Plough Hotel (stabling for cycles), —George Sanderson, High st
Railway Inn—Jn. Ness, Bridge street
Scott, George, New Winton
Tower—John Crawford, Fowler st

Ironmonger and Hardwareman.

Templeton, David, High st

Joiners and Wrights.

Craise, George, New row
Dickson, Walter, (Joiner and Cabinetmaker), High st
Edmond, A. W. & D., (Builders and Undertakers), Post Office, Longniddry
Gibb, Janet, Church st
Henry, Andrew, Gladsmuir
Hogg, George, Longniddry
Robertson, James, Ormiston
Wight, James, Elphingstone

Market Gardners & Fruit Growers.

Allan, Peter, Longniddry
Brander, Robert, Ormiston
Dickson, Andrew, Ormiston
Dickson, James, Church st
Dickson, James, Ormiston
Hadden, George, Longniddry
M'Neill, James, Tranent
Rennie, William, High st
Scrymgeour, James, Church st
Yorston, George, Tranent

Milliners and Dressmakers—see Drapers.

Painters and Decorators.

Crighton, D. & Son, High st
Millar, Joseph, High st

Plumbers and Gasfitters.

Templeton, David, R.P.C. High st
Wood, John, New row

Quarry Masters.

Wilson, Andrew, Bridge st
Wilson, John, Birsley

Slaters and Glaziers.

Gilchrist, John, Ormiston
Hood. James, High st
Hood, John, High st
Stevenson, Thomas, High st

Spirit Dealers—see Hotels and Inns

Surgeons.

Lindsay, Alexander, Ormiston rd
Ritchie, Daniel, Bridge st

Tailors and Clothiers.

Black, M., Church st
Millar, W. & G., (and Drapers),

High st
Morrison, Duncan, (and Gent's Outfitter), High st

Miscellaneous.

Bankers—Royal Bank, Tranent
Brick and Tile Maker—Andrew White, Ormiston
Chemist—Thomas Ness, High st
Contractor — Robert, Courtney Bridge st
Hairdresser—T. Baldwin, High st
Horse Slaughterers—Walker & Son Birsley
Miller — Pet Learmout, Seton Longniddry
Saddler—George Anderson, High st
Timber Merchant—Adam Souness, Ormiston
Watchmaker—John Meiklejohn, High st

TYNNINGHAME—SEE EAST LINTON.
WEST BARNS—SEE DUNBAR.
WEST SALTON—SEE SALTON.
WHITEKIRK—SEE EAST LINTON.
WHITTINGHAME—SEE EAST LINTON.

BERWICKSHIRE.

THIS is the most south-easterly county of Scotland ; it is bounded on the east by the North Sea, and on the west by the counties of Edinburgh and Selkirk ; on the north by the county of Haddington, and on the south by Northumberland and Roxburghshire. It measures from east to west thirty-five miles, and from north to south twenty-two, and its area comprises 267, 161 statue acres, or 464 square miles. In point of size, Berwick ranks as the twentieth Scottish county.

Berwickshire is divided into three districts, namely Merse, Lammermoor and Lauderdale. The Merse is the largest and most valuable district, and embraces that tract of low land between the Lammermoor Hills on the north, and the river Tweed on the south, having Lauderdale for its western boundary. Lammermoor consists of nearly 90,000 statue acres. The district of Laduerdale contains about 67,000 statue acres. The eminences of Berwickshire—those of the greatest altitude above the level of the sea —are Soutra Hill, 1,716 feet ; Crib Law, 1,615 ; Clint Hill ; 1,544 : Meikleless Law, 1,531 ; Tippet Knowes, 1,323 ; Dirrington Law, 1,309 ; and Twin Law, 1,260.

The exports of Berwickshire consist of great quantities of corn, coal, sheep and eggs ; and these indeed, may be considered as the extent of its commerce. Berwickshire is strictly pastoral and agricultural; the principal crops are wheat, barley, oats, beans and turnips, the latter being extensively cultivated. Manufactures finds its chief seat at the principal town, Berwick

The principal lines of railway in this county are the North British and its many branches, and the North-Eastern.

Berwickshire comprehends (exclusive of Berwick town), thirty-three parishes and two parts of parishes ; and contains one royal burgh, Lauder-Berwick-upon-Tweed is a royal burgh, and sends one member. The presen. member for the county is H. J. Tenant, Esq. The lord lieutenant of the county is the Earl of Home. Population, 32,257.

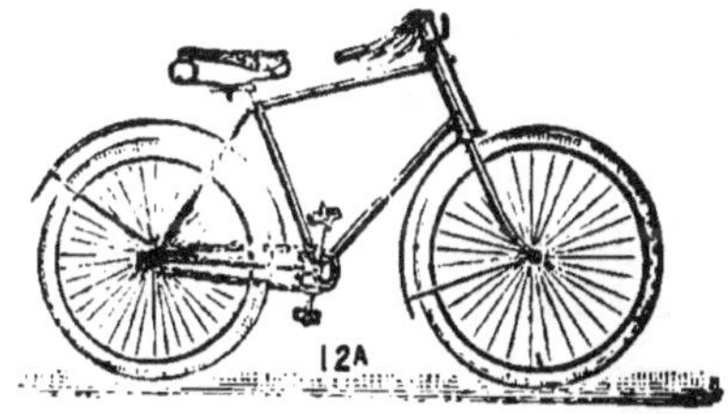

G. SMITH,

TWEEDSIDE CYCLE DEPOT,

BERWICK-ON-TWEED.

Maker of THE BORDERER CYCLES.

Agent for the leading Makers of Cycles. Lowest Prices for Cash.

WRITE FOR A QUOTATION.

Machines Sold on the Hire Purchase System, or let out on Hire by Day, Week, or Month. Second Hand Machines always in Stock at very Low Prices. Repairs and Alterations to Machines and Tyres.

EVERY MACHINE WARRANTED.

Lamps, Bells, and Sundries of every description.

Sewing, Wringing, Washing, and Mangling Machines and Perambulators, at equally low prices.

H. G. M'CREATH & CO.,

Manure Manufacturers,

Grain, Cake, and Seed Merchants.

BERWICK-ON-TWEED.

Telegraphic Address—"M'CREATH."

GEORGE M'ADAM,

Registered Plumber and Sanitary Engineer,

28 HIDE HILL,

BERWICK-ON-TWEED.

ABBEY SAINT BATHANS see—**CRANSHAWS.**
ALLANTON see—**CHIRNSIDE.**
ANCROFT see—**BERWICK.**
AUCHENCROW see—**RESTON.**
AYTON see **EYEMOUTH.**

BERWICK-ON-TWEED,

Ilncuding ANCROFT, NORHAM, SCREMERSTON, SPITTAL, TWEEDMOUTH, and Neighbourhoods.

BERWICK-UPON-TWEED is a corporate and parliamentary borough and seaport, 334 miles N. by W. from London, 64 N. by W. from Newcastle-upon-Tyne, from Edinburgh it is 58 S.E. and from Glasgow 103 E. by S. It stands on the north side of the river Tweed. The exportation of coal from the mines in the neighbourhood forms an important feature in the commerce of the port, while that of grain, manure, and salmon caught in the Tweed.

The weekly market is on Saturday, and one for fat cattle every alternate Monday. A fair is held on the last Friday in May for horses and cattle. Population, 13,378.

TWEEDMOUTH is a populous parish, forming a part of the borough of Berwick. It is situated about a quarter of a mile from Berwick. The North Eastern Railway has a station here.

SPITTAL, a village in the parish of Tweedmouth, about three-quarters of a mile from Berwick, and comprises in that parliamentary borough, is situated at the mouth of the river. The curing of herring is carried on here extensively, and there is a manufactory of spades and shovels, chemical and manure works. EAST and WEST ORD are hamlets in the parish of Tweedmouth.

ANCROFT is a village and parish in the county of Northumberland, 5½ miles S.W. from Berwick. Cheswick is a hamlet in this parish.

SCREMERSTON is a village in the county of Northumberland, 3 miles S. from Berwick, its post town

NORHAM is a village in the parish of its name, in the county of Northumberland, situated 7½ miles W. from Berwick. Felkington, Grindon, Horncliffe, Loan End, Longridge, Norham Mains, Shoreswood, Thornton, and Twizel are townships in this parish.

Business Directory.

Accountants.
Bogue, George, 14 Sandgate
Millar, Alexander L., Sandgate

Aerated Water Manufacturers—see also Brewers.
Elliot, John, (and Agricultural Chemist), 30 Hide Hill

Agricultural Implement Makers—see Engineers, &c.

Apartments—Furnished.
Bell, Esther, 3 Sandgate
Laidler, Mrs. S. A., Quay Walls

Architects and Surveyors.
Cookburn, John, jnr., 48 Castlegate
Gray, William, 2 Ivy place
Stevenson, James, North road

Auctioneers and Valuators.
Embelton & Son, Horncliff mains
Lambert, Robert, Tweedmouth
Miller, Alexander L., Sandgate

Baby Linen and Fancy Repositories.
Strother, Miss, 18 Hide Hill
Watson, Miss Isabel, Bridge st

Bakers and Confectioners.
Cairns, John, 109 High st
Cochrane, Walter, Railway st
Cowe, John, Norham
Dudgeon, Margt 47 Walkergatelane
Geggie, John B., (Baker and Confectioner), 17, 19, and 21 West st
Graham, William, 81 Castlegate
Jenkinson Ths., 19 Walkergate lane
MacDonald, H. T., 25 Castlegate
Mason, Francis, 2 and 4 Church st —see adv
Oliver, James, Norham
Ormston, John James, (& Pie & Pastry Baker) 15 Church st
Pearson, Elias, 60 Church st
Scott, George, 20 Castlegate
Simmen, J. J., 31 Bridge st
Simpson, Stuart, E., 38 West st
Thomson, Ralph, 20 Bridge st
Trainer, Mrs., 18 Church
Whitie, William, Spittal

Banks.
British Linen Co., Sandgate
Commercial Bank Ltd., Hide hill
National Bank Ltd., Bridge-end
North-Eastern Banking Co., Ltd., 4 Queen's buildings
Savings Bank, Sandgate
Woods & Co., 22 Hide hill

Bicycle and Cycle Makers and Dealers.
Cowes, Henry, 27 Wool market
Devey, J. & Co., 114 High st
Smith, G., Tweedside Cycle Depot, Tweedmouth—see advt

Blacksmiths.
Black, George, Tweedmouth—see advt
Blackett, Thomas, Scremerston
Cairns, Thomas, Ladykirk
Cooper, Peter G., Weddell's lane
Davidson, John, Scremerston
Hay, Thomas, Tweedmouth
Jeffray, James, High greens
Murray, George, Ancroft
Purvis, James, Norham
Reid, Robert, Railway st
Renton, Adam, North road
Rule, George, Ord
Taylor, Robert, Tweedmouth
Watson, William, Cheswick
Weatherburn, Henry, Norham

Boat Builders.
Ainslie, James, Spittal
Berwick Salmon Fishing Co. Tweedmouth
Lee, Robert & Sons, Tweedmouth
Wood, Blake, 1 College place

Boiler Makers.
Black, George (Estd. 1790—steel and wrought iron boilers

and tanks) Tweedmouth—see adv
Riddle, S. & Sons, Tweedmouth iron forge—see adv

Booksellers, Stationers & Newsagents

Bates, Margaret, 24 Castlegate
Hall, James W., 36 West st
Henderson & Son (and Printers), 42 West st
Howman, A., Post Office, Spittal
Morris, T. W. (successor to David Cobb), (Printer, Stationer, and Bookbinder, and proprietor and publisher of "The Berwick and Border Railway Time Tables and Diary," and "Mill's Penny Popular Guide to Berwick and District"), 3, 5, and 7 Church st —see advt
Plenderleith, J. W. (Bookseller, Stationer, Bookbinder, and Newsagent), 75 High st
Richardson, Agnes, Spittal
Rutherford, Henry J., Town Hall buildings
Smith, W. H & Son, Railway statn
Vance, Andrew H., 12 Bridge-end

Boot and Shoe Makers.

Blackey's, 40 Bridge st
Cairns, Robert, 60 High st
Davis, Patrick, Tweedmouth
Dickinson & Son, 35 High st
Fish, Alex. & Son, 133 High st
Gray, Jane, 49 West st
Gray, John, & Co., 26 High st
Mosgrove, John, 52 High st
Nicholson, Benjamin, 6 Parade
Noble, John, Spittal
Parkes, James, 1 High st
Purves, John, 30 Wool market
Richardson, George, Norham
Robinson, Thomas, 45 Church st
Swan, Ralph, Norham
Tyler, H. P., 2 Bridge End
Wilson, William, 57 High st
Winlaw, Adam, 5 High st

Brassfounders—see Ironfounders.

Brewers, Maltsters, and Aerated Water Manufacturers.

Border Brewery Co., Silver st
Johnston & Co., Governor's yard
Young, W. & W., (Maltsters) Pier road

Butchers.

Brown, George, Tweedmouth
Dixon, James, (& wholesale) Tweed st
Dod, William S., 40 High st
Edminson Brothers Spittal
Foreman, Henry, Norham
Hick, F., late Strecker, (Pork Butcher, Ham and Bacon Curer and Sausage Maker), 56 High st
Hogarth, W. & J., 85 High st
Marshall, S., Norham
Middlemas, Robert, Bridge st
Robertson, Hugh, Chapel st
Robson, Isaac, Castlegate
Ross Brothers, 36 Hide hill
Ross, Thomas, Spittal
Taylor, H., (Pork), High st
Thompson, Robert, W., Norham

Cabinetmakers, Upholsterers, and Undertakers.

See also Joiners and Builders.

Brown, James, 14 Castlegate
Dickson & Son, 41 Bridge st
Hawkins, R. Y. & Son, 9 Hide hill
Hickey, J. G., 21 Hide hill
Hume & Son, 83 High st
Wilson, John, 17 Eastern lane
Wilson, John, Tweedmouth
Wilson, T. & Son, 127 High st
Wood, Robert & Son, 48 High st
Young, George, 15 Hide hill

Carting Contractors.

Johnson, James, Spittal
Johnson, Robert, Spittal

Cartwrights—see Joiners and Builders.

Chemists and Druggists.

Brigham, Sibbit, Tweedmouth
Carr, William Graham & Sons (Circulating Library), Hide hill
Craig, Nicol M., 63 High st

Elliot, John (Agricultural Chemist, & Aerated Water Manufacturer), 30 Hide hill
Hutchison, John, 5 High st
Lyle, William, 10 Hide hill
Wilson, James T. (trust. of) (Manufacturing), Spittal

China and Glass Dealers.

Dunlop, Isa., Spittal
Elliot, Henry, Spittal
Renwick, John, 5 Walkergate lane
Renwick, Thos, 18 Walkergate lane
Thompson Bros., 41, 43 High st
Watt, Alexander K., Tweedmouth
Wight, Thomas, Church st

Coach Builders,

Maule, Wm. & Co., Palace st
Oliphant, William J., 94 High st
Taylor, Robert, Tweedmouth

Coal Merchants and Agents.

Aird, Thomas, Railway station
Carr, William Graham & Son, Hide hill
Cormack, Joseph, Railway station
Fraser, James, 10 Chapel st
Logan, Adam, Quayside
Logan, William A., Hide hill
Mutter, Howey & Co., Railway stn
Palmer, James, Spittal
Rennie & Sons, Railway station
Scremerston & Shorewood Coal Co. (& Brickmakers & Lime Burners), Quayside
Shillbottle Coal Co., Railway statn
Sutherland, Mrs. George, Railway station

Cod Liver Oil Manufacturers.

Carr, William Graham & Son, 12 Quay walls

Confectioners—see also Bakers and Confectioners.

Marked 'e' are Manufacturing.

Cradon, T., 83 Castlegate
Oliphant, Samuel, 10 West st
Purves, Eleanor, 22 High st
Rutherford, Miss M. H., 34 Church street
e Towers & Bishop, 81 High st
Whitehead, Mrs R., Tweedmouth
Wilkinson, J., Church st

Conveyance by Water.

London and Edinburgh Shipping Co., 10 Quay walls J. R. M'Cromarty, manager—see advt

Corn, Grain and Seed Merchants.

Anderson, William, 47 Hide hill
Black, James R. & Co., Limited (& Oilcake Merchants and Bone Crushers,, 4 Love lane Telegraphic address—"Mancorn, Berwick"—see advt
Carter, Thomas & Sons, Sandgate
Edney, James M. & Co. 1 Bridge st
Johnson & Co., Governor's yard
Logan, David, Hide hill
M'Creath, H. G. & Co., Eastern lane—see advt
Martin & Scott, 48 Bridge st
Prentice, John jr., Silver st
Short, H. O. & Son, Tweedmouth
Waite Brothers, Hope nursery
Young, W. & W., Pier road

Dentists.

Aitkinson, Richard, Parade
Riddell, Robert, 19 Quay walls
Tyer, W. T., City walls

Dining and Refreshment Rooms.

Elliot's Hotel, Bridge st
Gilchrist's—Tweedmouth
Lyall, Andrew, 30 High st
M'Dougall, James, 22 Main street, Spittal
Shiell, David, 129 High st

Drapers, Dressmakers, Milliners, and Clothiers.

Bond, A. M., 123 High st
Cockburn, J. & E., 25 West st
Cook, Miss F., 54 Bridge st
Dunlop, J. & Sons, 61 High st
Finharty, Patrick, 118 High st
Gunn, Adam T., 19 High st
Henderson, John, Norham
Johnston & Co., 39 High st

Morrison & Nephew, 15, 17 High st
Nesbitt Brothers, 47 Bridge st
Paxton & Purves, 125 High st
Pringle, Phillis, Spittal
Redpath, Wm., West street and 51 Castlegate
Scott & Inglis, 5 West st
Spowart, Miss A. J., 48 High st
Thompson, M. P., Spittal

Dressmaker—see Drapers, &c., and also Milliners and Dressmakers.

Engineers and Millwrights.

Black, George (Established 1790), and Bone Crusher, Plates & Gasholders, &c.), Tweedmouth —see advt
Elder, William, Tweedmouth
Purvis, J., 62 Castlegate
Riddle S. & Sons (& Boiler-makers), Tweedmouth Forge—see advt
Robertson & Co. Ltd., Tweedmouth

Fancy Goods and Toy Merchants.

Aitken, J. & C., 77 Castlegate
Galley, Miss A., 68 Church st
Gunn, Mrs A., 59 Castlegate

Farmers—see end of Directory.

Fishmongers, Game and Poultrg Dealers.

Cowe, James, 112 High st
Cowe, Peter, 34 Low Greens
Gow, James, 112 High st
Holmes, R. & Sons, 36 Bridge st
Wilkie, John, Town Hall buildings
Wilkie, John (Fish and Egg Merchant), Spittal

Fishing Tackle Manufacturer.

Steven, Robert C. (and Umbrella Maker and Wire Worker), 15 West st

Fruiterers and Greengrocers.

Craig, James, 36 Walkergate lane
Harbottle, Thomas, 94 High st
M'Donald, J-, 52a High st
Miller, Andrew, 26 Hide hill
Panlin, J., 36 Church st

Turnbull, M. J., 35 Bridge st—see advt

Grocers and General Merchants.

Atkinson, Thomas, 71 Castlegate
Allan, A., Spittal
Allan, William & Son, 45 High st
Ayton, Fred, Cash Supply Stores, High st
Barnes, Miss B., Tweedmouth
Blench, Joseph W., 6 Bridge end
Briggs, John, Norham
Burn, W., Norham
Chisholm, George, Scremerston
Christison, Henry L., 1 Bridge end
Cowe, Wm. & Sons, 64 Bridge st
Craik, Margaret, Tweedmouth
Craise & Son, 50 Hide hill
Davidson, E., Spittal
Davidson, John, 113 High st
Dodds, R. & Son. 19, 21, 23 Highst
Elliot, John & Co., Woolmarket
Foster, James, Norham
Gallagher, John, 88 High st
Gordon & Gollan, 79 High st
Gregson, Robert, 74 High st
Gunn, John M., 27, 29 West st
Industrial Co-operative Soc., Tweedmouth
Kennedy, Thomas, Post Office, Norham
Lilico, J. E., Norham
Lipton, Thomas J., 28 Bridge st
Lisle, C., Horncliffe
London & Newcastle Tea Co., High street
Nicholson, Wm., Scremerston
Oliver, Walter, Duddo, Norham
Paxton, Elizabeth, 10 Bridge st
Pratt, J. F., Tweedmouth
Richardson Brothers, 11, 13 High st
Richardson, Miss Alice, Norham
Romanes, R., Norham
Russell, James & Son (& Drapers), 53 High st
Simpson, E. & W., 11, 13 West st
Skelly, R. D. (Wholesale Tea, Coffee, and Provision Merchant), 44 Church st
Stoddard, John (Tallow Chandler), 91 High st
Tait, Christopher, Tweedmouth
Watson, Elizabeth G., 69 Castlegate

Weatherburn, Alex., 6 Castlegate
Willson, Walter, 14 Hide hill

Hairdressers.

Burns, W. D., 13 Hide hill
Suthern, George, 33 Hide hill

Hatters, Hosiers, and Glovers.

Lawson, Alexander, 51 High st
Moore, J., 11 Hide hill
Purvis, William, 9 West st

Herring Curers.

Boston, Brothers, Spittal
Cowe, John, Spittal
Edminson & Sons, Spittal
Evans, George Henry, Quay
Sayer, R. & Son, Ness st

Hotels and Inns—see also Spirit Dealers.

Black Swan—James Campbell, Rail way st
Blenheim Hotel — Wm. Douglas, Spittal
Hen & Chicken—Hugh Lymburn, Sandgate
King's Arms—John Carr, Hide hill
King's Arms — William Spiers, Tweedmouth
Mason's Arms Commercial Inn (Horses and Carriages on hire), Robert Brown, proprietor, Norham
Red Lion—J. Henderson, High st
Royal Hotel — Margaret Herriott, proprietrix, 36 Castlegate
Roxburghe Hotel — Henry J. W. Greenwood, Spittal
Salmon—Robt. T. Hogg, 77 High st
Spittal—John Barrie, Spittal
Station—Henry Roberts, Tweedmouth
Union—Robt Russell, Tweedmouth
Victoria Hotel—Robert Porter, proprietor, Norham

Ironfounders—see also Engineers.

Black, George, Tweedmouth—see advt
Craik, Geo. & Sons, High greens
Johnston, Thomas (brass), High st
Riddle, S. & Sons, Tweedmouth Forge—see adv

Ironmongers and Hardwaremen.

Caverhill & Co., Limited, 71 High street
Manderson, Charles G., 22 Church street
Sidey, Robert W., Tweedmouth
Spaven, Adam, 14 Bridge st
Thompson Brothers (and Oil and Colourmen), 41, 43 High st
Wilson & Son, Victoria buildings

Joiners and Builders.

Marked e are Cartwrights.

Brigham, William, Tweedmouth
Burn Alexander C., Spittal
Cockburn & Son (Joiners), Castlegate
Currie, Andrew & Son (Joiners, Undertakers, and Boat Builders), Norham
Dalgetty, Alexander (Joiner), Golden square
Davidson, Thomas, Ord
Graham, Mark, Tweedmouth
Henderson Brothers, 28 Church st
Jeffery, Alexander (Joiner), Twizel
Lowrie, Robert, Horncliffe
M'Call, John, High greens
Ord, John, 4 Wallace green
Renton, George, North road
e Robson, John (Joiner, Boatbuilder and Undertaker), Norham
e Smart, Wm., Scremerston
e Taylor, Robert, Tweedmouth
e Thomson, Ralph, 106 Castlegate

Land and Estate Agents.

Bolam, George, 72 Ravensdowne
Bolam, Robert G., Castlegate
Cook, Stephen M., 28 Hide hill
Willoby, E., 3 Bridge st

Laundries.

Anderson, Mrs., Wallace green
Border Public Steam Laundry, Hatter's Lane—Foster Lamb, proprietor—see adv

Linseed Cake and Oil Manufacturer

Young, Matthew, Palace st
Telegraphic Address—"Palace"

Maltsters—see Brewers and Maltsters.

Manufacturers.

Black, Thos. & Son (Spade) Spittal
Singer (The) Manfg. Co., 64 High st

Manure Manufacturers & Merchants

Black, James R. & Co., Limited (and Bone Crushers, Corn, Seed, and Oilcake Merchants), 4 Love lane—Telegraphic Address, "Mancorn, Berwick"—see advt
Dixon, James & Co., Spittal
Gilroy, James & Son (Manure and Potato Merchants), Sandgate
Holmes, Bros., 36 Bridge st
Johnson & Co., Governor's yard
Leitch, George, Norham
M'Creath, H. G. & Co. (and Grain, Cake, & Seed Merchants), Eastern lane — Telegraphic Address, "M'Creath"—see adv

Millers.

Dodd, Alex. & And., Twizel mill
Short, H. & Son, Tweedmouth
Turnbull, David, Bridge mill, Ancroft

Milliners and Dressmakers—see also Drapers, &c.

Davidson, Miss, West st
Fish, Eleanor D., 5 Woolmarket
Geggie, Miss (and Mantlemaker), 38 and 44 Eastern lane—see advt
Pringle, Miss, 11 Sandgate
Schooler, Miss M. (and Fancy Drapery), 22 Bridge st
Scott & Schooler, Misses, 23 West street
Spowart, Miss Isabel (Dressmaker), 43 High st

Millwrights—see Engineers and Millwrights.

Newspapers, Publishers, and Printers.

Berwick Advertiser—Estd. 1808—published Friday, 1d—circulates throughout Northumberland Berwick, and Haddington Shires and Border Counties—H. R. Smail, proprietor, West st
Berwickshire Advertiser — Estd. 1893—published Tuesday, 1d—circulates throughout Berwickshire and the Border Counties—H. R. Smail, proprietor, West st
Berwick Journal and Berwichshire News—Gibson F. Stephens, 25 High st
Berwickshire Gazette and Border Counties Gazette—George Turner 11 Sandgate

Painters and Decorators.

Crow, Henry F., 83 High st
Crow, John, 72 High st
Crow, Thos. & Co., 60 Bridge st
Gilchrist, George, 41 West st
Gladston, Mrs M., Spittal
Taylor, Robert, 18 High st

Photographers.

Green, William, 9 Castlegate
Herriott, James, 8 Castlegate

Plasterers and Slaters.

Renwick, T. (Slater), 46 Church st
Rule, Peter, Tweedmouth
Rule, Thomas, Norham
Russell, Mrs., Palace st
Sidey, Alexander, Tweedmouth
Weatherston, Joseph, 126 High st

Plumbers, Gasfitters, and Tinsmiths.

Baldwin, Thomas, 84 High st
Blyth, C. (tinsmith), 35 Walkergate lane
Hay, John R,, 120 High st
Hope, James, Tweedmouth
Lamb & Son, 13 Wool market
M'Adam, George (Registered Plumber and Sanitary Engineer), 28 Hide hill—see advt
Sidey, Robert W., Tweedmouth
Smith, George (and Hardware Merchant and Bicycle Agent), Tweedmouth—see adv
Teesdale, William, Spittal
Wood, John (and Hardware), Spittal

Potato Merchants.

Gilroy, James & Son (and Manure Merchants), Sandgate

Printers—see also Booksellers, &c., and also Newspapers, Publishers &c

Martin, George, 44, 46 West st
Morris, T. W. (successor to David Cobb), 3, 5, 7 Church st
Whyte, James, Sandgate

Rope and Sail Makers.

Davidson, James S., Tweedmouth
Davidson, John, Well close square
Mark, James, 11 Quay walls
Moor, James (Rope), Ravensdowne
Wilson, George W., Castlegate

Saddlers and Harness Makers.

Harvey, Robert, 65 Castlegate
M'Lennan, William, 39 Castlegate
Paxton & Son, 8 Hide hill
Scott, T., Hide hill
Smith, John M., Norham

School—Catholic.

St. Mary's Convent (First Class Boarding and Day School for Young Ladies), M. Aloysia Dunn Revd. Mother—see advt

Seed Merchants—see Corn and Seed Merchants.

Shipping Companies.

London and Edinburgh Shipping Co., 10 Quay walls J. R. M'Cromarty, manager—see advt

Ship and Insurance Brokers.

Heron, Henry T., Quay
Sinclair, Benjamin G., Ness st

Solicitors.

Douglas, R. B., 7 Quay walls
Dunlop, John, 5 Quay walls
Gray, James (Solicitor, & Commissioner for Oaths), 8 Sandgate
Maclagan, Philip S., 11 Bridge st
Sanderson & J. K. Weatherhead, 1 Quay walls
Sanderson, Stephen G, 1 Quay walls
Smith, Thomas C., 9 Church st
Weatherhead, William & B., Palace green
Weddell, J. C. & R., 4 Palace st
Willoby & Peters, 36 Ravensdowne

Spirit Dealers—see also under Hotels and Inns.

Baird, Alexander, Scremerston
Bedford, Charles, Tweedmouth
Bolton, Mary, "Corporation Arms," Whitadder Bridge, near Berwick
Borthwick, Johnston, Low greens
Bowman, Robert, 26 Church st
Bradford, R., Tweedmouth
Brady, James, 33 Walkergate lane
Brown, Jane, 91 Castlegate
Burke, Christopher, 40 Chapel st
Chappel, A., 110a High st
Crombie, Agnes, Low greens
Crombie, Ann, Spittal
Daniel, Mrs. A., 18 West st
Davidson, John, 117 High st
Davis, Patrick, 28 West st
Dickinson, Mrs Ellen, Norham
Dods, William S., 38 High st
Douglas, James, Ord
Douglas, Robert, Tweedmouth
Drysdale, John, Spittal
Ewart, Barbara, 4 High st
Gallagher, John, 4 Chapel st
Grieve, John R., Tweedmouth
Hall, John, Spittal
Hay, Hannah, 122 High st
Heslop, Thomas, Tweedmouth
Hunt, Margaret, Spittal
Jackson, N., Spittal
Johnson, James, 5 Silver st
Kerss, William, Sandgate
King, Thomas, Tweedmouth
Krenkel, W. C., 8 Church st
Liddell, Wm. (Black Bull), Silver st
Lillico, William, Sandgate
Lillie, Robert, 32 West st
Linkie, James, 75 Castlegate
M'Donald, Walter, Spittal
M'Gregor, Mrs E., 19 Castlegate
Marshall, Margaret S., 13 Bridge st
Moore, George, Hide hill
Murray, Thomas, 12 Church st
Murphy, Ann J., Low greens
Naple, Thomas, Tweedmouth

Ormiston, M., Tweedmouth
Patrick, John, Tweedmouth
Pott, William, 56 Church st
Pringle, Andrew, Ancroft
Reid, Mrs. Mary, Ann-Sandgate
Renwick, Margaret, 95 High st
Richmond, S.. (Fishers Arms), Horncliffe
Robertson, Margaret, Norham
Robertson, John, Folly Norham
Rutherford, Hugh, (accommodation for Cyclists), Meadow House, Northern Road, near Berwick
Robson, Peter, 89 Castlegate
Robson, Alexander, 103 Castlegate
Smith, James, 105 High st
Spiers, Margaret P., 90 Castlegate
Spiers, John, 57 Castlegate
Stangroom, Bridget, 40 Walkergate lane
Stephenson, William H., 27 Church st
Stoddart ,John, (& Grocer), 93 High st
Strother, J. A., 24 High st
Swinton, G. R,, 19 Church st
Taylor, A. H., Tweedmouth
Thompson, Ellen, Tweedmouth
Thompson, Jane, Soittal
Tindle, James, (The Old Hen and Chicken's Inn), 29 Bridge st
Todd, William, Tweedmouth
Trotter, David, 35 Chapel st
Wakefield, William, Tweedmouth
Webster, W., Spittal
Wilson, Henry, " Sun Inn" Woolmarket
Winter, Robert, Tweedmouth
Wright, Fred, Spittal

Steam Plough Proprietors.

Black, John, Norham
Hope, John, Tweedmouth
Oliver, M. T. & G., Norham

Stonemasons and Builders.

Ainsley, John, Norham
Beveridge, Michael, Tweedmouth
Briggs, John, Norham
Gray, & Sons, Ravensdowne
Storrar, John, Spital
Wilson, John, Tweedmouth

Young, John, Norham

Stone Quarry Owners.

Gray & Sons, Ravensdowne
Hall, John, East Ord

Surgeons.

Cahill, David F. S., 10 Parade
Fraser, Charles L., 46 Church st
Fraser, Thomas, 58 Ravensdowne
Heagerty, Daniel, Tweedmouth
Mackay, William B., 23 Castlegate
Maclagan, Charles G., Ravensdowne
Paxton, John, Norham

Tailors and Clothiers—see Drapers and Clothiers.

Burn, Robert, Norham
Campbell, James, 50 Church st
Craik, Robert, (and Hatter), 4 Hide Hill
Donaldson, Robert A., 25 Eastern lane
Dunlop, John R., 97 High st
Forsyth, Thomas, Post Office, Ancroft
Harens, Theodore, 16 Bridge st
Hepworth & Son, Ld., 45 Bridge st
Johnson, James, Spittal
Kinleyside, Peter R., 9 Eastern lane
Leeds Clothing Co., 22 West st
Martin. Adam, 14 West st
Ord, Edward, Norham
Pringle & Son, 11 Sandgate
Richardson Bros., 11 & 13 High st
Robertson, Thomas. Norham
Scott & Son, Tweedmouth
Storie, William, 35 Castlegate!
Turnbull, James & Son, 35 West st

Temperance Hotels—see Dining Rooms.

Timber Merchants,

Allan Brothers, Tweedmouth
Sinclair, Benjamin G., Ness st

Tinsmiths—see Plumbers, &c.

Tobacconists.

Ainsley, J. E., 35 High st
Ainsley, William, 27 Bridge st

Cooper, Thomas (hairdresser), 98 High st
Elliott, John, Bridge st

Veterinary Surgeon.

M'Gregor, J. D., M.R.C.V.S., 1 Tweed st

Watch and Clock Makers.

Dryden, J. H., 48 Church st
Garland, H. S., 27 High st
Harvey, Robert C., 65 Castlegate
Lee, Robert P., Castlegate
Macpherson, —., 67 High st
Pearson, William, 49 Bridge st
Ross & Ross (and opticians), 62 Bridge st—see advt

Wine and Spirit Merchants—Wholesale.

Alder, W. & Son, 17, 19 Hide hill
Grey, James, 44, 46, 48 Hide hill
Logan, William A., Hide hill
Noble, John, 8 Bridge end

Miscellaneous.

Basket Maker — Adam Forbes, Church st
Bill Poster—William Hogg, Wallace green
Curriers and Leather Merchants—L. T. & J. Fleming, 101 High st
Dyers—Mossman & Son, 38 Castlegate
Furniture Dealer—Joseph Ewart, Walkergate lane
General Dealar—J. White, 80 Church st
Lime and Cement Merchants—Luke & Co., Ballast Quay

BIRGHAM—SEE COLDSTREAM
BLAINSLIE—SEE LAUDER.
BOONHILL—SEE EARLSTON.
BUNKLE—SEE CRANSHAWS.
BURNMOUTH—SEE EYEMOUTH.
CHANNELKIRK—SEE LAUDER.
CHESWICK—SEE BERWICK.

CHIRNSIDE,

CHIRNSIDE BRIDGE and ALLANTON.

CHIRNSIDE is a parish of 5,553 acres, lying in the eastern part of the Merse. The village is 50 miles E. by S. from Edinburgh, 13½ N.NE. from Greenlaw, 9 N. W. from Berwick, and 6 N. from Duns. Population, 915

Less than a mile west of the village is the hamlet of CHIRNSIDE BRIDGE.

ALLANTON, a village in the parish of Edrom, 1½ miles south from Chirnside, and 7 miles from Duns.

Business Directory.

Bakers and Confectioners.
Graham, John, Allanton
M'Kay, John, Chirnside
Taylor, Mrs., Chirnside

Blacksmiths.
Dippie, Alexander, Chirnside
M'Bain, John, Chirnside
Oliver, Andrew, Allanton
Waite, Alexander, Chirnside

Boot and Shoe Makers.
Heugh, James, Chirnside
Heugh, Mrs W., Chirnside
Hogg. A., Chirnside
Oliver, Thomas D., Allanton

Builders—see Stonemasons, &c.

Carrier.
Johnston, James M., Chirnside

Contractors.
Lothian, Thomas, Chirnside
Turnbull, John (Contractor and Traction Engine Proprietor), Chirnside

Drapers—see Grocers.

Engineers and Millwrights.
Denholm, David, Chirnside
Steele, George, & Sons, Chirnside
Steele, Peter, & Son, Chirnside

Fancy Repository.
Wood, Jane, Chirnside

Farmers—see end of Directory.

Fleshers.
Philip, A., Chirnside
White, T. & W., Chirnside

Grocers and General Merchants.
Marked 'e' are also Drapers.
Amos, John, Chirnside
Buglass, William, Chirnside
Cockburn & Co. (& Bakers), Chirnside
Craig, J. F. (Licensed), Chirnside
Dickson, Miss, Allanton
Grieve, William, Allanton
Henry, Archibald, Chirnside
Knox, Mrs., Chirnside
Lockie. J., Chirnside
e Lugton, Miss M. E., Chirnside
Mabon, Adam, Chirnside
Miller, Isabella, Chirnside
Patterson, James, Chirnside
Purves, James, Allanton
Scott, Elizabeth, Chirnside
e Scott, Mrs., Chirnside
Veitch, John, Chirnside
Waite, Mrs., Chirnside
Watt, James, Chirnside

Hotels, Inns, and Posting Establishments.
Red Lion—Hector Haig, Allanton
Red Lion—Robert Paton Chirnside
The Waterloo Hotel (Good Fishing and Accommodation for Anglers)—Henry G Bush, proprietor, Chirnside

House Furnisher.
Kerr, John G., Chirnside

Joiners and Wrights.
Edgeley & Sons, Chirnside
Jeffrey, W. & J., Chirnside

Paper Makers.
Trotter, Y. & Son, Limited
Chirnside bridge, Ayton

Millers.
Gillies, John, Edington mill
Taylor, J. & G., Ninewells mills

Plasterers—see Slaters & Plasterers.

Saddler.
Spence, Archibald, Chirnside

Slaters and Plasterers.
Fortune, Thomas, Chirnside
Fortune, William, Chirnside
Hilson, Alexander, Allanton

Stonemasons and Builders.
Craig, Samuel, Chirnside
Gibson & Dickson, Allanton
Paterson, James, Allanton

Surgeons.
M'Vie, Samuel, Chirnside
Stuart, Charles, Chirnside

Tailors and Clothiers.
Brunton, Alexander, Allanton
Ferguson & Son, Chirnside
Ferguson, T., Chirnside
Laing, G., Chirnside
Middlemas & Sheriffs, Allanton
Purves, William, Allanton
Turnbull, James, Chirnside

Traction Engine Proprietor.
Turnbull, John (& Contractor) Chirnside

Miscellaneous.
Bankers—Commercial Bank, Ltd., Chirnside
Chemist—Robert H. Henderson, Chirnside
Cooper—William Glen, Allanton
Painters—Broomfield & Gibb, Chirnside
Watchmaker—W. Simpson, Chirnside
Wool Manufacturers—Martin & Co. Chirnside

CHIRNSIDE BRIDGE—SEE CHIRNSIDE.

COCKBURNSPATH

IS a parish of 12,652 acres, population 1112, on the sea coast, the village being 35½ miles E. from Edinburgh, 14 N. from Duns, 8 S.E. from Dunbar, and 21 N.W. from Berwick, and on the line of the North British Railway.

Business Directory.

Agricultural Implement Maker.
Anderson, John, (& Blacksmith), Cockburnspath

Baker.
Johnston, David C., Cockburnspath

Blacksmiths.
Anderson, John, (and Implement Maker), Cockburnspath
Malcolm, John, (and Registered Plumber), Bilsdean

Builders and Joiners.
Geddes, George, Cockburnspath
Innes, James, Cockburnspath
Turner, James, Cockburnspath

Drapers—see Grocers, &c.

Farmers—see end of Directory.

Grocers, Drapers, and General Merchants.
Aitchison, Robert, (licensed), Cockburnspath
Storey, Ralph, Cockburnspath

Hotel and Posting House.
Cockburnspath Inn, (Head Quarters of C.T.C.), William French, Proprietor, Cockburnspath

Joiners—see Builders and Joiners.

Plumber.

Malcolm, John, (Registered Plumber and Blacksmith), Bilsdean

Tailors.

Laing, Thomas, Cockburnspath
Pringle, James, Cockburnspath

Miscellaneous.

Bookseller—Miss Jessie Ogg, Post Office, Cockburnspath
Bootmaker—James, Rentor, Cockburnspath
Coal Merchant—George France, Cockburnspath
Miller—William Nesbit, Dunglass Mill
Slater—Thomas Bolton, Cockburnspath
Surgeon—Donald Macdonald, Cockburnspath

COLDINGHAM

IS a parish of 24,021 acres, lying on the coast of the German Ocean. The village, a burgh of barony, is 45 miles S.E. from Edinburgh, 21 N.E.E. of Greenlaw, 17 S.E. of Dunbar, 13 N.N.E. of Duns, 11 N.N.W. of Berwick, and 4 from Ayton. The village has been much resorted to within late years by sea-bathers. Population 492.

Business Directory.

Bakers.

Cormack, James, Coldingham
Gray, Archibald, Coldingham
Thornburn, George, Coldingham

Blacksmiths.

Craik, G. & J., Coldingham
Simpson, J., Coldingham

Boot and Shoe Makers.

Buglas, Peter, Coldingham
Gray, David, Coldingham
Kerr, James, Coldingham

Coach Builder.

Chisholm, T., Coldingham

Contractors.

Chisholm, A., Coldingham
Thornburn, R. & Sons, Coldingham

Drapers.

Beattie, James (Tailor), Coldingham
Gedde, G. M., Coldingham

Farmers—see end of Directory.

Flesher.

Duncan, Robert, Coldingham

Grocers and General Merchants.

Cairns, William (Licensed), Coldingham
Laing, George, Coldingham
Robertson, John W. (Draper), Post Office, Coldingham
Smith, Miss, Coldingham
Wood, John (and Posting Master), Coldingham

Horse Hiring and Posting Establishments.

Douglas, James, New Inn, Coldingham
Wood, John (and Grocer and General Merchant), Coldingham

Hotels, Inns, and Posting Houses.

Anchor—John Hood, Coldingham
New Inn and Posting House—Jas. Douglas, proprietor, Coldingham

Joiners and Wrights.
Corsar, David, Coldingham
Lindores, John, Coldingham

Slaters and Plasterers.
Gillies, John, Coldingham
Wilson, Robert, Coldingham

Tailors and Clothiers.
Blair, John, Coldingham
Laing, James, Coldingham

Miscellaneous.
China & Glass Dealer—Janet Robertson, Coldingham
Dairykeeper—Mrs R. Crow, Coldingham
Surgeon - J. M'Dougal, Coldingham
Watchmaker—James Buglas, Coldingham

COLDSTREAM,

Including the parishes and villages of CORNHILL, ECCLES, BRIGHAM, LEITHOLM, WARK, and Neighbourhoods.

COLDSTREAM is a town and burgh of barony in the parish of that name. The town is 47 miles S.E., from Edinburgh, 14 S.S.W. from Berwick, 10 S.E. from Greenlaw, 10 S. from Duns, and 9 N.E. from Kelso situated on the north bank of the Tweed. Justice of the Peace courts are held monthly, and Sheriff's Small Debt courts four times a year.

The parish contains 8,220 acres. Population, 1,535.

CORNHILL is a village and parish in Northumberland, 2 miles E. of Coldstream, of which the latter place is the nearest railway station There is a cattle market held here on alternative Mondays. Acreage 4944. Population, 634.

ECCLES is a village and parish 6 miles from Coldstream. Nearest railway station is Greenlaw, 5 miles distant. Acreage 12,418.

BIRGHAM is a village on the Tweed in the parish (Q.V.) of Eccles, 3½ miles S.W. of Coldstream.

LEITHOLM is a village in the parish of Eccles (Q.V.) 4½ miles N.W. of Coldstream.

WARK is a village (in Northumberland), in the neighbourhood of Coldstream.

Business Directory.

Agricultural Implement Maker.
Robertson, T. J., (and Blacksmith—Cycles Repaired) Cornhill

Bakers and Confectioners.
Black, John, High st
Haig, William, Market st
Middlemiss, John, Market place
Palmer, Thomas, High st
Turner, William, High st

Banks.
Bank of Scotland, High st

British Linen Co., High st

Blacksmiths.
Baird, Brothers, High st
Dalgleish, James, High st
Hogg, Archibald, Newtown
Kerr, J., Wark
Logan, John, Wark
M'Dougal, James, Eccles
Marshall, James, Cornhill
Mills, William, Leitholm
Murray, James, Duke st
Ormiston, Alexander, Orange lane
Robertson, T. J., (and Implement Maker—Cycles Repaired), Cornhill

Booksellers, Stationers, and News-agents.
Nesbitt, John, (& Printer), High st
Scott, Robert, High st

Boot and Shoe Makers.
Henderson, William, High st
M'Dougal, Alexander, Leitholm
M'Dougal, Henry, Leitholm
M'Queen, Andrew, High st
Pitt, Adam, Post Office, Eccles
Proud, William, High st

Builders—see Stonemasons, &c.

Cabinetmaker, Undertaker, and Upholsterer.
(See also Joiners, &c.)
Cairns. William R., (and Bedding Manufacturer), Duke st—see advt

Chemists and Druggists.
Elliot, W. M., High st
Wilson, George, High st

China, Glass, &c., Dealers.
Cockburn, Alexander, High st
Mowat, Mrs, Market st
Neilans, David, Market st

Contractors.
Hardie, W., (Carting), Market sq
Noble, A., New road
Roland, John, (Carting), Market sq

Smith & Son, (building), Market pl

Corn and Meal Merchants.
Leith, James, (meal), Cornhill
Playfair, Robert, High st

Drapers, Hosiers and Haberdashers.
Burns, John, High st
Hedley, Miss, Dun's road
Henderson, Wm. & Son, High st
Marshall, Miss, Leitholm
Robson, W. C., Leitholm

Engineers and Millwrights.
Dodds, James, Home place
Shiel Brothers, Market place

Farmers—see end of Directory.

Fishing Tackle Makers and Dealers.
Beloe, William L., Home place
Hendry, William, Birgham

Fishmongers, Game Dealers, and Poulterers.
Crombie, W., High st
Donaldson, Mrs, High st
Hunter, R., Market st
Simpson, J., Market place

Fleshers.
Allan, James, High st
Brydone, William, Market st
Hoy, William, Leitholm
Lillico, Richard, Market place
Neilans, John. High st

Game Dealers—see Fishmongers, &c

Grocers and General Merchants.
Marked e are Spirit Dealers.
Carlisle, George, High st
e Carmichael, R. & Son, (licensed), High st
e Davidson, J. & A., (& Brewers), Duke st
Easton, A., Donaldson Lodge, Cornhill
Elliot, John, Cornhill
Jeffery, Nicholas, Cornhill
Johnstone, Mrs., Leitholm
e Kerse, John & Son, High st

Kinghorn, William, Birgham
Landreth, R., (& Bookseller), High st
Leishman, Janet, (& Draper). Eccles
e Meikle & M'Dougal, Market place
Mein, W., Duke st
Murray, R., High st
Neilans, David, Market st
Robertson, Thomas, Eccles
Rutherford, T., High st
Scott, John, (licensed), Market st
Simpson, A. W., Market square
Simpson, M., Leitholm
Thomson, Robert, Post Office, Birgham
Wilson, J., High st
Wood, William, Leitholm

Hotels, Inns, and Posting Establishments.

Black Horse Hotel, (& Stabling), A. Taylor, Leitholm
Collingwood Arms—Mrs. M'Laughlan, Cornhill
Commercial—James Tully, High st
Crown (Temperance), J. Dickson, Market square
Ferguson, A., Leitholm
Fisherman's Arms—Ann Hume, Birgham
Kerse, Mrs., High st
Newcastle Arms—A. Scott, High st
Plough—Robert Dunlop, Leitholm
Robertson, Mrs, (Private Hotel), High st
Salmon—T. Slight, Newtown
Stenhouse, Archibald, Market st
White Swan—John Tully, High st

Ironmongers and Hardwaremen.

Murray, R., High st
Neilans, David, Market st

Joiners and Wrights.

Briggs, J., Duke st
Broomfield, John, Leitholm
Brownlee, Alexander, Cornhill
Gray, J. & A., Duke st
Hislop, James, Leitholm
Kerse, Charles, Eccles
Luke, Alexander, Hassington
M'Dougal, James, Wark
M'Dougal, Robert, Birgham
Renton, John, Newtown
Redden, Walter, (and Undertaker), High st
White & Elliot, Duke st

Miller.

Hume, Thomas, (Groat and Meal Miller), Lees Mill, High st

Milliners and Dressmakers.

(See also Drapers).
Foster, Miss E., High st
Hogarth, Mary, Eccles

Painters and Decorators.

Bruce, Robert, High st
Hogarth, Peter, High st

Plasterers—see Slaters & Plasterers.

Plumbers, Gasfitters, and Tinsmiths

Ford, Mrs A. (Sanitary), Duns road
Ford, Thomas B. (Sanitary), High street

Poulterers—see Fishmongers.

Refreshment Rooms.

Smith, John (accommodation for Bicycles), Coffee House, High street

Schools.

The Academy, Coldstream—Principal, Miss D. J. MacLean (Diploma de Paris)

Slaters and Plasterers.

Pearson, George, Duke st
Rule, Robert, Market place
Wood, William, Leitholm

Solicitors.

Deas, William A., High st
Porteous, James, High st

Spirit Dealers—see Hotels and Inns.

Stonemasons and Builders.

Johnston, John, Eccles
Marchline, William, Leitholm
Middlemass, John, Eccles

Smith & Son, Market place

Surgeons.
Dinsmore, G. H. T., Tweed terrace
Dobie, David R,, High st
Henderson, George, High st

Tailors and Clothiers.
Aikman, J., High st
Cameron, Alexander, High st
Hardie, James, High st
Logan, William, High st
Marshall, Samuel, Leitholm
Reid, William, Cornhill

Toy and Fancy Goods Merchants.
Dickson, John, High st
Donaldson, Mrs A., High st
Scott, Ann, Market place
Wood, James, High st

Veterinary Surgeons.
Harle, G. A. M., High st

Hepburn, W., Duns road

Watchmakers and Jewellers
Scott, Thomas, High st
Turnbull, R., High st

Wrights—see Joiners.

Miscellaneous
Bill Poster—R. Learmonth, Dukest
Coal Masters—Armiston Coal Co., Cornhill
Horse Dealer—W. Hardie, Market place
Photographer — G. W. Gibson, High st
Posting Master—J. Ford, High st
Saddler—Andrew Haig, High st
Seedsmen—Hogg & Wood, Market place
Thrashing Machine Proprietor — Wood & Nisbet, Birgham

CORNHILL—see COLDSTREAM.

CRANSHAWS,

Including ABBEY SAINT BATHANS, BUNKLE WITH PRESTON, ELLEMFORD, and LOMGFORMACUS.

CRANSHAWS is a parish of 8,708 acres, lying amongst the Lammermoor hills, 30 miles E. by S. from Edinburgh, 15 S.E. from Haddington and 12 N.W. from Duns. Population 85.

ABBEY SAINT BATHANS is a parish 7 miles from Duns, situated in the midst of the Lammermoor hills, containing 4,797 acres.

BUNKLE and PRESTON is a united parish containing 9,189 acres. Population 672.

LONGFORMACUS parish in the Lammermoor district, contains 19,532 acres. The village is 7 miles from Duns. Population 324.

ELLEMFORD, 3 miles from Longformacus, is in the same parish.

Business Directory.

Blacksmiths.

Dippie, Alexander, Preston
Hendry, William, Bunkle
Luke, David, Longformacus
Middlemas, David, Bunkle
Scott, James, Longformacus
Whitehead. R., Abbey Saint Bathans

Dressmakers.

Hislop, Mrs. C., Longformacus
Patterson, Mrs. C., Longformacus

Farmers—see end of Directory.

Grocers and General Merchants.

Anderson Alexander, Longformacus
Dickson, David, Bunkle
Hislop, Mrs. C., Longformacus
Mack, John, Longformacus

Joiners and Wrights.

Blackie, James, Longformacus
Broomfield, James, Preston
Mack, R., Abbey Saint Bathans

Tailors.

Johnstone. Thomas, Bunkle
Patterson, William, Longformacus

CUMLEDGE—SEE DUNS.

DUNS,

Including the Parishes and Villages of CUMLEDGE, EDROM, GAVINTON, IN LANGTON, and Neighbourhoods.

DUNS is a burgh of barony, and the largest town in the shire (Berwick not being taken in as strictly belonging to the county); it is 45 miles E. by S. from Edinburgh, 15 W. from Berwick, 11 from Ayton, ond 8 N.N.E from Greenlaw. It is a station on the North British Line from Reston to St. Boswell's. A justice of the peace court is held on the first Monday of each month, and a sheriff's court eight times in the year, viz., the last Friday in January, February, March, May June, and November, the second Friday in July, and the first Friday in October, at both of which debt claims of limited amount are adjudicated. A civil court is also held every Friday, except during the vacations, which are arranged by the sheriff. The parish of Duns contains 11,39? acres. Population 2,199.

EDROM is a parish and village, the latter 3½ miles east from Duns. It is a station on the Duns branch of the North British Line. The parish of Edrom contains about 9,545 acres. Population 1,861.

LANGTON is a pari h comprising the village of Gavinton, the latter situated 2 miles from Duns. The acreage of the parish of Langton is about 7,139. Population 417.

Business Directory.

Architects and Surveyors.
Duns, George, West cottage
Fortune, George, Kilmany House, Bridgend
Menzies, John, Bankhead

Auctioneers and Valuators.
Swan, R. G. & W. B., (and Cattle Salesmen), Market place and Reston

Bakers and Confectioners.
Buckham, Miss M., 23 Castle st
Cockburn, Adam, Easter st
Crawford, William, North st
Curle, William & Son, Golden square and South st
Darling, Thomas, Castle st
Hill, John, Langtongate st
Middlemiss, John, Gavinton
Rhind, Alexander, North st
Scott, James, North st
Veitch, William, Castle st
Wood, Andrew, Easter st

Banks.
Bank of Scotland, Newtown st
British Linen Co., Newtown st
Royal Bank of Scotland, Market pl

Blacksmiths.
Blaikie, J., Riselaw
Darling, Thomas, Edrom
Frisken, James, Gavinton
Grierson, H., Millburn
Johnston, Robert, North st
Kirkcaldy, John, Newtown st
Lugton, Charles, Pinkie
Polwath, Alexander, Easter st
Robertson, J. & A., Castle st
Whitehead, Thos., Gourlay's wynd
Young, Peter, Willis wynd

Booksellers, Stationers, Printers, & Newsagents.
Buckham Miss M., (and Tobacconist), Castle st
Kerr, Mss. J., Castle st
Swan, & Co., Market st
Wilkie, J. M., Market place
Williamson. John, Murray st

Boot and Shoe Makers.
Charles, William, Market place
Cormack, Alexander, Market place
Cowe, Robert, Market place
Forbes, Alexander F., South street
Gray John & Co., Castle st
M'Gregor, Horace, Black Bull st
M'Inroy, Alexander, Bridgend
More, John, Castle st
Mosgrove, J., Market place
Paterson, David, Castle st
Pringle, James, Easter st
Taylor, William, North st

Builders—see Stone Masons.

Cabinetmakers, Upholsterers and Undertakers.
Dewar, James, 1 Murray st
Dods, Robert, South st

Chemists and Druggists.
Gunn, William, Market square
Honnam, C., Market st

China and Glass Merchants.
Haggerty, Mrs. Jessie, Castle st
Norris, Mrs. Easter, st

Coal Merchants and Agents.
Alexander, R., Clouds st
Alexander, W. & Sons, Railway stn
Lowe, J., Railway Station
Swan & Falconer, Railway station
Swan, & Pringle, Railway station

Confectioners.
See also Bakers and Confectioners.
Beattie, Mrs. John, Castle st
Forsyth, John, North st
Lauder, A., South st

Corn and Meal Merchants.
Aitchison, William, North st

Wilson, P., Castle st

Cutler.

Polwarth, Alexander, Easter st

Drapers, Milliners, and Clothiers.

Brown, Robert, Market place
Dunlop, D., Market place
Rankine & Aitchison, Murray st
Robson & Oliver, Market place
Wilson & Son, Market place

Dressmakers—see also Drapers, &c.

Brunton, Miss, Currie st
Rodgers, Miss, 47 Castle st

Fancy Goods and Berlin Wool Repositories.

Ford, Miss, Castle st
Leask, Miss A., North st
Neilson, Mrs., Market place

Farmers—see end of Directory.

Fleshers.

Duns, Thomas, Market place
Guy, Robert, Castle st
Miller, A., Golden square
Simpson, Richard, Easter st
Tait, Robert (Family Butcher), Black Bull st

Grocers and General Merchants.

Those Marked e are Spirit Dealers.

e Alexander & Co., South st
Anderson, William, Newtown st
e Baillie, James, Market place
Bell, A., North st
Blackhall, Alexander, Mordington
e Brown, T. K., Market place
Cockburn, John, Market place
Forsyth, A. & I., Newtown st
Halliday, Mrs., Easter st
Hyslop, Mrs., Castle st
Lyall, Mrs., Gavinton
M'Inroy, Mrs., Easter st
e M'Intosh, George, Market place
Malcolm Brothers, Market place
Mathieson, J. W., Bridge end
Millar, George E., Lantongate st
Paxton, Francis, Newtown st
Polwarth, Alexander, Easter st
e Robertson, Thomas, South st
Ronaldson, Janet, North st
Scott, James, Castle st
Swan, James, South st
Thomson, Mrs., Castle st
Veitch, David, Market place
Watson, James, Gavinton

Hairdressers and Perfumers.

Aird, Robert. 3 Murray st
Aikman, P. J., Market square

Hatter and Hosier.

Garden, A. M., 8 Market place

Horse Hiring and Posting establishments.

Hislop & Skirving, 25 Castle st
M'Alpine, James, WhiteSwan Hotel, Market st

Hotels, Inns, and Posting Houses.

Black Bull Hotel, James R. Meikle, Proprictor, Black Bull st
Cross Keys, Wm. Darling Castle st
Commercial Temperance Hotel, Misses Liddell, Black Bull st
Eliot, J., (Temperance), Easter st
Horn Inn—Mrs Black, Newtown st
Hunt Inn—Mrs. Cowe, (Good Stabling), Newtown st
Plough Inn, Alexander G. Thomson, North st
Royal Hotel—George Martin, Proprietor, Market place
Smith, James (Temperance), Easter st
Wallace, A. (Temperance), South st
White Swan Hotel—(Posting in all it Branches), James M'Alpine, Proprietor, Market st

Insurance Company.

Prudential Assurance Co. Limited, George Allen, Agent, 23 South st

Ironmongers and Harewaremen.

Falconer, Allan, Castle st
Graham, George, Market place
Lamb, William G., Market place
Rae, John C., Market st
Stevenson, Richard, Market place

Joiners and Wrights.
Clazie, John, Langtongate st
Crombie, James, Bridge end
Douglas, Thomas, Gavinton
Hume, John, Gourlay's wynd
Kerr, John, Edrom
Kinlayside, James, Bridge end
Laurie, Andrew, Gavinton
M'Intosh, W., Willis wynd
Mack, James Johnsfield
Scott, James N., Castle st

Millers,
Blaikie, Wm. & James, Putton mill
Borthwick, M.. Edrom
Hastie, Michael, Cockburn mill
Pitt, John, H., Manderstone mill
Swanton, James, (threshing), Duns mill
Weir, William, Langton mill

Milliners—see also Drapers &c.
Stuart, Misses, 10 Murray st
Stewart, Mrs., Regent st

Painters and Decorators.
Harper, David, Market place
Hume, James, Newtown st
Tindall, A., (Photographer), Bridge end

Photographers.
Bruce, George, Easter st
Lothian, Adam, Castle st

Plasterers—see Slaters and Plasterers.

Plumbers, Gasfitters, and Tinsmiths.
Blyth, John, North st
Newbigging, Peter, Newtown st
Young, George, Black Bull st

Saddler and Harness Maker.
Edgar, Thomas R., South st

Schools—Boarding and Day.
Gun, Mrs. & the Misses, Newtown House
Verhaegh, Misses, E.S. (Boarding & Day School Murray), place

Seedsmen, Nurserymen and Florists.
Hogg & Wood, Railway station
Kinghorn & Co., Market place

Slaters and Plasterers.
Aitchison, John, Castle st
Kirkcaldy, James Easter st
Whitehead, James, Castle st

Solicitors and Notaries.
Crawford, A., Newtown st
Deas, Adam, Langtongate st
Gibson, John, Murray st
Kellie & Millar, Market place
Millar, J., Castle st
Robson & Ferguson, Market place
Somers. T. A. M., Market place
Wilson, Joseph, Newtown st

Spirit Dealers—see Hotels and Inns

Stonemasons, Builders, and Contractors.
Cooper, James, Gavinton
Dods & Hogg, Langtongate st
Spears, John, Gavinton

Surgeons.
Campbell, A. J., Duns
Campbell, W. W., Westwood
M'Watt, John, Morelands,
M'Watt, Robert C., Haymount
Wilson, James L., Wellfield

Surveyors—see Architects and Surveyors.

Tailors and Clothiers.
Dewar, A., Newtown st
Dunbar, Richard, Castle st
Fergnson, Daniel, South st
Newbiggin, John, Currie st
Ovens, Brothers, Easter st
Rae, John, Gavinton
Swan, Andrew, North st
White, Alexander, Castle st

Temperance Hotels—see Hotels &c.

Tobaccanists.
Buckham, Miss M., 23 Castle st
Rhind, Alexander, Golden square

Veterinary Surgeons.
Biair, William, Newtown st
Lothian, William North st

Watch and Clock Makers.
Aitchison, William, 16 Castle st
Edington, James. North st
Gibson, George, Easter st
Jeffrey, Peter, Langtongate st

Miscellaneous.
Coach Builders—Fair, Heggie & Co Castle st
Engineers—T. Brown & Son, Clock-mill
Fishmonger — William, Martin Castle st
Refreshment Rooms—Thomas Wilson, 9 Murray st
Rope Maker — Robert, Dods, Easter st
Saw Millers — Brownlee & Co., Railway station

EARLSTON,

LEGERWOOD, REDPATH, and Neighbourhoods.

EARLSTON is a parish and village, the latter 31 miles S.E. from Edinburgh, 11 W. by N. from Kelso, 18 S.W. from Duns, 15 N. from Jedburgh, 10 S.W. from Greenlaw, 8½ N.E. from Galashiels, and 7 S. from Lauder. There are two fairs—on the 29th of June, and the third Thursday in October, for cattle and horses, and a cattle and sheep market every alternate Monday ; also a corn market weeky during the winter and every alternate Monday during the summer. REDPATH is a village in this parish The parish of Earlston has an area of 8,968 acres. Population 1060.

LEGERWOOD parish contains 8,789 acres. Population 475. The village of Legerwood is three miles from Earlston. BOONHILL, in this parish, was a signal station during the time of war.

Business Directory.

Bakers and Confectioners.
Cathrae, William, Earlston
Watson, Mrs. D., Earlston

Banks.
Commercial Bank of Scotland, Ltd. Earlston—A. G. Sinclair, agent

Blacksmiths.
Brotherston, J. & A., Earlston
Lee, Robert, Earlston
Rutherford, John, Legerwood
Waldie, Robert, Earlston
Wilkie, James, Earlston

Booksellers, Stationers, and Newsagents.
Dodds, Ralph, Earlston
M'Donald, T., (& Printer), Earlston
Smith, Mrs. Dawson, Earlston
Weatherby, John P., Earlston

Boot and Shoe Makers.
Ballantyne, James, Earlston
Nichol, Thomas, Earlston
Smith, Robert & Son, Earlston
Young, Archibald, Earlston

Builders—see Joiners, &c.

Cartwrights—ser Joiners, &c.,

Coal Merchants and Agents.
Gray, William, Earlston
Spark, David, Earlston

Corn and Meal Merchants.
Dodds, Ralph, Earlston
Smith, Robert, & Son, Earlston

Drapers and Clothiers.
Clendinnen, Thomas, & Sons, Earlston
Miller, John, Earlston
Wallace, David, Earlston

Farmers—see end of Directory

Fishmongers, Game Dealers, and Poulterers.
Maltman, Alexander, Earlston
Mauchlan, Adam, Earlston
Moffat, Thomas, Earlston

Fleshers.
Kerr, Miss, Earlston
Miles, Mrs W., Earlston

Game Dealers—see Fishmongers, &c

Grocers and General Merchants.
Marked e are also Spirit Merchants.
Baird, Alexander, Earlston
Co-operative Soc. Ltd., Earlston
e Crockett, Mrs, Earlston
e Dodds, Ralph, Earlston
Jamieson, David, Earlston
Kerr, John, Earlston
Kerr, Mrs William, Earlston
Readman, Mrs, Earlston
e **Smith, Robert, & Son** (and Ironmongers, Corn, and Spirit Merchants), Earlston

Hotels, Inns, and Posting Houses.
Black Bull—Walter Scott, Earlston
Red Lion—Family and Commercial Hotel and Posting Establishment—Posting in all its branches—Robert Smart, proprietor, Earlston
Walker's Temperance—Earlston
White Swan Hotel—(good stabling)—Walter Keir, proprietor, Earlston

Ironmongers and Hardwaremen.
Dodds, Ralph, Earlston
Smith, Robert & Son, Earlston

Joiners and Wrights.
Gray, John, Earlston
Kerr, John, Earlston
Laidler, John (Joiner & Cartwright), Legerwood
Rodger, Wm. & Sons (Builders), Earlston
Wallace, G. & R., Earlston

Manufacturers.
Clendinnen, Wm., Earlston
Roberts, Dunn, & Co., Earlston

Millers.
Halliday, Francis, Bridgehaugh
Kinghorn, John, Mellerstain

Painters and Decorators.
Fisher, George & Son, The Green, Earlston

Poulterers—see Fishmongers, &c.

Refreshment Rooms.
Smith, Mrs. W., Earlston
Walker, S. & I., Earlston

Spirit Dealers—see Hotels.

Tailors and Clothiers.
See also Drapers and Clothiers.
Hunter, George, Earlston
Laurie, Thomas, Earlston

Watchmakers and Jewellers.
Lochhead, D. D., Earlston
Pringle, George, Earlston

Miscellaneous.
Chemist—John Cairns, Earlston
Plumber & Slater—Andrew Murdison, Earlston
Printer—Wm. Norrie, Earlston
Saddler—John M'Donald, Earlston
Surgeon—John Young, Earlston
Timber Merchants and Sawmillers—A. R. Brownlie, Earlston

EDROM—SEE DUNS.
ELLEMFORD—SEE CRANSHAWS.

EYEMOUTH.

Including AYTON, BURNMOUTH and Neighbourhoods.

EYEMOUTH is a seaport and burgh of barony in the parish of its name, 50 miles E. from Edinburgh, 21 north east from Greenlaw, 21 S.E. from Dunbar, 10 north from Coldstream, 13½ from Duns, 8 N. from Berwick, and 3 from Aytoun station, on the North British Railway.

Fairs are held on the first Thursdays of June and October. The parish of Eyemouth embraces an area of 1,004 acres. Population, 2667.

Ayton is a parish and village, the latter 2½ miles from Eyemouth, and 8 N.W. from Berwick, on the left bank of the Eye, on the main line of railway between Edinburgh and the South. The parish contains 3,699 acres.

A justice of the peace court is held here monthly, and a sheriff's court for the recovery of small debts is held four times a month. Population 1,826.

BURNMOUTH is a fishing village. It is 2½ miles from Ayton, and 6 from Berwick. It is a Coastguard Station, close to the entrance to the village, on the North British line.

Business Directory.

Bakers and Confectioners.

Armitage, T. G., Ayton
Armitage, Thomas, Eyemouth
Cairins, Alexander, Ayton
Chrystal, John, Eyemouth
Chrystal, William, Eyemouth
Fairbairn, David, Eyemouth
Gibson, Alexander, Eyemouth
Gibson, James, Eyemouth
Lothian, J. M., Ayton
Paterson, P., Eyemouth
Scott, R., Eyemouth
Wood, Joseph, Eyemouth

Banks.

Commercial Bank of Scotland, Ltd. Ayton and Eyemouth
Royal Bank, Ayton and Eyemouth

Blacksmiths.

Ewart, David, Ayton
Ewart, Mrs Mary, Eyemouth
Kinghorn, George, Ayton
Luke, James, Eyemouth

Booksellers. Stationers, and Fancy Dealers.

Donaldson & Co., (and Printers), Eyemouth
Henderson, John, Ayton
Tait, Mrs. A., Ayton

Boot and Shoe Makers.

Aitchison, John, Ayton
Allan, J. & W. Ayton
Bruce Brothers, Ayton
Edington, Archibald, Ayton

Ford, John, Eyemouth
Lothian, J. M., Ayton
Nisbet, James, Eyemouth
Parker, Ben, Eyemouth
Paterson, James, Eyemouth
Swanson, David, Ayton

Carting Contractors—see Coal Merchants.

Coach, Van, and Cart Builder.
Heron, John, (& Joiner), Ayton

Coal Merchants and Carting Contractors.
Colin, George, Eyemouth
Colie, John, Burnmouth
Dalgetty, Robert, Ayton

Drapers and Clothiers.
Burgon, R., Eyemouth
Dougall, James & Co., Eyemouth
Forsyth, J. G., (& Grocers), Eyemouth
Geddes, G. M., (Draper, Milliner, Clothier, and Outfitter), Ayton
Henderson, Alexander, Ayton
Hume, David, Eyemouth
Paterson, W., Eyemouth
Marshall, Robert, Ayton

Farmers—see end of Directory,

Fish Curers.
Aitchison, George, Eyemouth
Aitchison, Robert, Burnmouth
Crawford, James, (Salesman), Eyemouth
Dickson. Peter, Eyemouth
Dougal, David, Eyemouth
Glen, Alexander, Eyemouth
Johnston, John, Eyemouth
Meek, David, Eyemouth
Philips & Turner, Eyemouth
Robertson, B. & Son, Eyemouth
Wotherspoon, Robert, Burnmouth

Fleshers.
Armitage, Peter, Ayton
Armitage, Thomas, Eyemouth
Burgan' Alexander, Eyemouth
Purves, William, Ayton

Grocers and General Merchants.
Aitchison, Ann, Eyemouth
Boig, Ralph A., Eyemouth
Brack, Andrew, Eyemouth
Burgon, Mrs., Eyemouth
Carter, Andrew, Eyemouth
Colin, R. (and China Dealer), Eyemouth
Dougal, James & Co., Eyemouth
Dougal, John, Eyemouth
Forsyth, J. & G. (and Drapers), Eyemouth
Graden, Thomas, Eyemouth
Greig, James, Ayton
Grieve, George, Eyemouth
Hume, Mrs G., Eyemouth
Knox, Isaac H., Ayton
Livingstone, James K., Ayton
Martin, Alexander, Burnmouth
Nisbet, Mrs Ann, Eyemouth
Patterson, John, Eyemouth
Robertson, Alexander (and Spirit Merchant), Eyemouth
Sinclair, David, Ayton
Scott, William, Eyemouth
Spratt. A. (& Game Dealer), Ayton
Stewart, Walter, Eyemouth
Waddell. Robert, Eyemouth
Young, A., Eyemouth

Hotels, Inns, and Posting Houses.
Black Bull—David Lawson, Ayton
Cross Keys Hotel—Thomas Erskine, proprietor, Eyemouth
Flemington Inn—R. R. Buchanan, Burnmouth
Home Arms—Walter Flett, Eyemouth
Red Lion—Robert Greig, Ayton
Martin, Alexander, Burnmouth
Royal—John Hogg, Eyemouth
Ship—George Purves, Eyemouth
Whale Inn—James Hughes, Eyemouth
White Swan Hotel—William Scott, Eyemouth

Joiners and Wrights.
Henderson, John, Ayton
Heron, John (& House Carpenter, Coach, Van and Cart Builder), Ayton
Nisbet, George, Ayton

Wicks, George, Ayton
Waddell, Robert (Cabinetmaker), Ayton

Millers.

Bell, Mrs Robert, Netherbyres
Gibson, Peter, Eyemouth Grain mills
Nisbet, William, Ayton

Painters and Decorators.

Black, Robert, Eyemouth
Hume, R. M., Ayton
Shearlaw, A., Ayton

Plumbers, Gasfitters, and Tinsmiths

Christie, John, Ayton
Sweeney, P., Eyemouth

Sawmill Proprietor—see also Timber Merchants.

Paterson, Archibald, Eyemouth Sawmills

Solicitors.

Doughty, J., Ayton
Wood, John, Eyemouth

Surgeons.

Connachie, James, (v.s'), Ayton
Forsyth, James, Eyemouth
Jeffrey, J., P., Ayton

Tailors and Clothiers.

(See also Drapers and Clothiers).

Aitchison, A., Eyemouth
Aitchison, John, Eyemouth
Aitchison, Peter, Eyemouth
Dalgetty, John, Ayton
Geddes, G. M,, (and Draper, &c.), Ayton
Henderson, Alexander, Ayton
Miller, Adam, Eyemouth
Purves, R. N., Eyemouth
Whitlie, J. & J., Ayton

Timber Merchants and Sawmill Proprietors.

Allan Brothers, Eyemouth
Nisbet, William, Ayton

Miscellaneous.

Chemist—R. A. M'Ivor, Eyemouth
Game and Poultry Dealer—J.Spratt Ayton
Mill Board Manufacturer—William Martin, Ayton
Oil Merchants—John Currie & Cox, Eyemouth
Saddler—J. Davidson, Ayton
Slater & Plasterer—Robert Winter, Ayton
Stonemason — William Paterson, Ayton
Watchmaker — Thomas Morison, Ayton

FELKINGTON—SEE BERWICK.
FOGO—SEE POLWARTH.

FOULDEN AND MORDINGTON.

FOULDEN is a parish containing 3278 acres, and village, the latter is 52 miles E. by S. of Edinburgh, 10 E, of Duns, and 5 N.E of Berwick. Population 351.

The parish of MORDINGTON, containing 2939 acres, lies in the south-eastern corner of the county. At the boundary of the parish, with the liberties of Berwick, is the toll-bar and hamlet of Lamberton. Population 324.

Business Directory.

Blacksmiths.
Jeffrey & Son, Mordington
Jeffrey, Thomas, Foulden

Boot and Shoe Makers.
Jeffrey, Peter, Mordington
Mason, William, Foulden

Farmers—see end of Directory.

Grocers and General Merchants.
Blackhall, Alexander, Mordington
Weatherston, Foulden

Joiners and Builders.
Cook, Charles, Mordington
Laurie, Robert, Foulden

GAVINGTON-IN-LANGTON—SEE DUNS.

GREENLAW, GORDON, AND HUME.

GREENLAW is a burgh of barony, is 37 miles S.E. from Edinburgh. 20 W. from Berwick, 12 E. from Lauder, 7½ S.W. from Duns, and 10 N.W. from Coldstream. A sheriff court and one for the recovery of small debts are held monthly; the justices' court sits at Duns. The parish of Greenlaw contains 12,149 acres. Population 668.

GORDON village is 5 miles from Greenlaw, on the road from Edinburgh to Kelso. The parish contains 9,713 acres. Population 843.

HUME is a small village, situate 3 miles south from Greenlaw; it is a joint parish with STITCHEL (Roxburghshire). The joint parish contains an area of 6,898 acres. Population 366.

Business Directory.

Bakers and Confectioners.
Cossar, David, Greenlaw
Dodds, James, Gordon
Edington, Thomas, Greenlaw

Blacksmiths.
Aitkin, George, Hume
Brownlee, Thomas, Greenlaw
Dickman, G., Greenlaw
Matthewson, George, Greenlaw
Robertson, T., Greenlaw
Waldie, Robert, Gordon

Booksellers, Stationers, and Newsagents.
Lindsay, Thomas, Post Office, Greenlaw
Miller, Henry, Greenlaw
Smith, Stephen, Gordon

Boot and Shoe Makers.
Common, George, Greenlaw
Douglas, Robert, Greenlaw
Hermiston, Misses (and Drapers, &c,). Greenlaw
M'Dougall, William, Greenlaw

Smith, Stephen, Gordon
Spence, R., Gordon
Stark, William, Greenlaw
Whitelock, William, Greenlaw
Young, Adam, Gordon

Builders—see Joiners, &c.

Cartwright.
Spence, William, Greenlaw

Coal Merchants and Agents.
Aitchison, William, Greenlaw
Alexander, W. & Son, Greenlaw
Redpath, George, Greenlaw
Weatherhead, Mrs., Gordon

Contractors.
Mercer, James, Gordon
Temple, D., Hume

Drapers and Clothiers.
Brown, George, Gordon
Cockburn & Son, Gordon
Fairbairn, May, Greenlaw
Hermiston, Misses (& Boot and Shoe Makers), Greenlaw
Miller, Henry, Greenlaw

Farmers—see end of Directory.

Fish Merchants.
Dillon, P. (& General Merchant), Gordon
Tait, Jacob, Greenlaw

Fleshers.
Gladstone, Robert, Gordon
Lillico, A., Greenlaw
Rogerson, George, Greenlaw

Glass and China Merchants.
Lamb, James, Gordon
Robertson, Mrs., Gordon
Spence, William, Greenlaw
Young, Alexander, Greenlaw

Grocers and General Merchants.
Allan, James & Sons, Gordon
Anderson, James, Greenlaw
Blackie, Thomas, Greenlaw
Fleming, John, Gordon
Frisken, Peter, Gordon
Lunham, George, Hume
Newton, Robert, Gordon
Stoddart, John, Greenlaw
Veitch, David, Greenlaw, and at Duns

Hotels, Inns, and Posting Houses.
Castle Hotel (First-Class Family and Commercial; Posting in all its branches), Mrs. Turnbull, Greenlaw
Cross Keys, John Darling, Greenlaw
Gibson, John, Gordon
Railway—James Diffey, Gordon

Joiners and Wrights.
Allan, J., Greenlaw
Brownlee, James, Hume
Burton, James, Greenlaw
Henderson, James, Greenlaw
Hunter, James, Gordon
Leitch, Adam, Hume
Smeaton, A., Greenlaw
Spence, William (and Cartwright), Greenlaw
Steel, Henry, Greenlaw

Rabbit and Mole Catcher.
Clapham, James, Greenlaw

Surgeons.
Little, George, Gordon
Marr, James, Greenlaw

Tailors and Clothiers.
Happer, George, Greenlaw
Lamb, Thomas, Greenlaw
Storrie, William, Gordon

Watchmaker.
Weston, G., Greenlaw

Miscellaneous.
Bankers—Royal Bank Greenlaw
Cattle Salesmen—J. Rogerson, & Son, Greenlaw
Chemist—David Leitch, Greenlaw
Manufacturer—W. Shearer, Greenlaw
Millwright—Andrew Hislop Greenlaw
Painter—John Broomfield Greenlaw
Saddler—Peter Cockburn Greenlaw

Slater—A. Lyal, Greenlaw

Tile Maker—William Tully, Hume

GORDON—see GREENLAW.
GRANTHOUSE—see RESTON.
GRINDON—see BERWICK-ON-TWEED.
HORNCLIFFE—see BERWICK-ON-TWEED.
HORNDEAN—see SWINTON.
HOUNDSLOW—see WESTRUTHER.
HOUNDWOOD—see RESTON.
HUME—see GREENLAW.

HUTTON AND PAXTON.

ARE villages in the parish of Hutton and district of Merse, Hutton is 7 miles from Berwick its post town, and Paxton 5 miles distant from Berwick its post town. Tho parish contains 5,516 acres. Populrtion, 815.

Business Directory.

Blacksmiths.
Jeffery, William, Hutton
Wilkie, John, Paxton

Boot and Shoe Makers.
Allan, William, Hutton
Allan, William, Paxton
Armstrong, Alexander, Paxton
Sherlaw, Adam, Hutton

Farmers—see end of Directory.

Grocers and General Merchants.
Allan, Mary Ann, Hutton
Briggs, John, (Grocer, Flour, and General Merchant) Paxton—sec advt
Ford, Walter, Hutton
Huntly, George, (Family Grocer, and Meal Merchant), Paxton

Hotels and Inns.
Cross Hotel—Adam Moffat Paxton
Tait, Alexander, Hutton

Joiners and Builders.
Bain, Alexander, Paxton
Dunbar, T. Hutton
Ford, Benjamin, Hutton
Pringle, John,Paxton
Schooler, Benjamin, Paxton
Schooler, John, Paxton

Tailors and Clothiers.
Armstrong, James, Paxton
Whittle, Benjamin, Hutton

LADYKIRK—SEE BERWICK-ON-TWEED.
LAMBERTON—SEE FOULDEN.

LAUDER,

Including the Villages of BLAINSLIE, CHANNELKIRK, OXTON, and THIRLSTANE.

LAUDER is a royal burgh, and the capital of its parish, district of Lauderdale: 25 miles S E. of Edinburgh, 35 w. of Berwick, 21 N. of Jedburgh, 22 s.w. of Coldstream, 20 s.w. of Duns, 17 s.w. of Kelso, 12 w. of Greenlaw, 7 N. of Earlston, and 6 miles from the Stow station on the North British Railway. A justice of peace court, and sheriff's small debt courts are held here. The parish of Lauder contains 34,898 acres. Population 763.

BLAINSLIE, is a village in the parish of Melrose (Roxburghshire), 7 miles from Melrose, 4 miles of Earlston, and 2½ of Lauder.

The parish of CHANNELKIRK, containing 14,191 acres, is situated among the Lammermoor hills, where they divide the counties of Edinburgh and Haddington from Berwick. Population 545.

The village of OXTON is 4 miles from Lauder.

Business Directory.

Bakers and Confectioners.

Matthewson, Ronaleyn W., Post Office, Oxton
Pow, William, Lauder
Runciman, William, Lauder
Shaw, Thomas, Lauder

Blacksmiths.

Carruthers, John, Blainslie
Hardie, John, Lauder
Murray, John, Oxton
Park, James, Blainslie
Reid, Alexander, Oxton

Boot and Shoe Makers.

Cowan, John, Oxton
Harvey, David W., Lauder
Lothian, Alexander, Blainslie
Somerville, William, Lauder

Builders—see Joiners, &c.

Chemist and Druggist.

Scroggie, John H. Post Office Lauder

Confectioners.

Anderson, Miss H. (& fancy goods), Lauder
Thornburn, Elizabeth, Lauder

Drapers and Clothiers.

Aikman & Co., Lauder
Black, William, Lauder
Cossar, James, Lauder
Swan, Mrs. Helen, Oxton
Waddell, Andrew H. (tailor) Oxton
Wallace, David, Lauder

Fancy Repositories.

Anderson, Miss H., Lauder
Wight, Mrs.. Lauder

Farmers—see end of Directory

Fleshers.

Brodie, Alexander, Lauder
Henderson, Mrs T., Lauder
Ridpath, John, Lauder

Grocers and General Merchants.

Marked thus e are also Wine and Spirit Dealers.

Bain, David George, (grocer & wine & spirit merchant), Lauder
Graham, William, (grocer, wine merchant, seedsmen, and Ironmonger), Lauder
e Liddell, John, Lauder
e Matthewson, Ronaleyn W., Post Office, Oxton
Monro, A., Lauder
Park, James, Blainslie
e Reid, James, (licensed), Lauder
Robertson, Catherine, Blainslie
Walkinshaw, Mrs M. A., Oxton

Horse Hiring and Posting Establishment

Kerr, Robert Black Bull Stables Lauder

Hotels, Inns and Posting Houses.

Black Bull—John Sanderson Lauder
Carfraemill Inn—G. Henderson, Oxton
Commercial Inn—Thomas Wilson, Lauder
Eagle Hotel, (Family Commercial and Posting), Allan Davidson, proprietor, Lauder

Ironmongers and Seedsmen—see Grocers, &c.

Joiners, Builders, and Wrights.

Anderson, George W., Lauder
Bell, William, Oxton
Chisholm, George, Blainslie
Gill, Andrew, Lauder
Robertson & Son, Blainslie
Scott, William, (joiner and Van Builder), Blainslie

Millers.

Brown, William, Lylestone
Kinghorn, James, St. Leonards

Saddlers and Harness Makers.

Davidson, William, Lauder
Waddell, Robert, Lauder

Solicitors.

Broomfield, G. L., Lauder
Romanes & Rankin, Lauder

Surgeons.

Mair, John (v.s.), Lauder
Skinner, David, Lauder

Tailors & Clothiers—see Drapers &c

Van Builder.

Scott, William (and Joiner), Blainslie

Miscellaneous.

Bankers—Bank of Scotland, Lauder
China Dealer—Mrs Allen, Lauder
Cooper—George Cockburn, Lauder
Painter — George B. Westwood, Lauder
Plumber—Archibald Darling, Lauder
Tobacconist—James Rae, Lauder
Watchmaker—W. Murray, Lauder

LEGERWOOD—SEE EARLSTON.
LEITHOLM—SEE COLDSTREAM.
LOANEND—SEE BERWICK-ON-TWEED.
LONGFORMACUS—SEE CRANSHAWS.
MORDINGTON—SEE FOULDEN.
NORHAM—SEE BERWICK-ON-TWEED.
NORHAM MAINS—SEE BERWICK-ON-TWEED.
ORD (EAST AND WEST)—SEE BERWICK-ON-TWEED.
OXTON—SEE LAUDER.
PAXTON—SEE HUTTON.

POLWARTH and FOGO.

POLWARTH is a parish of 3,000 acres in the district of Merse. The village is 40 miles from Edinburgh, 4 from Duns, and about 3 from Greenlaw. Population 503.

The parish of FOGO, which lies to the south of Polwarth, the village of Fogo, and the hamlet of CHESTERS are in this parish. The parish contains 4,652 acres. Population 420.

Business Directory.

Farmers—see end of Directory.

General Merchants and Traders.

Comb, R. (Blacksmith), Fogo
Grant, A. (Mason), Polwarth
Grant, Miss (Grocer), Polwarth
Hamilton, John (Joiner), Fogo
Hunter, David (Tailor), Fogo
M'Dougal, Andrew (Blacksmith), Polwarth
Watson, W. (Implement Maker), Polwarth

PRESTON—see CRANSHAWS.
REDPATH—see EARLSTON.
RENTON—see RESTON.

RESTON,

Including AUCHENCROW, GRANT'S HOUSE, RENTON, HOUNDWOOD, and Neighbourhoods.

RESTON and AUCHENCROW are two villages in the parish of Coldingham, the former being 3 miles from Coldingham, the same distance from Ayton, and 9 from Duns; the latter lying between Reston, and Chirnside about 2½ miles from each place. A station on the North British Railway is in the village of Reston.

GRANT'S HOTSE is a village in the same parish as the above, 7 miles from Coldingham, 8 from Ayton, and 5 from Cockburnspath. Reston is a small hamlet a mile distant.

Business Directory.

Auctioneers and Valuators.
Swan, R. G. & W. B. Reston and Duns

Blacksmiths.
Fulton, John, Auchencrow
Jeffrey, Peter, Reston
Liddle, William, Reston
Whitlie, Mark, Houndwood

Boot and Shoe Makers.
Anderson, Henry, Reston
Colvin. Robert, Reston
Mason, Peter, Auchencrow
Shearlaw, Thomas, Grant's house

Builders—see Joiners &c.

Coal Merchants and Agents
Aitchison & Logan, Reston
McLauchlan, Thomas, Reston
Wallace Brothers (Coal Agents and Wire Fence Contractors), Grant's house
Wightman, Thomas, Reston

Drapers.
Fair, Edward (and Grocer), Grant's house
Fortune, Miss M. (& Grocer), Post Office Auchencrow

Farmers—see end of Directory.

Fish, Game, and Poultry Dealers.
Cassels, David, Auchencrow
Scott, James Reston

Flesher.
Stothart, Robert, Reston

Grocers and General Merchants.
Aitchison, James, Reston
Anderson, William, Grant's house
Fair, Edward (and Drapers), Grant's house
Fortune, Miss M. (&Draper). Post Office
Johnston, Adam, Reston
Johnston, Alexander, South Renton
Liddle, Miss, Reston
M'Lanchlan, John, Reston
Scott, George R., Post Office, Reston

Hotels, Inns, and Posting Houses.
Cross Keys—Robert, Reid, Auchencrow
Grant's House Hotel (and Posting), David, Hay, Grant's house
Red Lion—J. F., Brown, Reston
Wheatsheaf—Nicholas French, Reston
White Swan—Thomas M'Lauchlan, Reston
Wight, Thomas, Houndwood

Joiners, Builders, and Wrights.
Fair, W. & J,, Grant's house
Lawrie, Michael, Auchencrow
Turner, James, Grant's house
Watt & Wilson, Reston

Millers.
Bell, Andrew, Howburn
Denholm, Robert, East Reston mill
Wilson, Charles, Reston mill

Tailors and Clothiers.
Laing, John, Auchencrow
Ponton, Francis, South Renton Grant's house
Shearlaw, William, Grant's house
Swan, Walter J., Reston

Temperance Hotel.
Young, Andrew, (and Posting House), Grant's house

Wire Fence Contractors.
Wallace Brothers, Grant's house

Miscellaneous
Baker—Alex. Gilles, Reston
Masons—Campbell & Sons, Grant's house
Solicitor—J. S. Mack, Reston
Surgeon—Leslie Crooke, Rsston

SCREMERSTON—SEE BERWICK-ON-TWEED.
SHOREWOOD—SEE BERWICK-ON-TWEED.
SIMPRIM—SEE SWINTON.
SPITTAL-SEE BERWICK-ON-TWEEED.

SWINTON and SIMPRIM.

Including WHITSOME, and HORNDEAN.

THE parish of SWINTON and SIMPRIM is in the district of Merse, and contains 5,561 acres. Population, 847. The village of Swinton, 45 miles S.E. of Edinburgh, 12 S.W. of Berwick, and 6 N. of Coldstream.

The village of Simprim is in this parish. Whitesome, including the parish of Hilton, contains 4,896 acres. Population 573. The village of Whitsome is 3 miles from Swinton.

The parish of LADYKIRK contains 3,380 acres. Population 334. The village of HORNDEAN belongs to this parish.

Business Directory

Bakers.
Denham. George, Swinton
Gibson, George, Whitsome

Blacksmiths.
Briggs, George, Swinton
Briggs, John, Swinton
Kinghorn, Abram, Whitsome

Boot and Shoe Makers.
Guthrie Brothers, Swinton
Henderson & Son, Swinton
Patterson, A., Whitsome
Patterson John, Post Office Swinton
Robertson, James, Horndean

Builders—see Joiners, &c.

Drapers—see Grocers &c.

Dressmakers.
Sprott, Miss, Swinton
Stenhouse, Miss Mary, Horndean

Farmers—see end of Directory.

Grocers and General Merchants.
Marked 'e' are also Drapers.
Chrystal, George, (and Tailor), Swinton
Craig, William, Swinton
Denholm, Robert, Swinton
Grieve Jas., Post Office Whitsome
e Hendry, William, Swinton
e M'Kenzie, William, Swinton
Middlemas, E., Whitsome
Rodgers, Mrs., Whitsome
Short, Mrs., Swinton
Whitelaw, William, Swinton
Wood, Margaret, Horndean

Hotels, Inns, and Posting Establishments.
Salmon Inn—William Wood, Horndean
Wheatsheaf Inn—John Chalmers, Swinton

Joiners, Builders, and Wrights.
Middlemas, Andrew, Whitsome
Spence, Archibald, Whitsome

Spence, David, Swinton
Stewart, Robert, Swinton

Stenhouse, William, Horndean
Thompson, William, Horndean

Saddler and Harness Maker.
Thompson, Richard J., (and Ironmonger), Swinton

Tailors and Clothiers.
Purves, John & Son, Swinton
Sives, David, Swinton
Young, William, Swinton

Miscellaneous.
Slater—George Rae, Swinton
Surgeon—F. J. Mackintosh, Swinton

THIRLSTANE—SEE LAUDER.
THORNTON—SEE BERWICK-ON-TWEED.
TWEEDMOUTH—SEE BERWICK-ON-TWEED.
TWIZEL—SEE BERWICK-ON-TWEED.

WESTRUTHER, HOUNDSLOW, AND NEIGHBOURHOODS.

WESTRUTHER is a parish in the Lammermoor district. The village is 32 miles S.E. of Edinburgh, 8 from Lauder, 6 W. by N, from Greenlaw, and 5 N. from Gordon. The parish contains 14,630 acres. Population 615. In this parish is the village of HOUNDSLOW.

Business Directory

Blacksmiths.
Brownlea, William, Westruther
Swanston, J., Houndslow

Farmers—see end of Directory.

Grocers and General Merchants.
Campbell, Ann, Westruther
Donaldson, James, Westruther
Lothian, A., Houndslow

Joiners and Wrights.
Gill, Thomas, Spottiswood
Mercer, A. & G., Houndslow
Ramage, Robert, Westruther

Miscellaneous.
Bootmaker — Robert Aldcoran, Westruther
Spirit Dealer—Thomas Mossman, Westruther
Tailor—G. Renton, Westruther

WHITSOME—SEE SWINTON.

FARMERS IN ROXBURGHSHIRE.

Ancrum District.

Beattie, Robert, Ashyburn
Blythe, Robert, Townhead
Brunton, James, Standhill
Davidson, George, (trus of), Sandystones
Davidson, George W. Clifton house
Drummond, A. & A., Longnewton
Elliot, John, Pinnacle
Fairbairn, John J., Greenend
Gillies, George, Chesterhall
Graham, Andrew S., Rawflat
Hymers William & John, Furlongs
Ingram, William, Copland
Jacks, Richard, West mains
Jeffrey, William, Belses mill
Knox, Bobert, Whitehouse
Mackay, Andrew, Springfield
Murray, Alexander, Barnhill
Ormiston, John, Palacehill
Paterson, John, Woodhill
Paton, Walter, New Belses
Pringle, Andrew, Belsesmuir
Rea, Andrew, junr., Chesters
Rutherford, James, Old Belses
Rutherford, William, Ancrum craig
Scott, John, Dudgeon
Stark, Andrew, Broom
Turnbull, James, Ancrum
Thomson, George, Hobton
Thomson, James, Croupyett
Weatherston, George, Wellrig

Denholm District.

Amos, George, Earlside
Ashcroft, Ann, Southberry fell
Ballantyne Robert E. & W. Middle
Beattie, George, Dykes
Bell, Alexander, Denholm
Blyth, Thomas, jr., Whitrigs
Blyth, Wm., (reps of), Whiteriggs
Borthwick, Alexander, Symieleuch
Brodie, Walter, Upper Tofts
Brydon, Walter, Winnington rigg
Bulman, Robert, Denholm haugh
Burns, Walter, Denholmhill
Davidson, John, (reps of), Adderstonshiel
Douglas, Captn. Palmer, Cavers
Dryden, John, Northberry field
Elliot, Robert, Cavers mains
Grieve, Robt. (reps of), Southfield
Haddon, Andrew, Honeyburn
Hamilton, William, Newmills
Inglis, Thomas, Nethertofts
Reid, John, Barns
Scott, Alexander, Kinninghall
Scott, William, Orchards
Smith, Thomas A. Kirkton
Taylor, William, Ashybank
Thornton, Robert, Shankend
Turnbull, William, Spittal
Turnbull, John, Acreknowe
Usher, Thomas, Courthills

Hawick District

IN HAWICK PARISH

Ballantyne, John, Sturches Mains
Burnett, Alexander, Greenside hall
Davidson Gilbert, Wester Boonlaw
Elliot, James, Burnhead
Elliot, W., (reps. of), Goldielands
Easton, George, Overhall
Elliot, Peter, Longbaulk
Grierson, Robert, Whitchester
Grieve, Charles J,, Branxholm park
Grieve, James, Linton
Grieve, John & James, Southfield
Grieve, Robert, (reps. of), Branxholmbraes
Glendinning, Scott, Boghall
Hall, Thomas C,, Scawmill
Hislop, Joha, Carilaw
Hogg, Mrs. Janet, Crumhaugh hill
Home, George, Newmill
Knox, David, Martin's house
Learmouth, Henry, Greenbraeheads
Lees, James, Fenwick
Lees, Richard, Drinkstone
Oliver, John, Borthaugh
Oliver, John, Wiltonburn
Purdom, Charles M., Whitehaugh
Reid, Thomas & Son, St. Leonards
Scott, Robert & Walter, Blackcleuch
Scott, Andrew, Newton
Scott, Walter, Pilmuir
Simpson, Walter, Flex
Sheil, James & Rutherford, Midshiells

Thomson, Walter, Muirfield

IN HOBKIRK PARISH.

Barrie, Walter, Stonedge
Bell, Rebert, Town o' Rule
Brockie, Thomas, Hawthornside
Bruce, Robert, Harwood
Hislop, William, Harwood
Mather, John A., Hallrule
M'Kinnon, Peter, Gatehousecote
Mein, J. & J., Billerwell
Oliver, Mrs. Agnes, Greenriver
Paterson, John S., Wauchope
Purves, George, Easter Fodderlie
Rewooick, Charles, Braidhaugh
Smith, Thomas, Tythehouse
Tancred, George, Bonchester
Taylor, William, Howahill
Turnbull, Walter, Midburn
Waugh, John, Highend
Young, Walter, Hartshaugh

IN MINTO PARISH.

Bell, Robert Horsley hill
Brunton, James, Standhill
Drawhill, William, Huntlaw
Hall, William P., Hassendean bank
Maxwell, John S. H., Teviotbank
Murray, Ralph, Barnhills
Nichol, George, Newlands
Rodger, James, Cleuchhead
Scott, John, Hassendean Common
Shiell, Rutherford, Hassendean
Tait, Charles, Deanfoot
Watson, Robert & Robert, junr., Townhead

IN ROBERTON PARISH.

Beattie, John, Todshawhaugh
Blythe, Thomas, Borthwickshiels
Brydon, John, Woodburn
Burnet Francis & George Bellendean
Davies Miss Hannah, Wolfcleuch-head
Hobkirk, James, Broadhaugh
Hunter, Robert, Chapel hill
Moffat, James, Craik
Nichol, William, Philhope
Oliver, John, Highchesters
Oliver, William M,, Howpasley
Riddell, William, E. & W. Park-hill
Scott, Charles, Milsington

IN TEVIOT HEAD PARISH.

Aitchison, William, Linhope
Borthwick J. & J. M. Limeycleuch
Bruce, Robert, Priesthaugh
Cairns, Thomas, Buiks
Elliot, Miss Margt., Cotterscleuch
Elliot, James, Ramseycleuchburn
Govanlock Robert, (reps of), Teind-side
Grieve, Miss Marion, Skelfhill
Hislop, William, Harwood
Hobkirk, James, Broadhaugh
Martin, John & John junr., Carlenrigg
Scott, Robert & Walter, Falnash
Stevenson, John M., & William, Commonside
Tullie, James & John, Bowan hill
Turnbull, Archibald, North house
Turnbull Mrs. Apalina Rashiegrain
Welsh, Thomas, (reps of) Hislop

Jedburgh District.

IN JEDBURGH PARISH.

Bathgate, Robert, Bankend
Davidson, Richard, Swinnie
Bell, J. & J., Lanton mill
Black, George, Monklaw
Black, James G., Netherwells
Brown, John, Hundalee
Brunton & Daykins, Howden
Charleston, Thos. T., Brundenlaws
Dodds, Thomas, Hardenpeal
Dodd, Henry, Overton hush
Dodds, John C., Woodend
Douglas, Andrew, Edgerstontofts
Ferguson, John, Plesants
Hall, John, Earlshaugh
Halliwell, John, Tudhope
Halliwell, John, Todlaw
Johnston, James S., Mossburnford
Laing, Robert, Kersheugh
Mein, James, A. W., Hunthill
Minto, George, Camphouse
Neil, James, Larkhall
Neill, Robert, Sharp law
Nichol, Robert & Son, Thickside
Ormiston, Samuel, Ulston
Peter, John S., Linthaughlee
Rae, John, Cleithaugh
Richardson Alexander, Linton craig
Rutherfurd, William, A. O. Edgerston house

Shiel, James, Old Jedwart
Stedman, James, Timpendean
Storie, James & Son, Remiston
Sword, Robert & Son, Lochend
Sword, John R., Woodend
Telfer, Charles, Edgerston rigg
Tully, Andrew & James, New mill
Wilson, Alexander, Hundelee
Young, William & Samuel, Bonjedward

IN BEDRULE PARISH.

Bell, David, Lanton
Pott, Gideon, Knowesouth
Scott, Mrs Mary A., Newton
Simpson, George (reps. of), Bedrule

IN CRAILING PARISH.

Dodd, Nicholas, West Nisbet
Ord, John (reps. of), Upper Nisbet
Pringle, John, East Nisbet
Rutherford, Walter, Crailing, Tofts
Scott, John, Ploughlands
Spence, Peter, Bracheads
Waddel, Alexander, Palace

IN HOWNAM PARISH.

Lilie, John, East Grange
Rae, William, Bearhope
Ross, Richard, Upper Chatto
Shiell, Ann, James & George, Hownam mains
Shiell, Robert, Yett
Simpson, John, Bughtrigg
Smith, Adam, Hownam, Howegate
Turnbull, James (reps. of) Hownam Grange
Turnbull, M. & Sons, Sharplaw
Watson, William, Chester house
Wyllie, James, Over Whitton

IN OXNAM PARISH.

Aitchison, A. & W., Easter Samieston
Brodie, Alexander, Swinside hall
Clay, John, Plenderleith
Coltherd Brothers, Dolphinston
Davidson, Thomas, Newbigging bush
Douglas, George, Wester Hyndhope
Douglas, John, Swinside townfoot
Elliot, John, Easter Hyndhope
Elliot, Robert, Riccalton
Gray, Adam, Kirkstyle
Hall, James, Newbigging birks
Johnston, William L., Oxnam neuk
Murray, Thomas, Falla
Riddell, William, Cappuck
Scott, Andrew, Middleknowes
Simson, John, Oxnam row
Stavart, Archibald, Cunzierton
Wylie, James, Cleughside
Wylie, James senr. & junr., Newbiggings

IN SOUTHDEAN PARISH.

Balfour, William, Wester houses
Bruce, Peter & Robert, Wester Foderlie
Common, James, Dykeraw
Douglas, George, Ruletownhead
Gibson, William, Woodhouse
Henry, William, Doorpool
Inglis, Robert, Walhoplee
Maben, William, Bairnkine
Macpherson, Donald, Wolflee
Mein, Thomas, Broomhill
Ord, Andrew, Falside
Purves, George and John, Easter Fodderlie
Roberton, Robert, Lustruther
Robson, John, Southdean Glebe
Scott, Thomas S. R., Lethan
Telfer, William, Roundabouts
Thornton, Thomas Ord, Hyndlee
Turner, James, Mervinslaw
Wallace, John, Chesters

Kelso Districts.

IN ECKFORD PARISH.

Clark, George B., Marchcleugh
Dow, John, Mainhouse
Greg, Thomas, Wooden
Hay, Athol S., Marlfield
Purdom, James, Blinkbonny
Scott, George, Mossower
Scott, John (reps. of), Cessford
Sinclair, C. G., Grahamslaw
Smith, Ralph C., Ormiston Mains

IN EDNAM PARISH.

Blair, John & David, Springhall
Hamilton, Gavinton, Highbridgehall
Ross, Richard, Newtonlees
Rutherford, Andw. & Peter, Ednam

Stevenson, William, Edenmouth
Tully, James. Fernhill
Turnbull, John, Hendersyde
Whitehead, George, Houndridge

IN KELSO PARISH

Brodie Alexander, Easter Muirdean
Douglas, Alexander, Wooden
Cowe, John, Kaimknowe
Kay, Robert, Softlaw
Montgomery, Mrs. Jane, Pinnacle-hill
Scott, James, Softlaw, East Mains
Scott, Robert. Spylaw
Scott, Robert, Maison Dieu
Smith, John, Galalaw
Tilley, James, Fairyhill
Tully, Mrs. Elizabeth, Wallacenick
Turnbull, John, jr., Berryhill
Watson, William, Softlaw

IN MAKERSTOUN PARISH.

Gibson, Thomas, Haymount
Massey, John, Manor hall
Murray, William Robert, Charter-house
Oliver, Adam & Thomas, Stodrig
Purves, James, Suckleridge
Rae, Robert, Muirdean
Scott, Hugh, Home
Watson, John, Greatridge Hall

IN ROXBURGH PARISH.

Broomfield, Robert, Sunlaws Hill
Dunn, David, Roxburgh Mains
Hogarth, John, Heiton Mill
Logan, Peter, Roxburgh
Mein, Charles, Roxburgh Barns
Murray, William, The Trows
Robertson, John, Kers Mains
Robertson, Robert, Ladyrig
Scott, Robert, Heiton, East Mains
Scott, William, Whitehill
Sinclair, C. G., Grahamslaw
Stenhouse J., Roxburgh, Newtown
Thomson, William H., Over Rox-burgh
Turnbull, John, Sunlaws Mill

IN SMAILHOLM PARISH.

Balmer, William, Millerstein
Forsyth, Robert, New Smailholm
Hayes, Robert & James, Covehouse
Hewitt, George, Sandy knowe
Ormiston, Wm., Smailholm mains
Purves, James, Town farm
Riddell, John, Spotmains
Storie, Thomas, Girnick
Wood, John & William, Rachelfield

IN SPROUSTON PARISH.

Clay, John, Kirkchester
Craig, John, Whitemore ha'
Dunn, William, Redden
Hunter, John, Lempithaw
Ogleby, George, Oldfield
Smith, William, Windywalls
Stark, Jesse, Mellerdean
Tully, James, Kerse Quarter
Turnbull, James, Eastfield
Watson, George, Lurdenlaw
White, Alexander, Knottylees

IN STITCHEL PARISH.

Bain, William & Thomas, Legars
Henderson, Thomas, Baillieknowe
Logan Brothers, Hume hall
Rae, Robert, Caldonbrae
Shiel, Andrew, Sweethope
Sinclair, Joseph, Eastfield
Wilson, William, Runningburn
Wood, John, Home farm

Lilliesleaf District.

IN LILLIESLEAF PARISH.

Alexander, George, Chapelmoor
Anderson, William, Cotfield
Bain, William & James, Bewlie hill
Elliot, Andrew, Hermiston
Elliot, Alexander, Harelaw
Elliot, James, Newhouse
Elliot, John, Middles
Gray, John, Firth
Hislop, Robert, Raperlaw
Hislop, Walter, Netherlaw
Hogg, George, West Riddell
Inglis, William, Boosmill
Johnston, Elizabeth, Hillhead
Newton, George, Greenhouse
Smith, Adam, Bewlie mains
Smith, George, Friarshaws
Stark, Andrew, Craggs
Sykes, James, West end
Tinline, George, Bellfield
Turnbull, James, Easter Lilliesleaf
Young, William, Dunstane

IN BOWDEN PARISH.

Ainslie, Thomas, Curling
Ainslie, James, Friarshaw muir
Anderson, James, Kaeside
Anderson, John, Midlem
Ballinghall, George, Clairlaw
Blaikie, William L., Holydean
Darling, John, Midlem
Dryden, George & James, Eastfield
Dryden, Gavin, Midlemmuir
Gray, Adam, Midlem castle
Head, George, Bowdenmoor
Inglis, James, Howdshall
Henderson, James, Broomilees
Jeffrey, David, Shawburn
Laidlaw, John, Kippilaw
Lambert, James, Midlem
Madder, James, Fanghill
Neill Alexander, Midlem
Ormiston, Walter. Langside
Roxburgh Thomas, Kippilaw mains
Russell, George, (trns of) Whitelee
Scott, John, Templehall
Scott, William, Hayfield
Smith, Adam, Eildon hills
Sword, William, Midlem
Thomson, George, Bowden
Thomson, Thomas, Bowden

Melrose District.

IN MELROSE PARISH

Anderson, James, Kaeside
Anderson, James, Friarshaugh
Blackie, William, S. Blainslie
Blackie, William, Nether Blainslie
Bone, Alexander, Craigsford
Brown, John, Newstead
Brown, Robert, Gattonside
Bruce, John, Easter Langlee
Clyde, Hugh, Bluecairn
Cochrane, Adam L., Sunnyside
Cossar, Thomas, Mosshouses
Curl, Alexander, Millmount
Davidson, William, Colinslie
Dickieson, John, Eildon
Dodds' Ralph & William, Overlangslaw
Elliot, John, Chapel mains
Fell, John, Leaderfoot
Fleming, John, Craigsford mains
Ford J. & J. & A., Middle Blainslie
Ford, Alexander, Mid Blainslie
Graham, Andrew, Newhouses
Grieve, William & Andrew, Drygrangemains
Gladstone, John & James, Wester Langlee
Hamilton George, Abbey hotel
Henderson, James, Broomilees
Hope, David, Easterhouse byres
Hogarth, James, Newtown
Hogg, George, New Blainslie
Hogg, William, Clackmae
Hume, Thomas, Nether Blainslie
Kidd, Henry, Lowoodmains
Lees, Andrew, Buckholm
Little, James, Kittyfield
Lunn, John & Robert, Middle Blainslie
Lunn, John, Upper Blainslie
Newton, William & James, Langlee mains
Nichol, Thomas, Darnick
Nisbet, Alexander, Allanshaws
Oliver, Robert, Bridgend
Ormiston, Adam, Tweedbank
Porteous, Ronald, Newtown
Porteous, Thomas, Leaderfoot
Rae, James, Colinslie hill
Renton Peter Sorrowlessfield mains
Riddell, James, Newstead
Roberts, George, Whitelee
Robertson, John, Cotgreen
Robertson. William, Hoebridge
Shiel, William, Gattonside
Smith, Adam, Dingleton mains
Spottiswoode, Robert, Allerley mains
Swinton, Thomas, Eildon mains
Swan, John & Son, Norton hall
Waldie, John, Gattonside
Waugh, Alexander, Gattonside
Young George B. Weterhouse byres
Young, William, Halkburn

Newcastleton District.

IN CASTLETON PARISH.

Armstrong, James, Riccarton
Barton, John, Burnmouth
Beattie, John, Braidlie
Davidson, Isaac, Castleton
Dodd, John T., Riccarton
Elliot, John, The Flatt
Elliot, Robert & Son, Powiesholm
Elliot, William, Mangerton
Elliot, James M., Kirkdean

Fenwick, Frank, Foulsheil
Fleming, Andrew & John, Roan
Foster, Robert, Whithaugh
Goodfellow, Peter, Mains
Hall, David, Larriston
Halliday, John, Demainholm
Holiday, John, Dinlabyre
Kyle, Wm & Thos, Leeshaugh
Kyle, James, Sorbietrees
Nichol, William, Dinley
Mason, Thomas, Milnholm
Murray, David, (reps. of), Whisgills
Paterson, James, Redbeugh
Potts, William, Under Burnmouth
Robson, Alexander, Yett
Routledge, Richard, Gorrenberry
Stavart, Archibald M., Saughtrees
Turnbull, Andrew & Thomas, South Greenholm
Turnbull, William & John, Tweedenside

St. Boswells District.

IN ST. BOSWELLS PARISH.

Bell, William, Laretburn
Dodds, Thomas, Weirgate mains
Dove, George, Crossflat
Fairbairn & Dodds, Hiltonshill
Fairbairn, John F., Fens
Graham, Charles, Whinfield
Hogarth, James & Son, Newtown
Porteous, Ronald, Hawkslee
Rae, James, Temple
Scott, Walter, Bankhead
Simpson, William, Merwick
Somerville, Robert, Charlesfield
Swan, John & Sons, Whitehill
Thomson, Andrew, Mainhill
Trees, George, Whitelee
White, George, Northfield
Wilson, James, Camieston
Wight, Peter, St. Boswells
Young, Robert, Thornielaw

IN MAXTON PARISH.

Bell, John, Ploughlands
Cunningham, Charles J., Muirhouselaw
Dove, George, West end
Porteous, Ronald, East-end
Rae, Robert, Morridghall
Ross Willm. & Richard, Rutherford
Smith, Thomas, Riddletonhill
Wight, Peter, Maxton

Yetholm District.

IN MOREBATTLE PARISH.

Cunningham, Charles John, The Tofts
Elliot, Robert Henry, Clifton
Elliot, Thomas, Attonburn
Howie, Thomas, Gateshaw
Johnstone, Alexander, Primside
Laurie, James & Thomas Woodside
Lillie, John, Burnfoot
Lillie, John C., Cliftoncote
Logan, Abraham, Whitton
Pearson, William S., Otterburn
Richardson, James (trus. of), Primside
Shiell, Robert, Sourhope
Smith, George (reps. of), Shielstock braes.
Smith, James, Belford
Smith, James R. C., Mowhaugh

IN YETHOLM PARISH.

Briggs, Hugh & Alexander, Lochtower
Bruce, Robert, Halterburn head
Calder, Adam, Halterburn
Dodds, John C. & Robert, Yetholm
Elliot, Robert Hy., Yetholm
Gowanlock, James, Duncan haugh
Guthrie, William, Hayhope
Hogg, William, Old Graden
Newton, James, Curbarn
Riddell, Adam, Greenlees
Scott, Alexander, Venchen
Scott, —., New Graden
Smith, John, Crookedshaws

IN LINTON PARISH.

Elliot, Robert Henry, Clifton park
Hogarth, James, Linton Bankhead
Murray, James, Linton
Oliver, Capt. William, Hoselaw mains
Scott, George & John, Frogden

FARMERS IN SELKIRKSHIRE.

Galashiels District.

Boyd, William B., Faldonside
Brownlee, James, Galashiels
Brydon, Adam, Netherbarns
Douglas, James, Lindean
Elliot, Andrew T., Newhall
Elliot, John, Meigle, Caddonfoot
Elliot, Walter, Hollybush
Erskine, Charles, Nether Whitlaw
Gladstone, John & James. Galabrig
Grieve, James, Fernalee
Hall, Robert, Kilnknowe
Hogarth, James, Galashiels
Laurence Bros., Caddonmill
Riddell, John, Rink
Scott, Wm. & Helen, Mossilie
Taylor, William, Over Whitlaw
Wyllie, James, Langhaugh mains

Selkirk District.

PARISH OF SELKIRK.

Bruce, James, South Common
Cleghorn, W. & T., Greenhead
Douglas, James, Bridgeheugh
Dunlop, Charles Walter, Whitemuirhall
Gifford, Thomas Linglie
Glendinning, Michael, Williamhope
Graham, John, Greenhill
Graham, Robert, Bridgelands
Grieve, J. & J., Howden
Hill, Thomas, Walter and John, Harehead
Inglis, John, Howdshall
Lang, Hugh M., Broadmeadows
Lindsay, William, Shaw mount
Linton, James, Hartwoodmyres
Linton, Simeon, Oakwood
Mitchell, Thomas, Howford
Plummer, Charles H. S., Sunderland hall
Pringle, Alexander, Yair
Pringle, Joshua & Thomas, Philiphaugh
Redpath, George, Broomhill
Redpath, James, Old mill
Turnbull, James, Fauldshope
Wilson, Thomas, The Shaw
Young, James, Smedheugh

PARISH OF KIRKHOPE.

Aitchison, William, Helmburn
Anderson, Thomas S., Ettrickshaw
Boston, James, Easter Deloraine
Brown, Adam, Hyndhope
Brydon, Robert & William, Whitehillshiels
Graham, George, Drycleuchlee
Grieve, Robert, Outer Huntly
Mitchell, James, Newburgh
Mitchell, Thomas (trus. of), Kirkhope
Mitchell, Thomas, Howford
Muirdead, Wm., Gavin, and Hugh, Gilmanscleuch
Scott, John, Wester Deloraine
Scott, Thomas & James, Singlie
Scott, Thomas, Langhope
Turnbull, James, Fauldshope

PARISH OE ETTRICK.

Aitchison, Wm. (reps of) Glenkerry
Anderson, James, Braidgarhill
Blake, Andrew, Shorthope
Brydon, George, Scabcleuch
Brydone, William, Annelshope
Dalgliesh, Simon, Potburn
Davidson, Gilbert, Ropelawshiel
Graham, Thomas, Wardlaw
Grieve, Charles J, Easter Buccleuch
Grieve, John & J, Wester Buccleuch
Grieve, William, Deephope
Howatson, John L., Ramsaycleuch
Kennedy, David, Chapelhope
Laidlaw, Alexander, The Gair
Little, John, Gamescleuch
Nichol, Thomas & James, Corslee
Paterson, John, Thirlstanehope
Pennycook, Robina, Over
Pott, George, Nether Pawhope
Purdom, Findlay, Tushielaw
Rutherford, Wm. & Thos., Riskenhope
Scott, Henry, Midgehope
Scott, Thomas, Cossar hill

PARISH OF ASHKIRK.

Bell, William S., The Woll
Cook, Andrew, Castleside
Davidson, John, Headshaw

Douglas, John, Easter Esenside
Easton, Andrew, (trus. of) Todrig
Elliot, James, Sheelwood
Graham, John, Greenhill
Gray, John, Ashkirktown
Grieve, James, North Synton
Grieve, William, Synton
Heard, George, Wester Essenside
Lawson, D. & T., Clerklands
M'Dool, Thomas & John, Ashkirk
Murray, William, Whitslaid
Paton, Edwyn, D., Synton
Pattison, Walter, Dimple knowe
Scott, James, Burnfoot
Scott, John C., Synton
Thomson, John, Synton mains

PARISH OF YARROW.

Anderson, James & John, Crosscleuch
Anderson, John, Cramilt
Barrie, Walter, Sundhope
Buccleuch, Duke of, Carterhaugh
Calder, Adam, Blackhouse
Cunningham, Charles J., Berrybush
Doeg, Robert Edwin, Tinnis
Douglas, James, George, & Archd., Catslackburn
Gibson, William, East Plora
Graham, William, Fawburnhead
Laidlaw, James, Bowerhope
Lindsay, James V., Whitehope
Linton, Andrew, Mounthanger
Linton, S. & S., Kirkstead
Macfarlane, James, Ashiestiel
Mitchell, James & John, Hawthorn
Mitchell, James, Henderland
Muir, George W., Shuttinglees
Muir, J. & G. W., Dryhope
Pretsell, J. & J. (reps. of), Syart
Scott, Alexander, Ladhope
Scott, Robert, Elibank
Tennant, Edward P., Birks of Evelane
Turnbull, Archibald, Eldinhope
Thorburn, William, Meggethead

FARMERS IN PEEBLESSHIRE.

Peebles District.

PARISH OF BROUGHTON, GLENHOLM AND KILBUCHO.

Alexander, Thomas & John, Burnfoot
Baxter, James & Thomas, Galzeat
Clark, Mrs G., Gosland
Clark, Thomas, Thriepland
Fowler, Margaret, Wrae
Gairns, Alexander, Cloverhill
Galbraith, Alexander, Rachan
Home, William, Kilbucho
Home, William, Southside
Hope, James, Kilbucho
Kay, James, Comlees
Kitchen, John, Parkgatestone
Lindsay, Mrs Margt., Howslack
Lochie, Thomas, Blendewing
Logan, Robert, Knowehead
Masterton, Ebenezer, Broughton green
Masterton, John, Bamphlat
Muirhead, Robert, Kilbucho
Newbigging, John, Langlaw hill
Newbigging, Thomas, Crossstone
Renwick Thomas Broughton knowe
Ritchie, G., Cardon
Todd, Thomas & James Bilbucho mains
Todd, J., Mitchellhill
Tudhope, John, Broughton place
Wilson, James, Burnetland

PARISH OF EDDLESTON.

Aitken, Thomas, Stewarton
Ballantyne, William, Wormiston
Cairns, J. & W., Burnfoot
Calvert, James, Burnhead
Douglas, George, Early pier
Ellis, James, Waterhead
Forrest, William, Harehope
Greenshiels, James, Cloich
Inch, William, Shiplaw
Kerr, John (reps. of), Westloch
Ketchin, John, Longcote
Mackenzie, Colin J, Partmore
Melville, Mrs. Margt., Darnhall mains

Minto, David F., Glebe
Patterson, John, Huttonknowe
Smart, John C., Cowieslynn
Stuart, Benjamin, Harcus
Tudhope, W. & J., Milkieston

PARISH OF DRUMMELZIER.

Aitken, William, Drummelzier pl
Dickson, William L., Drummelzier haugh
Lindsay, William F., E. & W., Stanhope
Martin, William, Dalwick
Mitchell, Thomson, Polwood
Stoddard, Thomas T., Patervan
Stuart, Walter, Kingledores

PARISH OF KIRKURD.

Noble, A. & W., Lochurd
Sanderson Adam, Netherurd mains, west
White, Mrs Jane A., Kirkurd

PARISHES OF LYNE AND MEGGET.

Purdie, James G., Hamildean
Ritchie, William, Lyne

PARISH OF MANOR.

Davidson, William, Kirkton
Hamilton, Andrew, Glenrath
Hamilton, William, Manorhead
Jeffrey, T. & J., Haswellsykes
Lambie, Thomas, Castlehill
Linton, Simon, Cademuir
Melrose, James, Bellanridge
More, James, Robert, and Alexander, Woodhouse
Wotherspoon, Thomas, Hindleshope

PARISH OF PEEBLES.

Ballantine, William, Upper Kidston
Cairns, John, Winkston
Cairns, William & John, Jedderfield
Erskine, Adml., Venlaw house
Fleming, William, Soonhope
Forrester, George & Thomas, Edston
Frier, M. & J., Kidston
Hay, Sir J. A. (reps. of), Haystoun
Hunter, James (reps of), Standalane
Macpherson & White, Heathpool-common
Macpherson, D. & D., Kirklands
Macpherson, Donald, Edderston
Paterson, William, Crookston
Patrick, A. & J., Mailingsland
Russell, Jas. (reps. of), Bonnington
Scott, James, Whitehaugh
Thom, Alexander, Chapel hill
Watson, James, Elliottspark

PARISH OF SKIRLING.

Alexander, John, Skirling
Brown, James, Candyburn
Clarkson, Alexander, Skirling
Dempster, James, Skirling
Frame, George, Clinwell
Gavin, Lawrie, Skirling mains
Henshilwood, George, Skirling
Noble, John, Skirling craigs
Noble, Robert, Skirling
Renwick, William, Skirling
Rough, John, Kirklawhill
Russell, John, South mains
Somerville, William, Skirling
Watson, James, Townhead
Watson, John, Muirburn

PARISH OF STOBO.

Gracie, Charles A., Easter Happrew
Inch, Robert, Easterknowe
Jackson, J, & J., Altarstone
Lindsay, Alexander B., Dreva
Tudhope & Lawson, Easter Dalwick
Turner, James, Wester Happrew

PARISH OF TWEEDSMUIR

Carruthers, John, Fruid
Gunn, Alexander, Crook
Hunter J. & W. (reps of) Glenbreck
Lyall, David, Hawkshaw
Montgomery, Sir G. G., Menzion
Scott, Alexander, Fingland
Thomson, Messrs, Ganoshope
Stodart, Thomas, Oliver
Thorburn, Walter, M.P., Badlieu
Thorburn, William, Talla
Tweedie, Alexander, Hearthstane
Watson, James, Tweedshaws
Welso, T., (trus of), Carcerhope

PARISH OF INNERLEITHEN.

Anderson, George, Nether Pirn
Brydon, A. & L., Tweed bank
Cunningham, George M., Whithop

Elliot, Walter, & Murray, John, Colquhar
Graham, William, Horsbrugh castle
Grieve, James, Blackhope byres
Hogg, James, The Lee
Kitchen Jas. P., Nether Horsburgh
Laidlaw, Walter, Holylee
Lennie, Alexander, St. Ronans
Martin, John, Caberston
Roxburgh, Mrs. Cath., Thornilee
Tait, William, Kirklands
Tait, W. & J.. Common

PARISH OF TRAQUAIR.

Beattie, Walter, Glenlude
Black, W. C., (reps of), Kailzie
Borthwick, James, Scotsmill
Dickson, William, Damhead
Gibson, John, Howford
Gibson, Thomas, Traquair
Gibson, William, Juniper bank
Gibson, William, West Bold
Gouinlock, Walter, Traquair knowe
Graham, William, Cardrona mains
Muir, George, W., Kirkhouse
Reid, Walter, Haughead

West Linton District.

PARISH OF WEST LINTON.

Adams, William, Fairslock
Alexander, William, Mendick
Barr, Alexander, Hartside
Barr, William, Hyndford
Bartleman, Archibald, Blyth
Cranston, James, Rutherfordmains
Dickson, George, (reps of), Kippet
Dobie, John, Deanfoot
Ferguson, George, Lintonbank
Finlayson, James, Medwyn mains
Finlayson, Peter, Castlelaw
Gibbon, James, Felton
Gordon, Charles, Hallmyre
Hamilton, William, Kittley knowe
Hardie, Alexander, West mains
Hunter, Walter, Tayhaugh
Kerr, John, N. Slipperfield
Lawson, William, Ingraston
Millar, William, S. Slipperfield
Murdock, David, Harlowinner
Nobles John, Farliehope
Robertson, Alexander, Noblehall
Stoddart, Mrs. Margt., Carlops
Tweedale, Robert, Howison hall
Watson, James, Blyth bank
Watson, William, Whitfield
Weir, Thomas, Robinsland
Young, George W. West Linton

PARISH OF NEWLANDS.

Ballantyne, John, Leadburn
Brown, Adam, Drochil
Brown, Thomas, Noblehouse
Carrick, John, Scotstonrig
Crighton, Mungo, Lamancha
Gibson-Carmichael, Geo., Callands
Hogg, Robert, Leadburn
Hume, John, Lamancha
Johnston, John, Scotston
Kerr, John, Leadburn
Lewis, Alexander, Lamancha
Murray, William, Lamancha
Muir, James. Romanno mains
Pate, William, Leadburn
Pate, Samuel, Macbie hill
Paterson, Alexander, Leadburn
Reid, James, Leadburn
Ross. John, Lamancha
Small, James, Scotstonknowe
Smith, George, Whim
Sommerville, James, Lamancha
Steel, —., Stevenston
Stewart, James, Romanno
Stewart, Thomas, E., Leadburn
Story, Daniel F., Flemington
Swinton, Adam, Leadburn
Thomson, Mrs. Anne, Leadburn
Wilson, William, Leadburn
Yorkston, James, Leadburn
Yeats, John, Lamancha

FARMERS IN HADDINGTONSHIRE.

Aberlady District.

Auld, Robert, Lochhill
Finlayson, William, Redhouse
Glendinning, James, Ballincrieff
Hope, Henry W., Luffness Mains
M'Laren, John, Ballincrieff
Murray, Alexander, Ballincrieff mains
Punton, Alexander, Aberlady mains
Sinclair, Gabriel, Aberlady
Toderick, Archibald, Spittal

Athelstaneford District,

Binnie, Thomas, Saltcoats
Gillespie, William, Athelstaneford mains
Mason, William G., West Fortune
Ogilvy, Mrs., Archerfield
Reid, James, Drem
Ronaldson, George, Kilduff mains
Skirving, Miss Helen, Muirton
Wath, James, Newmains

Dirleton District.

Dobbie, Alexander, M., Fenton
Donald, Andrew, Queenstonbank
Ford, William, Fenton Barns
Handyside, John B., West Fenton
Inch, John, Congalton, N. Berwick
Kerr, William, Ferrygate
Lees, John, Archerfield
Moffat, Mrs J., Williamston
Player, John, Muirfield
Robertson, James F., Newhouse
Thomson, Thomas D., Craigville

Dunbar District.

IN DUNBAR.

Anderson, George B., Meikle Pinkerton
Cowan, Walter, Summerfield
Cunningham, St Clair, Hedderwick hill
Craik, James, Friarscroft
Davidson, John and James, Wood Hall
Dods, George, Hedderwick
Fraser, John H., East Pinkerton
Fysche, Peter, Newtonlees
Hope, Harry, Oxwell mains
Hope, James, East Basns
Nelson, John, West Barns
Stobo, David, North Belton
Turnbull, Phipps., West Pinkerton
Wallace, Forbes, South Belton
Waugh, Robert (trust of), Eweford
White, George, Howmuir

IN SPOTT.

Anderson, George B., Boonslie
Anderson, James W. H., Pleasant
Bayley, Isaac F., Halls
Caverhill, J. & A., Bothwell
Murray, George, Brunt
Nelson, George, Wester Broomhouse
Stein, Mrs Mary J., Easter Broomhouse
Turnbull, Phipps., Pathhead
Watt, Miss A., Easter Doon

East Linton District.

IN GARVALD AND BARO.

Bruce, John & Robert, Newlands
Clapperton, James, Garvald mains
Edgar, Robert, Baro
Harper, James D., Snawdon
Kinnaird, John Andrew, Garvald Grange
Scouter, William, Garvald
Shiels, Robert, Carfrae
Stewart, John, Sanderlane
Wyllie, Alexander, Quarryford
Wyllie, Andrew, The Mains

IN PRESTONKIRK.

Aitken, George, Traprain
Bowe, John H., Drylawhill
Calder, Robert, Cardennis
Gray, William, Brownrigg
Haldane, Robert, Phantassie
Jamieson, James M., Beanston
Lee, Joseph, Markle
Mark, James, Sunnyside
Middlemas, A. R. & T., Crauchie
Pringle, John R., Luggate
Robertson, James, Beanston mains
Wallace, John, Over Hailes
Welsh, Alexander, Waughton
Whyte, Alexander, Nether Hailes

IN STENTON.

Hardie, J. & D., Bielgrange
Elliott, Walter, Pitcox
Jeffrey, James, Dewchrie
M'Gregor, John, Little Spott
Ogilvy, H. T. N. H., Beesknowe
Purves, Andrew, Preesmennan
Rankin, John, Ruchlaw, W. Mains
Stewart, Alexander, Meiklerigg
Turnbull, Phipps, Pathhead

IN WHITEKIRK.

Arthur, William, Stonelaw
Clark, James, Kirkland hill
Dale, Thomas, Scoughall
Ewart, Henry, The Lochs
Hope, Thomas P., Whitekirk
Howden, Mrs., Lawhead

IN WHITTINGHAME.

Darling, James, Priestlaw
Fortune, James, Stoneypath Tower
Kinnaird, James, Yarrow
Kinnaird, John, New Mains
Pringle, John & Robert, Luggate
Robson, John, Mayshiel
Smith, Charles & E. H., Papple
Stewart, Frank, Whitelaw
Stewart, John, Stoneypath

Fala and Soutra District.

IN FALA AND SOUTRA.

Allan, John, Fala-dam
Burton, James, Fala hall
Jones, John, Soutra mains
Pate, James, Soutra mains
Prentice, William, Fala mains

IN HUMBIE.

Burton, James, Boughtknowe
Inch, Adam, Pogbie
Pate, James, Mavishall
Ramsey, James, Newmains
Sharp, John, Leaston
Tod, William, Stobshiels

Gifford District.

Botram, Andrew, Townhead
Glendinning, George, R., Kidlaw
Hay, Alexander, Giffordvale
Little, Adam, Longyester
Matthison, Adam, Leehouses
Robertson, Alexander, Gifford
Wilson, James, & Robert, Sheriff side
Wood, Robert, Bankrug
Wyllie, Alexander, Longnewton

Haddington District.

IN BOLTON PARISH.

Clark, George D., Eaglescairnie
Maxwell, William, Cauldshiel
Nichol, T. & W., Under Bolton
Pringle, James, Upper Bolton
Sharp, John G., Ewingston
Shiel, George, Pilmuir
Stewart, Alex., Marvington
Trotter, George, Kirkland

IN HADDINGTON PARISH.

Ainslie, M. & M. S., Huntington
Alexander, Andrew M., Heathery hall
Andrew, Hugh, Lennox love
Barr, J., Clerkington
Briggs, Francis, Myreside
Brown, Malcolm, Ugston
Dignell, James, Blackhouse
Durie, John (trus. of) Barneymains
Elder, Hugh, East Bearfood
Elder, Thomas, Stevenson mains
Gibson, Walter, Compton
Gibson, William B., W. Coalston-mains
Golightly, Robert, Abbey
Irving, William, Amisfield mains
Haddingtonshire Lunacy Board, Hawthornbank mains
Howden, W. & A., Barberfield
Kirk, T. & J., Byres
Lawrie, James, Monkrigg
Millar, Daniel, West Garleton
Osborne, Walter (trus. of), Letham mains
Pringle, James, Harperdean
Reid, Henry, Gladshot
Riddell, George, Mungoswell
Steven, John, Begbie
Torry, George, Clerkingtonmains
Turnbull, W. M. & J., Gateside
Turnbull, William, Spittalrig
Tweedie, Alexander, Coats
Ure, John, Abbey mains
White, Thomas, Blinkbonny
Wilson, J. & S., Seggarsdean
Wyllie, Patrick, Westfield

IN MORHAM.

Ainslie, John jr., Morham mains
Blair, Thomas, Northrigg
Dickson, John, Morham muir
Dodds, John, Renton hill
Drysdale, Alexander, Mainshill
Wilson, James, Standingstone

Innerwick District.

Binnie, John, Oldhamstocks
Binnie, William A., Birnieknowe
Broadwood, Thomas, Crawhill
Brodie, James, Thornton loch
Caverhill, Andrew. Crichness Duns
Christison, William, Branxton
Christison, William, Lawfield
Clark, T. & R., Cromwell hall
Davidson, John, Woodhall
Clark, T. & R., Oldhamstock mains
Elliott, T. W. & W., Harehead, Duns
Foggo, George, Innerwick
Gregor, Charles E., Innerwick
Hunter, Richard, Thurston
Nelson, Charles, Skateraw
Riddell, William, Cocklaw
Smith, Alexander, Moneynut
Wilson. John, Oldhamstocks
Wyllie, James, Elmscleugh

North Berwick District.

Clark, John, Wamphray
Cockburn, David, Castleton
Howden, Charles, Highfield
M'Ewan, J., Reaside
M'Ewan, John jr., Balgone barns
Shepherd, Thomson S., Gleghornie
Suttie, Robert, Carperstone
Thomson, Robert, Chapel
Tweeddale, J. & J., Rockville
Tweeddale, James (trus. of), East Craig
Wallace, Andrew, North Berwick mains
Wilson, Peter, Rhodes
Wyllie, Robert, Heugh
Young, David S., Bonnington
Yule, Edward, Sheriff house

Salton District.

IN PENCAITLAND PARISH.

Ainslie, Archibald, Templehall
Dickson, John, West mains
Fletcher, John, Milton
Howden, Mrs Annie, Boggs
Kerr, James H. & Peter, Spilmersford mains
King, William, Wolfstar
Morrison, Andrew, Broomrigg
Neilans, T. P. & G., Huntlaw
Nisbet, Alexander & George, Wester
Peffers, Archibald, Fountainhall
Simpson, William, Spilmersford
Stoddart, John, Red mains
Stoddart, William, Wilton hill
Taylor, John B. Seaton, W Mains

IN SALTON PARISH.

Cadzow, Thomas, Samuelston mains
Fletcher, John, Townhead
Guild, Alexander, Greenhead
Hay, Peter, West Blance
M'Intosh, James, Greenlaw
Maxwell, John, Gilchriston
Monteith, John, Salton E mains
Staig, David, Barley field

Tranent District.

IN GLADSMUIR PARISH.

Black, George, Penston
Blair, Thomas, Hoprig mains
Cunningham, St Clair, Adingston
Dickson, Charles, Hodges
Finlayson, William, Redhouse
Fisher, G. & F., Midmains
Gaukroger, George, Southfield
Gemmill, William, Greendykes
Jackson, Alexander, West Bank
Mitchell, George, Longniddry
Parke, John, Hoprig
Ritchie, J. B., Samuelston
Ronaldston, —., Redcote
Simpson, Robert, Innlands
Smith, Andrew, Longniddry
Stevenson, Mrs, West Mains
Tweedie, Alexander, Coats
Wood, Miss (trus. of), Chesterhall

IN ORMISTON PARISH.

Ainslie, Robert, Dodridge
Dewar, David, Murrays
Dickson, James, West Byres
Johnston, Alexander, North Mains
Pace, Frederick, Ormiston mains
Thomson, William, Ormiston
Turnbull, Walter, Lynemount

IN TRANENT PARISH.

Adamson, David (reps. of), South Elphinstone
Aitken, James, Northfield mains
Binnie, Robert (reps of) Setonmains
Courtney, Willm, Portobello mains
Ferme, George, Rigginhead
Knox, Robert, Caerlaverock
Mackie, James, Kingslaw
Minto, P. (for J. Polson), Muirpark
Ritchie, William, Meetinghouses
Shields, James, Dolphinstone
Smith, Dvd W. E., N. Elphinstone
Stenhouse, Andrew, W. Windygoul
Stenhouse, James, The Myles
Taylor, James D., Bankton
Taylor, John B., Seton W. Mains
Watt, David, E. Windygoul
Wyllie, William, Tranent mains
Young, Jas. B., Elphinstone Tower

FARMERS IN BERWICKSHIRE.

Berwick-on-Tweed District.

Allan, John, Lithamshank
Bell, Robert M., Muirton Ord
Berry, James, Bates Strand
Blakey, William & Sanderson, Baldersburyhill
Brison, John, Billylaw Ord
Cairins, Thomas, Bogend
Christison, Henry, Conundrum
Cockburn, William, 3rd Outer Cow Close
Cowe, Hry, Springhill, Scremerston
Cowe, William, Tweedmouth
Crossman, L. Morley, Gainslaw hill
Dickson, James, 1st Horse close
Edgar, & Sons, Lowhaughs
Embleton Thomas Horncliffe mains
Fairbairn, Ralph, Ordmains
Fender William, Mordington mains
Forster, William, Fairney Flat
Gilroy, James & Son, Sunnyside, Tweedmouth
Hardy, Wm, Middle Scremerston
Hattle, Alexander, Grangeburn
Hay, Bros., Scremerston
Holmes, Sidney M., Murtonwhite Ord
Hosick, Daniel, Hutton mains
Kerr Joseph & Robert, Cumberland bower
Kirkup, Bros., Screamerston]
Lyle, William, Sanson leal
Marshall, Robert, Tweedmouth
Marshall, Robert, West edge
Marshall, Alexander, New East
Marshall, Thomas, West Ord
Martin, John, 3rd Horse closes
Mitchell, Nathaniel, High Lethan
Moffat, Joseph, Bonner's Stead, Tweedmouth
Nesbitt, Rbt, South Mains, Paxton
Renton, James, Camphill
Ross, Bros., Seaview, Spittal
Ross, James, Newwaterhaugh
Ross, Ralph, Stoneymoorriggs
Rutherford, Mark, Priorhouse Ord
Sanderson, Thomas, High Cocklaw
Short, Thomas B., Newmills
Smith, Mrs., Tweedmouthmoor
Todd, Peter, Scuddylaw
Tullock, Andrew, Brow of the hill
Waite, Peter, Castle hills
Younger, Mrs., Marshall meadows
Young, Andrew, South Ord

IN NORHAM.

Adams, W., Thornton mains
Allan, G., Emerick
Allan, J., Mount Carmel
Allan, W., Newburn
Burns, J., Greenlaw wells
Carr, D., Felkington
Darling, J., Boathouse
Friar, Emma, Grindonridge
Lumsden, G., Shoreswood
Mitchell, J., Westmains
Moore, W., Tiptoe
Smith, W., Thornton park
Tait, G., East Newbiggin
Tait, W., Shell acre
Wood, George R., Duddo

Chirnside District.

Baird, James, Maines
Blackadder, John, Ninewell mains
Cowe, Peter, Old Castle

Dalgleish, William, Blackburn
Darling, James, Chirnside mill
Everitt, Francis H, Edington mains
Gillies, John, Edington mill
Lindsay, Thomas H., Nether mains
Millican, Gilbert, Harelaw
Scott, James, Crofts
Scott, Peter, Westfield
Swiney, P. J. & A., Broadhaugh
White, Alexander, Causewaybank

ECCLES PARISH.

Aitchison, Wm., Kannes W mains
Barron, John & Thomas, Bellmount
Darrie, George, Hassington mains
Dawson, Alexander, Stonefoulds
Dawson, Peter, Grizzlerig
Elliot, Robert, Stoneridge mains
Hamilton, James, Bankhead
Hardy, William, Longrig
Hendry, William, Lochton
Hume, Thomas, Wormerlaw
Lagton, Robert, Hassington
Laidler, Joseph, Hume bank
Lawrie, Thomas, Harlaw
Lugton, Andrew, Pictlesheugh
M'Crae, Hugh, Blinkbonny
M'Dougal, John, Eccles Tofts
Mather, John, Easter Printonian
Nisbet, James, Lambden
Nisbet, James, Crosshall
Ormiston, Henry, Kennetsidheads
Ormiston, John, Battlehill
Redpath, John, Leitholm mill
Robeson, George, Springwells
Scott, Thomas, Mersington
Simpson, Alexander, Eccles farm
Simpson, James, Loanknowe
Smith, John, Lochrig
Stenhouse, Adam, Wester Printonian
Todd, George, Kaimes East mains
Waddell, Charles, Long Birgham
Waddell, James, Cloverhall
Waddell, James, Sainfoin
Waddell, John, Birgham
Watson, Robert, Eccles Newtown
White, Thomas, Whiterig
Wood, John & Wm., Mersington mill

Cockburnspath District.

Allan, William jr., Redheugh
Allan, William, Bowshiel
Hardy, James, Old Cambus West
Hood, James, Townhead
Hoprig, Frederick C., Hoprig
Johnston, George, Fulfordlees
Nesbit, William, Dunglass mill
Sanderson, Neinan, Old Cambus East mains
Scambler, William. Cockburnspath
Wallace, John, Penmanshiel
Wight, John, Eclaw
Wilson, John, Chapelhill
Wyllie, James, Pathhead

Coldingham District.

Brown, Margaret, Bogbank
Cairns, Alexander, Templehall
Cairns, James, Fleurs
Cairns, Wm., Coldingham law
Cormack, Robert, Coldingham hill
Dudgeon, Robert A., Northfield
Edington, James, Westerside
Edington, William, Dowlaw
Edington, James, Lumsdaine
Gunn (trus. of), Abbeypark
Hay, Messrs. Cairncross
Johnstone, William G., Alemill
Lugton, Peter, Buskenbrae
Lothian, Thos. & Peter, Bee Edge
M'Gall, John, Halidoun
Marshall, Adam, Huxton
Martin, Robert, Crosslaw
Morrison, Wightman, Myrtlehall
Patterson, Alexander, Springbank
Patterson, G. & A. M., Press mains
Scott, Robert F., Blackhill
Thorburn, Wm. & James, Eastlaw
Thorburn, Peter & Alex., Burnhall
Thornburn, Robert, Milldown
Thornburn, William, Abbey park
Westgarth, Charles, S Falaknowe
Wightman, Thomas, Comelybank
Wilkie, John, Pilsmuir
Wood, John, North Falaknowe

Coldstream District.

Briggs, Robert E., Rennehill
Calder, William A., Oxenrig
Forbes, George & John; Georgefield
Fulton, James, Skaithmuir
Fulton, John, Hatchednize
Hogg, Robert, Fireburnmill
Hood, Thomas, Coldstream mains

Hunter, James, Todhillrigg
Lewis, James, East mains
Lewis, James, Milne Graden
Lillico, Richard, Gallowsknowe
M'Donald, Daniel, Hawkslaw
M'Lean, David, The Crooks
Robinson, James C., Westmains
Smith, James F., West mains
Tait, George, Milne Graden mains
Tait, Geo. & Sommerville, James, Milne Graden mains
Tait, John, Castlelaw
Tait, James & John, Danchester
Thomson, James & Robert, Earnslaw
Turnbull, Michael & Thos., Little Togrigg
Watson, Robert, Ruthven
Wilson, Alexander, Marlfield
Winber, Ramsay, Earnslaw

Cranshaws District.

IN ABBEY ST. BATHANS PARISH.

Bertram, James, Blackerston
Caverhill, Jos., Abbey St. Bathans
Cockburn, George, Banhead
Cockburn, Messrs, Channo Bank
Cockburn, Robert, Paiteshill
Hogg, John, Quixwood
Hunter, William, Godscroft
Rankine, James J., Barnside
Scott, Thomas, Abbey St Bathans

IN BUNKLE PARISH.

Aitchison James, Primrosehill
Calder, Adam, West Blanerne
Calder Thomas, Billie mains
Edgar John, Sleighhouses
Elliot, John, East Cruicksfield
Fullarton, Robert, Hoardwell
Hogg, James, Blackhouse
Lumsdane Robert J., Lintlaw
Weatherhead, William, Preston

IN CRANSHAWS PARISH.

Elliot, William, Ellemford
Gillie, Alexander, Playhaugh
Johnston, Thomas, Ellemford
Stephenson, Richard, Cranshaws
Young, William, Smiddyhill

IN LONGFORMACUS PARISH.

Brodie, James, C., Longformacus
Craik, John, Caldra
Cowie, Peter, Blacksmill
Craw, James, Rawburn
Elliot, John, Castleshiel
Maclaren, John, Dronshiel
Pate, Andrew, Horsupcleoch
Smith, Andw., Rigfoot Whitchester
Trotter, John, Millican

Duns District.

IN DUNS.

Allan, James, Middlefield
Brash, John S., Woodend
Brash, James, Cairnhill
Clark, James, Rules mains
Cockburn, James, Knock
Denholm James & Wm., Broomhill
Elder, James, Wedderburn mains
Elliot, William, Racleughhead
Elliot, Robert, Turtleton
Elliot, David P., Grueldykes
Fortune, George, Windshiel
Fortune, John, Ninewar
Goodfellow, Adam, Peelrig
Hastie, Mrs. Isa, Cockburn mill
Hastie, Thomas, Checklaw
Hunter, John, Dunslaw
Johnston, Thomas, Kidshielhaugh
Ker, William, Ashfield
Laidlaw, Peter, Burnhouses
Lawrie, John H., Hardens
Lockie, W., Choiclee
Pitt, John Hope, Manderston mill
Purves, James, Castle mains
Robson, J., Millknowe
Smith, Andrew, Crumstane
Stephenson, Richard, Chapel
Swanston, James. Dunsmill
Swanston, Mrs, Dunsmill
Torrance, Thomas, Langtonlees
Webster, Mrs Eliz., Chalkielaw
Weir, William, Langton mill
Weir, David, Ladyflat
Wilkinson, John, Bridge-end
Wilson, James & W., Cockburn
Young, W., Smiddyhill

IM EDROM.

Cossar, Mark, Greenknowe
Codds, Robert, Blackadder bank
Elliot, David R., Nisbet hill
Elliot, Francis, Middle Stotts
Ford, Peter, Broomhouse mains

Forrest, Robert, Stuartslaw
Gray, Alexander, Belshiel
Hislop, Elspeth, Mid Edrom
Hume, Thomas, Nisbet mill
Kirkwood, Robert, Allanbank mill
Lumsden, E. S., East Blanerne
Lyall, Robert, Broomdykes
Middleton, Hilton, Kimmerghame mains
Miller, Thomas, Todheugh
Patton, Peter, Blackaddermains
Robson, James, Edrom mains
Sanderson, James, Crunklaw
Somerville, James A., Broomdykes
Speedy, James, Readyloch
Spence, George A., Whitelaw
Thomson, James, Mungoswalls
Trotter, Y. & Son, Limited, Chirnside Mill
Watson, William, Mary Gold
Webster, James, Edrom Newton
White, Alexander, Kelloe mains
Wightman, Alex., Mountpleasant
Wightman, W., Kimmerghame mill
Young, George, Blackadder mains, west

Earlston District.

Allan, David, Georgefield
Anderson, Mrs Annie, Town farm
Balmer, William, Mellerstain mill
Beattie, Michael, Kedslie
Bone, Miss Margaret, Grizzelfield
Brown, Alexander, Whitefield
Charlton, T., Lightfield
Elliot, Thomas. Cortcrooks
Elliot, William, Kirklands
Elliot, James, Chapel mains
Fairnbairn, John, Huntslaw
Gibb, Robert, Legerwood
Henderson, George, Huntly wood
Herbertson, Robert H., Fans
Hope, Col. Charles, Cowdenknowes mains
Hogg, John, Craighouse
Kedzie, Robert, Kirkhill
Keir, James, Earlston
Lillie, Allan, Yarside
Logan, James, Birkhillside
Logan, Robert, Legerwood
Lowson, James, West Morriston
Lowson, Thomas, Legerwood
Martin, David, Earlston
Mather, George, Earlston mains
Michael, Richard, Legerwood
Purves, John, Redpath east end
Wood, W. & J., Legerwood

Eyemouth District.

IN AYTON.

Bell, George, East Flemington
Brodie, Mrs, Chesterbank
Cockburn, William & John, Ayton mains
Fulton, John, Whitfield
Johnston, John, Greystonless
Leith, Wm. & Robert, Fairneyside
Logan, John, Flemington
Martin, William, Bleachfield
Middleton, William, Cocklaw
Nisbet, William, Ayton Mill
Scott, Peter, Whiterigg
Smith, Alexander, Brenderguest
White, Eli. C., Aytonlaw

IN EYEMOUTH.

Brown, James, High laws
Brown, M. & P., Houndlaw
Brown, Thomas, Killilaw
Gray, Charles, Aiksop
Hair, George, Deerslaw
Johnston, Archibald, Linthill
Paterson, Archibald, Eyemouth
Paxton, James, Killilaw mains
Purves, Misses C. & M., Deanhead
Whitelaw, Peter, Under Killilaw

Foulden District.

Bogue, William, Greenfield
Brown, John, Moorpark
Craw, Henry, West mains
Davidson, William, St Johns
Fender, And. (exors. of), Foulden Deans
Fender, William, Mordington
Hill, George, St Johns
Landels, George, Nunlands
Millican, Gilbert, New mains
Milne, William, Newton
Rae, William, Burnbank
Sanderson, James B., Fouldenhill
Speedie, George, Foulden Castle

Greenlaw District.

IN GREENLAW.

Brockie, John, Gordonbank

Broomfield, Wm. J., Old Greenlaw
Burton, James, Angelraw
Craise, James, Slagden
Dods, Walter, Woodhead
Dods, William, Elwartlaw
Hewat, James, Easter Howlaws
Inglis, Alexander, Greenlawdean
Majoribanks, Frank B., Rowchester
M'Dougal, G., Bedshiel
M'Dougal, George, Ecclestofts
Nisbet, George, Rumbleton
Nisbet, James, Lambden
Paterson, Thomas, Catmoss
Robertson, John, Clerkinville
Smeaton, Andrew, Whiteside
Spark, John, Hexpath
Turnbull, John, Crumrig
Walker, Andrew, Cowrig
Watson, Andrew L., Hallyburton

IN GORDON.

Allan, James, Greenlees
Curle, James, Evelaw
Gibson, James, Westruther mains
Guy, Robert, Broomiebank
Henderson, Robert, East Gordon
Hogg, Alexander, Macksmill
Hogg, Thomas, Darling, Middlethird
Lyal, Alexander, Greenknowe
Lyall, Robert, Cammerlaws
M'Dougal, George, Bassendeans
M'Dougall, James, Gordon cottage
Miller, Henry, Bassendean hill
Moon, Mrs Annie, Lightfoot
Rutherford, Andw., Rumbeltonlaw
Shiel, Andrew, Byrelaws
Virtue, Alexander, Fawside
Watson, John, Harlow

IN HUME.

Bain, W. & T., Legars
Bertram, William, Hume Mill
Brotherston, Thomas, Hume byres
Clark, W. & W. & Jas., Coldside
Johnson, Alexander, Todrig
Logan, John, Hume hall
Roberton, John, Fallside hill
Shepherd, David H., Mill place
Telly, W. & T., Fallside hill
Wilson, J. & A., Stennuir

Hutton District.

Barclay, Alex., Fishwicks mains
Brunton, James, Clarabed, Paxton
Henderson, Walter, Spittal West mains
Hogg, James, Hutton mill
Hope, Peter Kin., Sunwick
Hosick, Daniel, Hutton mains
Lyle, John, Hutton croft
M'Leod, John, Nansfield
Marshall, James, Broad meadows
Milne, Robert, Spittal mains
Murray, George, Nabdean, Paxton
Murray, William, Fishwick
Nisbit, Robert, South mains, Paxton
Purves, Robert, Clairvale, Paxton
Tait, Alex., Hutton hall mill
Thorburn, William, North mains, Paxton
Torrance, Robert, Hutton hall barns
Whiteman, Alex., Clarabe, Paxton
Whitlie, John Chesterfield, Paxton
Younger, Robert, West Fishwick, Hutton

Lauder District.

Bathgate, Simon, Justicehall
Beattie, James, Thornydykes
Bell, James, Oxton mains
Bertram, James, Addingston
Blackie, Thomas, Headshaw, Oxton
Brodie, Walter, Threeburnford, Oxton
Bruce, Robert, Thirlestane
Brydon, Thomas, Burncastle
Dickinson, William, Longcroft
Dykes, James, Kirktonhill, Oxton
Elliot, James, Chapel mains
Fleming, John, Bowerhouse, Oxton
Forsyth, Peter, East mains
Fortune, Robert, Midburn, Oxton
Gilchrist, John, Burnfoot
Graham, W. & J., Trabroun
Halliday, F. & A., Bridgehaugh
Henderson, George, Ca-frae mill, Oxton
Hunter, Robert, Herriotshall, Oxton
Hunter, Simon, Whitslaids
Johnston, James, Huntington
Kinghorn, James, St. Leonards
M'Dougal, George, Blythe
M'Dougal, Mrs Jane, Lylestone

Mill, George, Hindsidehill
Mill, John, Dods
Nisbet, William, Trabroun
Outerston, Peter, Blackburn
Purdon, James T., Raccleuch
Runciman, George, Wantonwalls
Sharp, Andrew, Overhowden
Shaiving, Thomas, Glengcit, Oxton
Stobbie, Mrs Jane, Kelphope Oxton
Thomson, Andrew, Collielaw
Torrie, A., St. Leonards
Tweedie, David, Netherhowden
Weddell, John W., Lauderbarns
Waldie, R., Muircleuch
Walker, John, Howletsha
Wright, George, Carfrae, Oxton
Young, A. & G., Shielfield

IN MERTOUN.

Anderson, Geo. & Wm., Spadeslee
Davidson, Wm., Bemersyde, Eastend
Fairbairn, Archd., Bemersyde, Westend
Gray, David, Dalcove mains
Haig, Peter, Hallidean mill
Lawrie, John, Dryburgh Orchard
Ormiston Bros., Dryburgh mains
Storie, George, Millfield
Whitehead, Alexander, The Third

IN NENTHORN.

Black. John, Gurick
Brownlie, Thomas, Whitehill
Carlow, Alexander, Blinkbonny
Logan, Summer, Harrietfields
Purves, Robert, Mellowlees
Ritchie, George, Burnbrae
Simson, George, Courthill

Polwarth District.

Clark, George, Cairns Mill, Fogo
Elder, David, Broomy park
Fairbairn, Henry, Polwarth mill
Hood, Thomas, Bogend, Fogo
Humphreys, Henry, Caldra, Fogo
Johnston, John and J., Sisterpath, Fogo
Lambie, John, Fogorig
Mather, James, Printonan, Fogo
Paxton, John Peter, South croft
Purves, William, Ryselaw
Robertson, John (trust. of), Clerkenville, Fogo
Robertson, George, (trus. of) Harcus, Fogo
Robertson, W., Fogo, Eastend
Sanderson, & Sons, Fogo
Taylor, James, Polwarth, Rhodes
Wilson, James, Cothill

Reston District.

Aitchison, James, Greenburn, Auchencrow
Allan, John, East Renton
Bell, Alexander, West Greenfield
Bertram, James, Henghead
Calder, T., Auchencrow mains
Caverhill, Joseph M., Hillend
Cockburn, W. & R., Howburn
Cockburn, William, Reston mains
Cookson, Charles L., Lemington
Craise, Robert, Swinewood
Darling, Adam, Fairlaw, Auchencrow
Fairbairn, Wm. W. & Peter, Reston hill
Fender, William, Mont Alban
Fergie, John, Warlaw Bank, Auchencrow
Hay, J. & G., Cairncross
Hogg, James, Horsley
Hogg, James, Blackhouse
Johnston, George, Stoneshiel
Logan, Adam S., Ferney Castle
Mack, Joseph, Berry Bank
Nesbit, Alex. & Mary Gold, Auchencrow
Sanderson, William, Greenhead
Storey, Ralph, Swansfield
Swan, Robert B. & W., Perryhaughs
Wood, John & Thos., Anchencrow

IN GRANTSHOUSE.

Aitchison, James, Strafonton
Bird, George, Rentonbarns
Cockburn, George, Whitebarn
Cowe, Peter, Butterdean
Dickson, A., Shannonbank
Fullerton, William, Howpark
Murray, Thomas & James, Brockholes
Rankin, Thomas, Barnside
Saunderson, Robert, Harelawside
Wight, J., Nethermonynut

Wight, J., Greenwood

Swinton District.

IN SWINTON PARISH.

Bowhill, Thomas, Harcarshill
Brodie, John, Mountfair
Calder, Thomas, Swintonhill
Davidson, George, Simprin mains
King, Alfred, Swinton
Landels, Mrs Ann, Longbank
Mather, M., Swinton mill
Simpson, Peter, Butterlaw
Trotter, J. J., Crowfootbank
Whillans, Aaron, Bridgend

IN LADYKIRK PARISH.

Aitchison, George & William Fellowshills
Black, James, New Ladykirk
Davidson, Alexander, Ladykirk shiels
Davidson, Thomas, Ramrig
Fairburn, Ralph, Waltershead
Lyall, Thomas, Old Ladykirk
Mills, William, New Horndean

IN WHITSOME PARISH.

Alder, Thomas, Heritage
Balsillie, Andrew C., Dykethead
Brodie, John P., Mountfair
Dodds, Robert, Blackadder bank
Edgar, John & Samuel, W Newton
Fleming, James, Winfield
Craws, Jas. (exors, of), Whitsome mill
Robeson, William A., Longrig
Tait, James, East Newton
Torranee, George, Leetside
Torrance, Thomas, Whitsome laws

Westruther District.

Allan, James, Whiteknowe
Beattie, James, Thorny dykes
Bryson, Andrew, Whiteburn
Clay, John, Wedderlie
Curle, J., Evelaw
Gibson, James, Westruther mains
Grieve, Adam, Flass
Guy, John, Westertown
Lyall, Robert, Cammerlaws
M'Dougal, George, Bassendean
Mills, George, Hindside mill
Outerson, George, Jordanlaw
Walker, John, Howlets'ha
Watson, John, Harelaw

T. W. MORRIS,

(Successor to David Cobb),

Printer, Stationer, and Bookbinder,

DAILY & WEEKLY NEWSPAPERS, MAGAZINES & PERIODICALS.

Proprietor and Publisher of " The Berwick and Border Railway Time Tables and Diary," and Mills's Penny Popular Guide to Berwick & Distric

3, 5, and 7, CHURCH STREET,

Berwick-on-Tweed.

Mason's Model Hygienic Bakery,

(The Largest and most complete Bakery in Town),

Sole Agent for **Oliver's Patent Brown Bread,** as used in the Dairy Department of the Health Exhibition,

2 & 4 Church Street, BERWICK-ON-TWEED

JOHN R. WHITECROSS

GROCER and WINE MERCHANT,

West End, North Berwick.

Full particulars of Furnished Houses and Apartments to Let Free on Application.

Telegrams—Whitecross, West End, North Berwick

PRATT & PRINGLE,

Cycle Agents and Repairers

Accessories kept in Stock. Cycles on hire.
General Stabling for Cycles.

Manufacturers of Steam Traps for Tweed Mills and Dishorning Machines.

North Berwick and East Linton.

www.ingramcontent.com/pod-product-compliance
Lightning Source LLC
Chambersburg PA
CBHW030557270326
41927CB00007B/967